John C. Hirsh is Pro[illegible] American Literature at Georgetown University. He has published extensively on late medieval literature and spirituality, including *The Revelations of Margery Kempe: Paramystical Practices in Later Medieval England* (Brill, Leiden 1989).

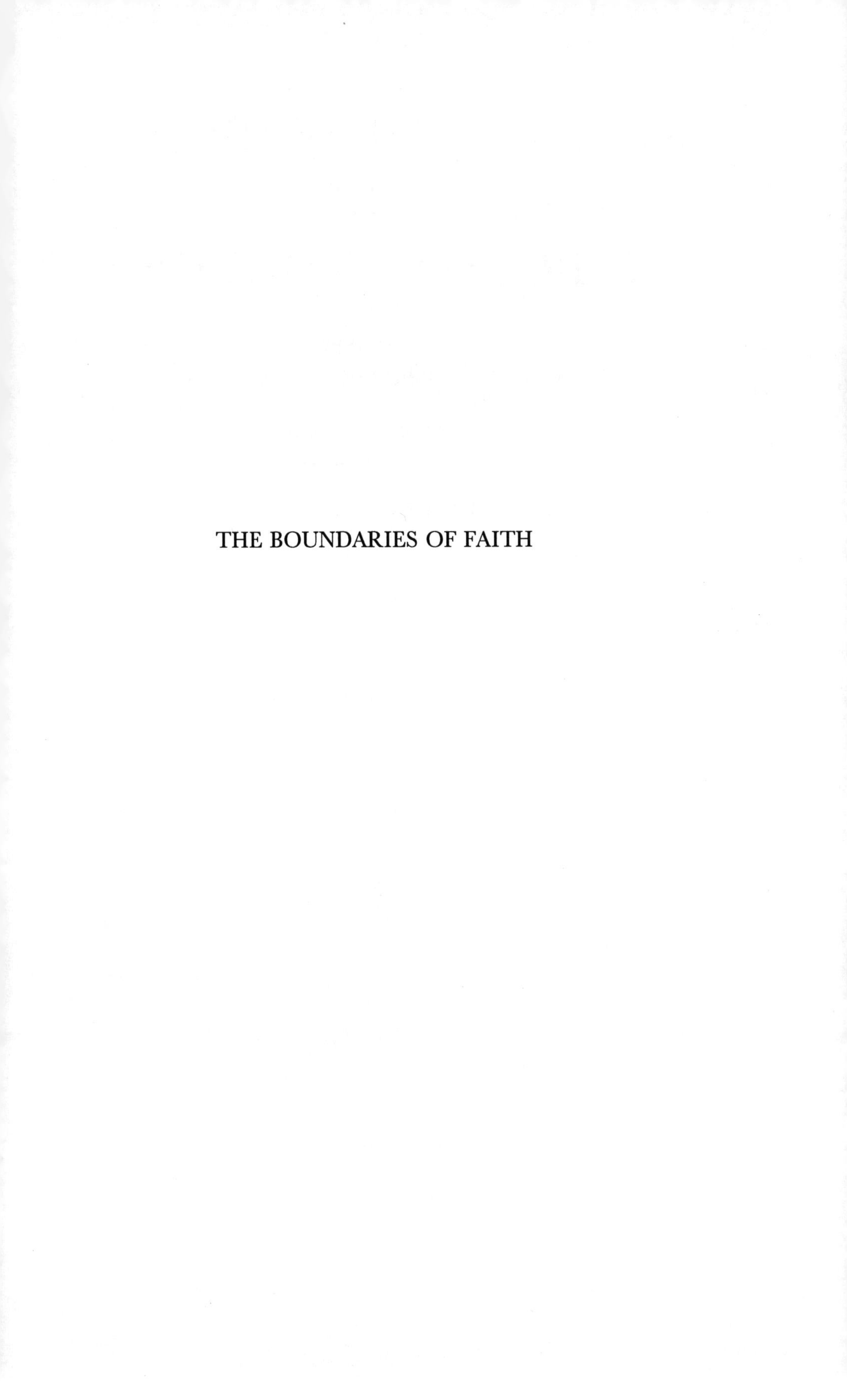

THE BOUNDARIES OF FAITH

STUDIES IN THE HISTORY OF CHRISTIAN THOUGHT

VOLUME LXVII

JOHN C. HIRSH

THE BOUNDARIES OF FAITH

THE BOUNDARIES OF FAITH

THE DEVELOPMENT AND TRANSMISSION OF MEDIEVAL SPIRITUALITY

BY

JOHN C. HIRSH

E.J. BRILL
LEIDEN · NEW YORK · KÖLN
1996

The paper in this book meets the guidelines for permanence and durability of the Committee on Production Guidelines for Book Longevity of the Council on Library Resources.

Library of Congress Cataloging-in-Publication Data

Hirsh, John C.
The boundaries of faith : the development and transmission of medieval spirituality / by John C. Hirsh.
p. cm. — (Studies in the history of Christian thought, ISSN 0081-8607 ; v. 67)
Includes bibliographical references and index.
ISBN 9004104283 (alk. paper)
1. Spirituality—England—History—Middle Ages, 600–1500. 2. Mysticism—History—Middle Ages, 600–1500. 3. Mystics—England. 4. Women and religion—England—History. 5. English literature—Middle English, 1100–1500. I. Title. II. Series.
BR750.H57 1996
274.2'05—dc20 95-24728
CIP

Die Deutsche Bibliothek - CIP-Einheitsaufnahme

Hirsh, John C.:
The boundaries of faith : the development and transmission of medieval spirituality / by John C. Hirsh. – Leiden ; New York ; Köln : Brill, 1996
(Studies in the history of Christian thought ; Vol. 67)
ISBN 90-04-10428-3
NE: GT

ISSN 0081-8607
ISBN 90 04 10428 3

PRINTED IN THE NETHERLANDS

to surrender an image of God that has become too familiar

Jean Sulivan

Once you're here, however, whether you want to or not, you have to ask the question: does all of this have a meaning, and if so, what? The more I think about it, the more I realize that the final and decisive answer is not to be found in external factors that rely on so-called information, for no mere information can give me an answer to that question. Ultimately I can only find an answer—a positive answer—within myself, in the meaning of things, in my hope. What, in fact, is man responsible to? What does he relate to? What is the final horizon of his actions, the absolute vanishing point of everything he does?... Ever since childhood, I have felt that I would not be myself—a human being—if I did not live in a permanent and manifold tension with this "horizon" of mine, the source of meaning and hope—and ever since my youth, I've never been certain whether this is an "experience of God" or not.

Václav Havel

To the Memory of Thomas F. Walsh
of Georgetown University

to the
Children of Sursum Corda
in Washington D.C.

and to the
Head Teacher, Staff and Children
of Hermitage School, Wapping

CONTENTS

PREFACE

This book has been written over a period of about eight years, and in the course of writing it I have incurred many debts. Several of the chapters began as papers presented to the Old and Middle English Seminar which Professor Douglas Gray and Professor Malcolm Godden direct at Oxford University, and I am grateful for the invitation to offer them, and for the questions and advice which they brought forth. During 1993 I held a Visiting Fellowship at Pembroke College, Oxford, which allowed me time to work on several of the chapters. I am most grateful to Pembroke for the election, and to its then Master, Sir Roger Bannister, to the late Dr. David Fleeman, Senior Fellow in English, who graciously and gallantly engaged and assisted me, and to all the fellowship, for gracious hospitality and welcome support during the time I was in Oxford.

At Georgetown I am grateful for the support of the Medieval Studies Program, ably directed by my dear friend and colleague Professor Penn R. Szittya. From Georgetown too I have had a sabbatical leave which assisted greatly with the writing of the book. I am grateful to the staff of Georgetown's Lauinger Library, and in particular to the Woodstock Collection, for much help over the years. While I was in Oxford I used extensively the British Library, the Cambridge University Library, and especially the Warburg Institute, where I benefited from conversations with Dr. Jill Kraye, as I had earlier with Professor Joseph Trapp and the late Charles Schmitt. In Oxford, I must record special thanks to David Vaisey, Bodley's Librarian, for good advice and fine hospitality during the period of my fellowship. During my stay in Britain I spent a month in Rome, and am most grateful to the authorities of the Biblioteca Apostolica Vaticana, particularly the Prefect, Rev. Leonard E. Boyle, O.P., for permission to work in that collection. I have debts as well to Msgr. Walter Edyvean of the Congregation for Catholic Education and Director of the Villa Stritch, and to Rev. Henry Bertells, S.J., Librarian of the Biblicum, for hospitality, advice, and many courtesies while I was in Rome.

More recent debts are not less deep. I am particularly grateful to the Editor of "Studies in the History of Christian Thought," Professor Heiko Augustinus Oberman, whose work I have long admired, not only for including the book in a series which offers a particularly appropriate context for works often examined in textual and bibliographical terms, but also for the attentive, careful, and meticulous reading he gave the manuscript. The changes which he indicated, and which I willingly adopted, have improved it in every way. I am indebted too to Harry E. Cole for having read the text carefully, and for raising several valuable points with me, and to Valerie Babb, Anne Clark Bartlett, C. David Benson, Edward Bodnar, S.J., Grace Burford, R. Emmett Curran, S.J., Ian Doyle, Martin Irvine, George Keiser, Valerie Lagorio, John Pfordresher, James Reddington, S.J., Jan Rhodes, Elizabeth Robertson, Eusebio Rodrigues, Thomas Schubeck, S.J., James Slevin, Charles Tung and Mary Wack for interest, support and advice of various kinds over the several years this book has been in progress: but they are not responsible for its conclusions. Dean Robert B. Lawton, S.J., rendered necessary support when it was most needed. Individual chapters record particular debts to those who assisted with them, but I am very grateful to all who, by encouragement or intervention, sped me on my way.

Two of the chapters have appeared, in earlier versions, in collections of essays for which they seemed particularly appropriate: for both were conceived, from the beginning, as chapters of this book. The chapter now called "Feminism and Spirituality in Chaucer: the *Second Nun's Tale*" appeared in *Chaucer's Religious Tales*, Chaucer Studies XV, edited by C. David Benson and Elizabeth Robertson (Cambridge: D.S. Brewer, 1990), and the chapter now called "The Gods Appear: Representing the Divine in Quest Narratives" first appeared in *Vox Mystica: Essays on Medieval Mysticism in Honor of Professor Valerie M. Lagorio*, edited by Anne Clark Bartlett, William F. Pollard, Janet Goebel and Thomas Bestul (Woodbridge, Suffolk: Boydell & Brewer, 1995). I am most grateful for permission to reprint them here, albeit in somewhat modified form.

Georgetown University, Washington D.C. John C. Hirsh
December, 1995

INTRODUCTION

The title of this book—and the even more audacious subtitle—may require a word of explanation, if not of apology. For how is it possible either to delineate "the boundaries" of something as free of constraint as faith, traditionally one of the gifts of the Holy Spirit, or to record "the development and transmission of medieval spirituality" in so short a space—or indeed in any space at all? What follows is a series of *exempla* which are also explorations, and which surround a central ground which I have called, in a word which is at the heart of my investigations, faith.

Wilfred Cantwell Smith began a significant examination of this phenomenon by proposing that: " 'Faith,' ... shall signify that human quality that has been expressed in, has been elicited, nurtured, and shaped by, the religious traditions of the world. This leaves faith unspecified, while designating its locus. We do not yet say what it is, but indicate where we are to look in order to find out. Thus an inquiry becomes possible, historical and empirical. That it can also be rewarding will, we believe, become evident in the course of the investigation." [1]

Although the chapters which follow spring from a particular religious tradition, they are not circumscribed by it, and I have used the words "development" and "transmission" to indicate the many ways in which medieval faith changed, adapted and yet remained, influencing and informing those who achieved insight into its properties and responded to its imperatives. My interest thus has been not only with particular manifestations of faith, but also, and more particularly, with what meaning they held out (or hold out) for those who are concerned with them. It is in meaning, or at least within a search for meaning, that faith finally resides.

Even though interest in spirituality is increasing apace, there is still a lingering reluctance, particularly among medievalists who study devotional and religious texts, to admit into academic discourse those aspects of religion which involve individual responsiveness, commitment and belief, and in some quarters it is almost as though such

---

[1] Wilfred Cantwell Smith, *Faith and Belief.* (Princeton, N.J.: Princeton University Press, 1979), p. 6.

things are a properly ignored embarrassment, which should be quietly separated off from the scientific study of religious doctrine, ecclesiastical history, devout practices, the institutional church, the history of religious women, even mystical encounter—in a word, from all of the apparently external aspects of organized religion.

But even among those who agree that faith exists (or once did) there is a reasonable concern for the ways in which such matters are to be addressed: how is faith, when it exists, to be discussed? In what ways can its development be recorded and measured? How is its transmission to be understood? The external manifestations of religion are of course of great help in addressing these matters, but precisely because they are external they are to some extent limited. If it were possible to record every appearance of the *arma Christi* in Europe (or in any one country), what would be accomplished? Or if it could be shown that the new directions which emerged in late medieval northern European spirituality sprang directly from certain mercantile (and religious) contacts with the Low Countries, what follows next? In what ways do texts transform a culture, or a person?

It is possible (though too rarely done) to invoke either psychology or sociology in many of these cases, and to indicate the primary importance of (a not easily identified!) life history, or of social context, in all matters pertaining to religious inquiry. But even those approaches will only go so far since, although personal attitudes and social constructions are indeed deeply woven into the manifestations and conventions through which religious persons express themselves, the growth and movement of religious faith are not circumscribed by them, and remain singularly hard to ascertain, particularly when they are not identified more or less exclusively with the pronouncements of a few often-acknowledged minds.

Yet it is that which I have attempted here, offering an exploration of the ways in which values are established and remain, attitudes taken up, and assumptions grounded. I have called my book the "boundaries of faith" because I have become convinced that it is at the frontiers, internal as well as external, that religious attitudes become most apparent. It is quite true that one century's (or one person's) frontier is the next's capital (or orthodoxy), but as long as they exist, frontiers are usually unmistakable, and are, among other things, the point at which religious minds and religious persons meet, usually to mutual advantage, though not always with equal understanding.

Religion, however defined, is not static, is remarkably sensitive to context, and often reveals fidelity to a past from which it claims continuity. Yet historically it has also been a refuge, transcending person and culture in the interests of "truth," claiming a freedom from time and promising an end to history. It is within these tensions that spirituality develops and that its transmission takes place. What occurs is not the passing down of a text but of an attitude, not the repetition of a devout practice but (sometimes at least) the preservation of a belief, not the invocation of a saint but the grounding of an assumption. Nothing changes, everything changes. The religious person never reaches forward so confidently as when he or she reaches back, and some attitudes will perpetuate themselves whether or not there is a religious context to receive them. My book's subtitle is thus a continuing topic, and one which recurs, often in the form of an interrogation, in chapter after chapter; it does not refer to the impossible act of finally describing the religiousness of medieval persons, which, however, it often seeks to address.

This interest in faith was once more popular in academic circles than it has since become. When Bernard Lord Manning (1892-1941) published *The People's Faith in the Time of Wyclif* (1919), one of the first English studies to offer a sympathetic and systematic account of late medieval religious attitudes, he used the word "faith" in his title easily, and assumed (with his reader) a continuity between the late fourteenth and the early twentieth century which few now would accept.[2] But Manning believed in the reasonableness and good sense of those whom he studied (though he also credited them with a liberal amount of superstition), and argued that, changes having been made, these qualities contributed to, even led to, the Protestant tradition.[3] He

---

[2] Bernard Lord Manning, B.A., *The People's Faith in the Time of Wyclif* Thirwall Essay 1917 (Cambridge: Cambridge University Press, 1919; rpt. Hassocks, Sussex and Totowa, New Jersey: The Harvester Press/Rowman and Littlefield, 1975). The book examines "the ways by which religion was taught in the fourteenth century," (chapters 1-3); "the subject matter of popular religion," (chapters 4-9), and "three problems which agitated the popular mind: the social problem of poverty, the philosophical problem of free-will, and the religious problem of prayer" (pp. vii-viii). Manning was himself a committed Congregationalist, though with an inclination towards the Methodism which his father had abandoned not long after his son was born; in later years he developed a high regard for Anglicanism, while remaining true to his earlier attachments. See F. Brittain, *Bernard Lord Manning. A Memoir* (Cambridge: W. Heffer & Sons, 1942), pp. 1-10, and *passim.*

[3] "The true successors in modern Europe of Gregory VII and Innocent III and Boniface VIII, as we now begin to see, were John Calvin, John Knox and the English Independents" (p. 186). Though different in its methods, sources and approach,

remarked that the religious poetry of the fourteenth century had its nearest parallel in Charles Wesley's hymns, and that many of the religious attitudes of the late-medieval devout layperson or cleric were most nearly represented by the strictest of the modern day Dissenters. "The medieval Church is the mother of us all," he wrote in the final sentence of his book.

Underlying these beliefs were assumptions concerning the limitations of many medieval religious practices, and of the several medieval (and most later) ecclesiastical hierarchies. Against these strictures, however, Manning set a regard for "faith," and several of the chapters which follow may reasonably be read as responses to certain of his ideas. I have been concerned, for example, with the evidence of faith offered in certain of the texts I have discussed, and as a part of this concern I have sometimes considered, and sometimes assumed, a relationship between faith and religious belief. I have engaged this subject, however, less as a topic for discussion than as an attitude, and have addressed it empirically, like Manning, seeking evidences wherever they can be found.

Given this orientation, it would probably be well for me to indicate certain assumptions I have made (or avoided) in what follows. In English, the usual definition of religious faith involves some or all of the elements listed under the third meaning in the *Oxford English Dictionary*:

> 3. *Theol.* a. Belief in the truths of religion; belief in the authenticity of divine revelation (whether viewed as contained in Holy Scripture or in the teaching of the Church) and acceptance of the revealed doctrines. b. That kind of faith (distinctively called *saving* or *justifying faith*) by which, in the teaching of the N[ew] T[estament], a sinner is justified in the sight of God. This is variously defined by theologians ... but there is general agreement in regarding it as a conviction practically operative on the character and will, and thus opposed to the more intellectual assent to religious truths (sometimes called *speculative faith).* c. The spiritual apprehension of divine truths, or of realities beyond the reach of sensible experience or logical proof. By Christian writers often identi-

---

Manning's study is in its way a remote ancestor of works like Anne Hudson's important *The Premature Reformation. Wycliffite Texts and Lollard History* (Oxford: Clarendon Press, 1988). For a study with which Manning would have been in sympathy see Geoffrey Rowell, ed., *The English Religious Tradition and the Genius of Anglicanism* (Wantage, Oxon and Oxford: IKON and Keble College, Oxford, 1992), though the medieval chapters treat as well the discontinuity in the medieval/Anglican tradition.

> fied with the preceding; but not exclusively confined to Christian use. Often viewed as the exercise of a special faculty in the soul of man, or as the result of supernatural illumination."

This only partially defensible focus on the meta-rationality of faith may help to account for the general disinclination of many students, even students of devotional texts, to engage it. The fact that Manning did so, even though he was himself a part of the same culture which produced the *Oxford English Dictionary*, suggests something of the resilience which the concept holds, though a modern student of spirituality could be forgiven for finding the *OED* definition in certain ways quite misdirected. In a practical sense, faith, like the spirituality which it both influences and is influenced by, often appears in a largely social aspect, not a personal one, and one which is manifested in action, not in reflection. Unlike belief (which always involves a mental action) faith (from Latin *fides*) involves trust and confidence in others and a measure of loyalty. It is not merely a habit of mind, whether meta-rational or not, nor does it simply call forth a response from the will. Rather, from one point of view, it is itself that response: indeed it can be seen to be the first of many actions in which it issues. Those actions can take many forms, as the chapters which follow will indicate, though taken as a whole they illustrate the other-directedness of the topic, not its reflexive quality.

Faith is thus both immediately and ultimately concerned with others, and reaches out to engage them through identifiable means, both social and individual. Yet although both individual and group meanings are integral to any act of faith, these meanings do not exist apart from the persons who maintain them. The individual's apprehension of faith is thus complex, and is rooted both in personal and social constructions and in individual and group religious observance, even when these point in different directions. There is no particular reason to avoid any of these in academic inquiry.

What matters for the student of religious attitudes is the relationship of faith and belief, even as that relationship is defined in common discourse. From one point of view that relationship is relatively simple: belief is a statement of perceived fact, while faith involves a larger commitment. Belief can be discussed quite easily in academic (and other) discourse; faith is more difficult to engage. Augustine associated faith with an act of the will, though he insisted (as did subsequent commentators) that it comes from God as a gift, in an act of grace. In the classical definition, faith is an infused theological virtue; simple belief, when it resides in the will, is not.[4] Thus, "Credo Deo" suggests that I believe God who is revealing something to me; "Credo Deum" that I believe the truths about God; but "Credo in Deum" that I commit myself to the revealing God. Although the locus for that *credo* may reside in either the will or the mind or in both, the assent to faith is also and inescapably an ascent to faith, which, in engaging both the mind and the will, goes beyond (but not against) the rational moment, and inscribes meaning.

Cases alter practice, even devout practice, and it is usually with practice that students of history and literature are most concerned. Faith (like action) is often a response based upon a perception of reality which is founded in time and in culture. At once a part of history, it is also apart from it, though it is not exactly true that faith is founded on belief. "Faith is an almost priceless treasure," Smith observed, "and the modern world has been in desperate search of it. But the spectre of having to believe has stood in the way. Early in the century there were some who would have liked to believe but could not. The role of belief in the history of religious life has been turned quite upside down." [5]

Yet in the medieval period as in the modern, received tradition takes many forms, and both faith and belief are susceptible to mutual influence and to individual variation. In many cases the attitudes implied by devout practice give important evidence of the way the individual mediates between them, and what often emerges from this mediation is a form of spirituality.[6]

The chapters which follow explore some at least of the attitudes contained in texts (including literary texts, whose usefulness in exploring certain non-literary concerns I have accepted as a given) written

---

[4] See Smith, *Faith and Belief*, pp. 263 ff. on Augustine and pp. 78-9 and 142 on Aquinas. Smith points out that *credo* "began in Christian usage as a term to designate an act of self-commitment, in which the will is predominant ... . Later, *credo* came to be regarded by some as ... an act in which the mind plays a predominant role" (79). On late medieval attitudes which developed under nominalism see Heiko Augustinus Oberman, *The Harvest of Medieval Theology. Gabriel Biel and Late Medieval Nominalism* (Cambridge, Mass.: Harvard University Press, 1963), pp. 68-89.

[5] Smith, *Faith and Belief*, p. 124. See further chapter 6, "The English Word 'Believe'," pp, 105-27.

[6] The bibliography is enormous. On the history of the term (which is by no means a nineteenth-century French Catholic invention) see Walter Principe, "Toward Defining Spirituality," *Sciences Religieuses/Studies in Religion*, 12 (1983), 127-141.

between the eleventh and sixteenth centuries. These texts, together with the implications they contain and with the other evidences preserved from this period, seem to me to reveal the complex and sometimes contradictory qualities of medieval faith, but there are three major issues or themes which I touch on repeatedly throughout the book, and which I should like to indicate here:

1. The ways in which spirituality is rooted finally in religious persons, not in texts or practices or conventions.
2. The interaction of gender and spirituality.
3. The relationship of mysticism to spirituality.

The first point needs to be insisted upon if only to avoid the suggestion that the student of spirituality is concerned finally with external objects of whatever sort, texts, practices, devotions, and the like. On the contrary, what the student shares with the religious person is a search for meaning, and it is this which is at the heart of our program. But it is not only individual or psychological meaning which concerns us. Spirituality is usually communal in some or all of its aspects and implications, and a sense of community—as well as a sense of the individual—is rooted in many of the observances with which I have been concerned throughout the following chapters. The examination of a devout attitude will sometimes lead beyond the bounds of Europe, or even Christianity. A genuinely religious quest is rarely undertaken in one's own interests, at least not exclusively, but in the interests of others, too. Even a mystic's example is just that, and is intended for others, however *sui generis* the mystical moment itself may be.[7]

Gender is now widely studied in medieval circles, and students of visionary literature in particular have made important contributions to its dissemination. At the same time there is increasingly a tendency to examine it as if it were a separate discipline, and to examine less enthusiastically the ways in which it is connected to (or becomes a connection between or among) other aspects of medieval culture and religion, and this practice seems to me sometimes to lead to distortion. One of these chapters—by no means the only one concerned

---

[7] The bibliography here is not small either, but see Louis Dupré, "The Christian Experience of Mystical Union," *The Journal of Religion*, 69 (1989), 1-13 and for the development of mysticism, two recent studies by Bernard McGinn, *The Presence of God: A History of Western Christian Mysticism*, Volume I, *The Foundations of Mysticism*, and Volume II, *The Growth of Mysticism* (New York: Crossroad, 1991 and 1994).

with the relationship between gender and spirituality—concerns a fifteenth-century English work often referred to as an autobiography and now known universally as the *Book of Margery Kempe*. In that chapter I attempt to contextualize certain aspects of the *Book*, but in doing so I seek as well to articulate the ways in which gender functioned to inform Margery Kempe's spirituality, not to frustrate it. At the same time I have tried not to overstate the evident if proto-feminism present in that extraordinary text. The *Book of Margery Kempe* is one of those works which has been widely read and discussed, and I have often been struck by the way in which nonmedievalists have made important contributions to its criticism, particularly when they are discussing its feminism. The reasons for this are complex, but one seems to be that nonmedievalists are somewhat more inclined to allow that the feminist attitudes it represents may be more proto than modern. There is understandable temptation with a work like this one to turn it into a key for all locks: but its actual concerns are fairly specific. What the *Book* does address, sometimes with startling originality, is the issue of the relationship between gender and spirituality, a topic which is in its way as modern as any could wish, and the components of which are represented in the *Book* as neither mutually repressive nor starkly dissimilar.

The third larger issue which appears throughout the book is a concern for the relationship between the mystic and the world. My practice has been to lessen, not to increase, the distance between the two, while also retaining a sense of the mystic as a religious seer informed by, and often responsive to, theological teachings which impinge upon spirituality. I do not treat the mystic simply as a visionary whose utterances may be accounted for in largely secular terms, as now sometimes happens. Yet it has been with the effect of the mystic that I have been most concerned, and with the ways in which the mystic's spirituality at once springs from, and resorts to, those to whom he or she speaks or writes. This connectedness of mysticism, this ability of the mystic to explain, or at least to transmit, something of his or her experience has implications for the ways in which Christian spirituality has traditionally communicated itself. This prayer gives way to that one; this practice grows from those; this text, this devotion, this person echoes that. It is the same; it is different. But at certain moments this assurance breaks down, whether in the face of death, or cultural confrontation, or old age, or some other factor. But somehow, in Christianity at least, mystics are at the heart of everything.

I thus have been concerned with the development of the subject in prayer and in meditation ("The Origin of Affective Devotion," "Christ's Blood"); the role and importance of gender ("Is the *Book of Margery Kempe* a Feminist Text?," "Feminism and Spirituality in Chaucer"); and the inclusion of antecedent (and sometimes unexpected) sources, particularly when they contribute significantly to the spirituality of the text in question ("Buddhism and Spirituality in Medieval England," "The Gods Appear: Representing the Divine in Quest Narratives"). I have been concerned as well to identify religious values, and I have not hesitated to educe modern parallels when these seem to me appropriate and helpful ("The *Arma Christi* and Power," "The New World," "The Liberation of Mysticism"), though in all cases my concern has been with the spirituality which these concerns expose. I share the modern (and medieval) view that often spirituality can be identified in (but not exclusively with!) those whom society has marginalized, and as I have insisted in my title, it is with boundaries that I am often concerned. But the boundaries of spirituality do not exist between the spirit and the world, still less between heterodoxy and orthodoxy. Rather they exist between and among persons as they define their lives and consider their ends. They are concerned primarily with values and attitudes, and also, if to a lesser extent, with assumptions, as these manifest themselves in the programs of action which make up human life.

"Some while ago," Wilfred Cantwell Smith wrote, "in the *New York Times Book Review*, there appeared a critique of a novel ... by the American writer [Bernard] Malamud. The reviewer protested in passing against what he considered to be a pretentious remark: that 'to be Jewish is to be human.' He seemed deeply irritated by this. The protest was, I suggest, obtuse. One cannot understand Jews unless one understands both the truth and the profundity of that quoted observation. For Jews, if not for every man, to be Jewish is indeed to be human. To fail in understanding this is to misunderstand not only Jews, but humanity." [8]

---

[8] Smith, *Faith and Belief*, p. 136. The novel referred to was *The Fixer*, which was reviewed by George P. Elliott in *The New York Times* [Sunday] *Book Review* for September 4, 1966, p. 1.

The examination of religious attitudes requires this same grasp of the closeness of the bond between being human and being religious, and a willingness to admit it into discourse. Literary texts, perhaps more than any other, seem to be best suited to this task, and that is why they figure so prominently here, though I have not hesitated to reach out to others, and to the larger cultural circumstance which it seems to me these texts, these attitudes, inform.

CHAPTER ONE

THE ORIGIN OF AFFECTIVE DEVOTION

The relationship of an individual to his or her God is such an important aspect of late medieval—and much modern—Christianity, that it is difficult to think of it as "starting" anywhere. Attitudes of wonder and adoration were so widespread—at least before the nineteenth century—that they almost seem to be integral to any human encounter with the divine, and no one who partakes of these attitudes in any century would agree that they are in any real sense objectless. But during the Western medieval period these attitudes took on a particular character, one rooted both in structural formulations and in a certain responsiveness to the requirements of what came to be called the individual. The object of this first chapter is to consider both of these circumstances, as a way of beginning to address the larger concern for the role of faith in the development and transmission of medieval spirituality.[1]

I.

In the late ancient world a felt interest in holiness, conditioned, as Peter Brown has taught us, by prophecy, was indeed present, and changes having been made, ancient attitudes contributed to Christian perceptions. But an individual responsiveness which was not limited to a select group and which was expected, at least to a degree, of all was a manifestly Christian concern, and from the beginning such attitudes were linked to themes of conversion, repentance and personal salvation.[2] Attitudes were conditioned further by the doctrinal con-

---

[1] On the existence of the individual, see (among many places) the exchange between Caroline Walker Bynum, "Did the Twelfth Century Discover the Individual?," *Journal of Ecclesiastical History*, 31 (1980), 1-17, reprinted in *Jesus as Mother. Studies in the Spirituality of the High Middle Ages*, Publications of the Center for Medieval and Renaissance Studies, UCLA, No. 19 (Berkeley, Los Angeles and London: University of California Press, 1982, rpt. 1984), pp. 82-109, and *contra*, Colin Morris, "Individualism in Twelfth-Century Religion. Some Further Reflections," *Journal of Ecclesiastical History*, 31 (1980), 195-206.

[2] Peter Brown, *Society and the Holy in Late Antiquity* (London: Faber and Faber, 1982), *passim.*, but reprinting Brown's influential "The Rise and Function of the Holy Man

texts and individual practices supplied by the Christian community, particularly those influenced by Augustine, but the role of the individual Christian remained, though sometimes hedged in by religious convention and by social and economic status. Even those who could not abide the community reflected its presence. Banished from Rome in 385, Jerome would retire (as Brown remarks) to a "somewhat more distinguished city"—Bethlehem—there to pursue, or at least argue for, an asceticism which seemed a model for Christian holiness, so long as one did not much trouble about the presence of others.[3] But given a choice, most Christians (and others) would prefer Rome to Bethlehem, precisely because of its urban advantages. Augustine's spirituality becomes finally social when he becomes a bishop and has to account for a city.[4] From the beginning, Christian spirituality assumed the presence of others, whether as preceptors, colleagues, or subordinates. Armed with an acute sense of community, the Christian in late antiquity responded to the divine in a variety of ways, for the most part in keeping with his or her social or economic status. But the notion of a felt relationship between a

---

in Late Antiquity," originally published in the *Journal of Roman Studies*, 61 (1971), 80-101, here reprinted pp. 103-152. See too Garth Fowden, "The Pagan Holy Man in Late Antique Society," *Journal of Hellenic Studies*, 102 (1982), 33-59. The standard biography of St. Augustine, the closest connection between late ancient and the medieval world is still Brown's, *Augustine of Hippo, A Biography* (London: Faber and Faber, 1967), but see now Brown's *The Body and Society. Men, Women and Sexual Renunciation in Early Christianity* Lectures on the History of Religions Sponsored by the American Council of Learned Societies, New Series, Number 13 (New York: Columbia University Press, 1988), in which he argues that "the Christianity of the High and Later Middle Ages—to say nothing of the Christianity of our own times—is separated from the Christianity of the Roman world by a chasm almost as vast as that which still appears to separate us from the moral horizons of a Mediterranean Islamic community" (p. xvii). In earlier periods the difficulties of interpreting individual religious attitudes are proportionately greater: see E. R. Dodds, "The Religion of the Ordinary Man in Classical Greece," in *The Ancient Concept of Progress and Other Essays on Greek Literature and Belief* (Oxford: Clarendon Press, 1973), pp. 140-155.

[3] Jerome, *In Ecclesiasten*, Praef. in M. Adriaen, ed. *Corpus Christianorum* 72:249, cited by Brown, *The Body and Society*, p. 367 n.8, who points out that the alternate reading, *angustiori*, "somewhat smaller," is equally ironic.

[4] F. Van der Meer, *Augustine the Bishop. The Life and Work of a Father of the Church* trans. Brian Battershaw and G. R. Lamb (London and New York: Sheed and Ward, 1961), 129-198 and 453 ff. See too Peter Brown, *Augustine of Hippo*, pp. 244-258. Recently Susanna Elm has proposed that asceticism began as an urban movement, and one in which, until the fourth century, men and women participated together. *'Virgins of God.' The Making of Asceticism in Late Antiquity*. Oxford Classical Monographs. (Oxford: Clarendon Press, 1994).

divine being and a human agent is a medieval development, resting as it does on a concept of the individual which began to gain currency only in the eleventh century.[5]

But if spirituality was rooted in the city, devotion grew out of the monastery. Only in the monastery were personal attitudes acknowledged along with communal ones, thus setting up an opposition which would endure at the heart of Christian devotion for the next millennium. Chapter 20 of Benedict's *Rule* turns to the nature of the monk's spirituality:

> Whenever we want to ask some favor of a powerful man, we do it humbly and respectfully, for fear of presumption. How much more important, then, to lay our petitions before the Lord God of all things with the utmost humility and sincere devotion. We must know that God regards our purity of hearts and tears of compunction, not our many words. ('Et non in multiloquio, sed in puritate cordis et compunctione lacrimarum nos exaudiri sciamus.') Prayer should therefore be short and pure, unless perhaps it is prolonged under the inspiration of divine grace. ('Et ideo brevis debet esse et pura oratio, nisi forte ex affectu inspirationis divinae gratiae protendatur.') In community, however, prayer should always be brief; and when the superior gives the signal, all should rise together.[6]

The monastic influence remained in a tension, always present in Christian spirituality, between the requirements of the subject in prayer and those of the community of which he or she was a part.[7]

---

[5] Dodds notes that "Aristotle denies that there can be such a thing as *philia* between man and God, the disparity being too great; and in the *Magna Moralia* one of his pupils remarks that it would be eccentric (*atopon*) for anyone to claim that he loved Zeus. Classical Greece had in fact no word for such an emotion: *philotheos* makes its appearance for the first time at the end of the fourth century and remains a rarity in pagan authors" ("The Religion of the Ordinary Man," pp. 140-141).

[6] *RB 1980. The Rule of St. Benedict in Latin and English with Notes*, ed. Timothy Fry, O.S.B., *et al.* (Collegeville, Minnesota: The Liturgical Press, 1981), pp. 216-17. The passage may contain "an allusion to the monastic custom of prostrating for silent prayer after the psalm, even if no psalter collect was to follow....Thus the psalm (reading) awakened a response (interior prayer) that was sometimes gathered up into the words of a public prayer (psalter collect). This three-stage movement—reading, personal prayer, collect—was an important way for Christians to appropriate the deeper meaning of the psalms" (p. 413).

[7] Certain devout practices seem to call upon the practitioner to engage himself particularly deeply in prayer, in a way which may prefigure later devotions. See for example the Veneration of the Cross ceremony, recorded in British Library Cotton MS. A.xiv, and printed in *A Pre-Conquest English Prayer-Book (BL MSS Cotton Galba A.xiv and Nero A.ii (ff. 3-13)*, ed. Bernard James Muir, Henry Bradshaw Society vol. CIII (Woodbridge, Suffolk: The Boydell Press, 1988), pp. 143-46.

Both demands were absolute, and yet each acknowledged the requirements of the other. The tension between the denied self and the affirmed individual remained as important within the monastic enclosure as in time it was to become outside it.[8] Monks withdrew from the world, not from the human race, and their devotions sought the fullest expression of a spiritual love which assumed the presence of others, not only of the monk himself.

But evidence for monastic devotion is found less in the Psalter than in prayerbooks owned by individual monks, manuscripts which, in their citation, selection, and very existence break with the more formal organization of the monastic hours. These early prayerbooks sought to extend the boundaries of monastic prayer, and in doing so at once reflected and precipitated a new development in Western spirituality.[9] The method chosen appears disarmingly simple—the prayerbooks extended the adoration proffered to God and the honor accorded the Virgin and certain of the saints—but it also recognized and engaged the individual in prayer, treating him both as an individual, autonomous subject, and also as part of a Christian community which existed outside of time and space.[10] As the individual

---

[8] The central tradition was monastic, which involved both personal and social standing, at least from those who elected their profession. C.H. Lawrence, *Medieval Monasticism. Forms of Religious Life in Western Europe in the Middle Ages*, 2nd edition (London and New York: Longman, 1989, rpt. 1993), and Derwas J. Chitty, *The Desert a City. An Introduction to the Study of Egyptian and Palestinian Monasticism under the Christian Empire* (Oxford: Basil Blackwell, 1966): both focus on the spiritual life of monasteries. More specialized accounts of early monastic spirituality concerned with the self are numerous. See Kassius Hallinger, "The Spiritual Life of Cluny in the Early Days," in Noreen Hunt, ed. *Cluniac Monasticism in the Central Middle Ages* (London: Macmillan, 1971), pp. 29-55, and Gillian R. Evans, " *Mens Devota,* The Literary Community of the Devotional Works of John of Fècamp and St. Anselm," *Medium AEvum*, 43 (1974), 105-15. Chitty is now supplemented by Yizhar Hirschfeld, *The Judean Desert Monasteries in the Byzantine Period.* (New Haven and London: Yale University Press, 1992).

[9] Early English prayerbooks are listed in Beate Günzel, ed. *AElfwine's Prayerbook (London, British Library Cotton Titus D.xxvi+xxviii)* Henry Bradshaw Society volume CVIII (London: Boydell Press, 1993), "Manuscripts containing Private Prayers," pp. 205-6. MS Cotton Titus D.xxvi (a manuscript of the early eleventh century) contains an interesting text which the editor has called "Directions for Private Devotions," and printed on p. 143. It emphasizes both personal and social considerations, stressing, among other things, that the subject in prayer should conceive of God as "almighty," remember his sins and pray for God's mercy, and recollect how Christ suffered "for eall mancyn" [for all mankind], themes which would remain constant in Christian devotion for the next five centuries and beyond.

[10] See for example Barbara H. Rosenwein, *Rhinoceros Bound. Cluny in the Tenth Century* (Philadelphia: University of Pennsylvania Press, 1982), pp. 84-100 for the place of liturgy and the *Rule*, and a short but interesting sociological analysis of some at

begins to appear in the organization and reformulation of monastic prayerbooks, the first practical sense of the individual's responsiveness to God emerges clearly.

Early Carolingian prayerbooks had preserved relatively few private prayers specifically associated with the cross, that staple of devotions designed to engage individual affective feeling, and the prayers to the saints they contain are generally limited to the Virgin, the Apostles, and Confessors. A late ninth-century manuscript in the National Library in Rome, however, MS. Sessorianus 71, contains a rich assortment of prayers, including in its third part (folios 57 verso to 75), a number of prayers which reveal the depth and range of private prayers available to the Carolingian compiler.[11] A prayer to the Father is followed by one to the Son and by one to the Holy Spirit. A prayer to the Trinity follows (nos. 1-4). The sequence is then repeated (nos. 5-8). A prayer to Christ is followed by thirteen prayers to saints, among whom Augustine and Gregory figure prominently (nos. 9-24), and these by a new series of prayers to the persons of the Trinity (nos. 25-27). These are followed by a particularly suggestive sequence, which focuses on the sinfulness of the reader (no. 28), on Christ crucified (nos. 29-34), and on the Virgin (nos. 35-37). This section is in turn followed by a series of prayers to St. Michael Archangel (nos. 38-39), and those to saints Peter, Paul, Andrew, and all apostles (nos. 41—44). These then give way to prayers directed to saints Martin, Stephen, Benedict, Cassian, and all confessors (nos. 45—49). But what is extraordinary about all of the Carolingian compilations, including this one, is the way they record the prayers: grouped, for the

---

least of the structures present at Cluny. But the role of sin, so important in establishing a sense of self, retained its importance too. See H. E. J. Cowdrey, *The Cluniacs and the Gregorian Reform* (Oxford: Clarendon Press, 1970), "the especial preoccupation of eleventh-century Christianity with the 'remissio peccatorum' has never been satisfactorily explained by historians. But so far as its religious background is concerned, it seems to have been, in large measure, a consequence of the state of the penitential system of the Western Church at this particular juncture" (p. 121).

[11] See Dom. André Wilmart, O.S.B., *Precum Libelli Quattuor Aevi Karoloini* Prior Part (all published) (Rome: Ephemerides Liturgicae, 1940), *passim* for a collection of four such prayerbooks, and, for a treatment of MS. Sessorianus 71, Wilmart's remarkable study "Le Manuel de Prières de Saint Jean Gualbert," *Revue Bénédictine,* 48 (1936), 259-99, which contains, *inter alia*, an analysis of the prayers found in the manuscript. In recording where the individual prayers are elsewhere preserved—the list could not be complete in view of time and the circumstances in which Wilmart was working—the author performed a very great service, illuminating, really for the first time, the extent to which individual prayers circulated across Europe. Private prayers are discussed on pp. 276-86.

most part, according to the category—confessor, apostle, virgin—of saint supplicated or the aspect of the deity adored, prayer follows prayer with what seems to be almost studied disinterest in the devout reader's state of mind while reading the texts, though numbers 28-37, with their focus on the sinfulness of the reader, Christ's passion, and the Virgin, suggest the very beginning of an interest in the reader's devotional inclinations.

However briefly, then, MS. Sessorianus 71 has begun to suggest a new concern. Its selection of prayers—many very brief—follow an abbreviated psalter, itself an invitation to private reflection. The traditions of honor and worship, deeply rooted in monastic tradition, find full expression, as does the sense that the individual, before God, will now be moved to the deepest of recollections. He will pray, he will be moved to devotion, and in that movement the prayers in the manuscript will play their part. There is only a brief attempt to engage the individual in the Sessorianus manuscript, but there is for a moment a gingerly, even a grudging, sense that the manuscript has a use, and that that use is to move the subject in his or her devotions.

This concern for the devotional attitude varies, and what may be true in one manuscript will not be so in another. But it is not too much to say that in some manuscripts a disposition to prayer, though assumed, is now consciously addressed, as is the state of mind of the subject in prayer. These concerns become even more evident when the prayerbook is intended for a particular individual, particularly one who will attend to his devotions apart from his fellow monks. In these cases the compilers of devotional manuscripts, themselves monks, recorded the first examples of an individual response to God.

II.

There is among the Egerton manuscripts in the British Library a small (11.5 cm. x 7.8 cm.) Latin prayerbook of 140 folios, MS. Egerton 3763, which was written for Archbishop Arnulf II of Milan about 1000 A.D. Its present state (and its present binding) were effected in 1907 by the English collector W.C. Dysons Perrins, who recognized two parts of the manuscript in two different private collections and acquired them. The rebound manuscript was acquired by the British Museum in 1958, shortly before the sale of Dyson Perrins' remarkable library.[12]

Although descended from earlier prayerbooks, the Egerton manuscript represents a departure from them in size, format, and what can only be called identity. In spite of the ecclesiastical significance of its illustrious owner and its Benedictine associations, it is not precisely a monastic production. Rather, in its *orationes peculiares*, the series of fifty-nine private prayers which follow the psalter and, with six benedictions, conclude the manuscript, it stands well apart from most of its ancestors, for these prayers, connected as they are to the psalter which comes before, give unmistakable testimony to the existence of a rapidly developing affective spirituality now appearing in the West. The text of the manuscript, including the private prayers and the benedictions which conclude it, has been printed in its entirety by Dom Odilio Heiming, O.S.B., and the numbering of the prayers I follow here is the one present in his study.[13]

It is of course impossible to say that affective devotion begins in any one manuscript, or that it was the creation of a single person. But the Egerton prayerbook presents texts which, taken together, suggest a conscious effort to engage deeply the individual reader in his prayers and devotions. It is true that many of the prayers which make up the final section of the manuscript appear elsewhere, but even more clearly than in the Sessorianus manuscript, their organization, rather than their individual content, sets them apart. With no order to follow, the Egerton scribe (or possibly the scribe of his exemplar) arranged the articles according to what he understood to be the requirements and disposition of the reader, and the result is a new creation, one in which contrast and suggestion were central to the presentation of the text. The section of private prayers in the manuscript opens with eight prayers in which repentance for sin contrasts

---

[12] T.J. Brown, G.M. Meredith-Owens and D. H. Turner, "Manuscripts from the Dyson Perrins Collection," *The British Museum Quarterly*, 23 (1960/1), 27-38. Dyson Perrins' library was sold at Sotheby's in three separate sales, on December 9, 1958, December 1, 1959, and November 29, 1960. Ten of Dyson Perrins' manuscripts found their way into the British Museum (now the British Library) after his death on 29 January, 1958, two by gift, eight by private treaty. Egerton 3763 was one of those eight.

[13] The early work on Egerton MS. 3763 was by D. H. Turner, "The Prayer-Book of Archbishop Arnulph II of Milan," *Revue Bénédictine*, 70 (1960), 360-392, and Odilo Heiming, O.S.B., "Ein Benediktinisch-Ambrosianisches Gebetbuch des frühen 11. Jahrhunderts, Brit. Mus. Egerton 3763 (ehemals Dyson Perrins 48)," *Archiv für Liturgiewissenschaft*, VIII 2 (1964), 325-435, prints the text of the manuscript, including the fifty-nine "orationes peculiares," pp. 399-424. I am indebted throughout to both studies.

with an attestation of the truths of Christianity (nos. 1-8). Conditioned by repeated invocations to divine mercy, their effect is to dispose the reader to an awareness of his own sinful state and of past weaknesses, against which stands a present source of strength. The first prayer calls upon God for mercy, thus both acknowledging the presence of the individual and focusing his thoughts on his own past sins, and so on himself. The second turns more particularly to the (unnamed) sins themselves, *omnia peccata et crimina*, but the third turns from them to an acknowledgment of the power of the divine, and, by its tone of adoration, serves both to strengthen the subject in prayer, and to confirm him in his present reflection. Though brief, it comes at an important point in these opening devotions, representing a confirmation not only of God *omnipotens*, but also in the availability of that power. It is followed by two prayers (nos. 4-5), the first of which acknowledges sin, but sets against it the subject's dependence on Christ and on his Church, the second of which again attests to the availability of divine power. This complex series of acknowledgments, confessions, and confrontations issues in a long catalogue of sins in the sixth prayer, in which the settled and careful reader reviews a range of sin, fault, and failure, before turning to a prayer attributed to St. Augustine which will stand against the catalogue of transgressions he has just ennumerated. Throughout the first section of Egerton 3763 (nos. 1-32) the prayers have been organized into small clusters, usually with three or four to the group, and each containing a kind of turning point which controls the devotions before and after: the subject could read through and meditate upon them all, or restrict himself to one or two: but he would not escape the general orientation of the program, nor fail to be impressed by the contrasts which it develops. Thus the third prayer concerns God's power; the sixth reveals a list (and so the depth) of human weakness; the ninth turns to the history of Christian salvation, commencing with the Old Testament, a theme which the next three prayers (nos. 9-11) explore in full. No academic discourse, the second of this group (no. 10) applies the lessons of history directly to the subject in prayer, *Succurre mihi, deus meus, succurrite mihi sancti angeli*, linking the historic past of Abraham, Isaac, and Jacob directly to the subject in prayer.

This realization is particularly important for the next group of prayers (nos. 12-14), which are directly concerned with *seipso*, and in which the reader prays *Da mihi, domine, timorem tuum, compunctionem cordis, humilitatem mentis, conscientie puritatem* in a series of devotions which direct attention to the subject's person and to his spiritual state. The *credo* which the second of these three prayers contains clarifies the enlarged sense of self which it roots in reflection and meditation. This is a self which resides within a Christian community, and which takes its definition from an articulate sense of Christian teaching, rather than from the self alone. Yet even with this important qualification, the prayers reach well beyond the individual sense of guilt, already recorded, to a deeper consciousness of strength in community and personal place in an ordered, diverse universe.

Against this consciousness the next series of prayers (nos. 14-17) places a final *confessio* (no. 15) followed by a prayer, again attributed to St. Augustine, for mercy, and a final prayer on sin (no. 17): the four together constitute a review of all the themes elicited thus far. The subject group begins with a prayer attributed to "sancti Gregorii pape" (no. 18) which acts as a connecting prayer between groups. Like the prayers which precede it, it draws upon what has gone before, but turns to what will become the general themes of prayers 18-32, the Trinity and the Passion. The prayer leads into the first of the crossprayers (18a) which is linked to the Trinity: *Signa me pater. Signa me fili. Conserua me spiritus sancte*, and the two prayers are concluded by a third (no. 19) which, by its often repeated *miserere* begs for divine mercy. This request for mercy leads easily to a prayer to Jesus (no. 20), whose death brought salvation, and it is followed by three prayers to the Father (no. 21), the Son (no. 22), and the Holy Spirit (no. 23). The next prayer (no. 24) is directed to the Trinity. Thus ends the sequence which began with prayer 19, marking the shift from the Old Testament to the Trinity.

Though there is now a lacuna in the manuscript, prayers 25-26 return again to the Old Testament themes of prayers 9-11, emphasizing not their historical but their redemptive aspects: thus "St. Abel, St. Enoch, beatus Noae" and others prepare for the New Testament evangelists and those associated with Christ, who are also honored and petitioned. Prayer 25 is the first of the third grouping of prayers (nos. 25-32) that continues with a prayer attributed to St. Gregory, which also sounds the Old Testament theme, followed by six prayers (nos. 27-32) on the Holy Cross, which stand against the Old Testament reference of prayer 26, making explicit the implied typology of the sequence, an important addition to the program of prayer which has been developing.

This sequence now confirms this movement by presenting a prayer on the cross itself (no. 27) and to Christ on the cross (no. 28), and then turning to a sequence of three prayers in which the subject presents himself before the cross and places himself under its protection (nos. 29-31). The sequence leads to a final invocation, by the sign of the cross, to a sequence of prayers to saints (nos. 33-59) which do not have the same concern with the subject-reader of the earlier part (nos. 1-32).

Throughout this first part of the manuscript (nos. 1-32), however, certain dominant themes and attitudes have emerged and developed. The preparation of the subject (nos. 1-8), through the realization of sin, attestation of divine goodness, and comfort in God's power, has given way in the second part (nos. 9-24) to a series of prayers, primarily in groups of three, which has led from a historical realization of the past (nos. 9-11), to a concern for the Christian in his community (nos. 12-14), to a series on God's power over sin and his redemptive mercy (nos. 15-17) which culminates in his care for humanity (nos. 18-20) and an awareness of the power of the Trinity (nos. 21-24). This sequence is itself followed by the third (nos. 25-32), which begins again in the Old Testament (nos. 25-26) and culminates in Christ's cross (nos. 27-32).

These prayers were derived, as both Turner and Heiming have shown, from a number of monastic sources, but it is the order in which they have been presented that is most revealing. Not only do they represent a clear program of private devotion, but the history of the manuscript suggests that it derived from—but also departed from—north Italian Benedictine devotions which were themselves influenced by northern European and, in some cases, ultimately English sources.[14] But the Egerton manuscript departs from the earlier tradition as well. There is a sense in it that the reader has to contend with a world against which his prayerbook will give him both comfort and a refuge.

In important ways the church in Northern Italy was as embattled

[14] Turner notes that "seven ... prayers [in the manuscript] can be traced back to Anglo-Saxon books, whilst the majority were common in texts of the Carolingean era. Compared with the more strictly Frankish collections of prayers, Egerton 3763 ... show[s] an increase in devotion to the Cross and the Saints" (p. 368), and goes on to remark that "[i]t is the peculiar position of Egerton 3763 to stand in time and content at the beginning of that development of private devotion and prayer which was the great contribution of the 11th century to the history of the spiritual life" (p. 389).

as it was anywhere in the early eleventh century,[15] and though the badness of the times is a universal convention, it is not difficult to believe that, against the corruptions of time and place, the effects of Cluniac reform and northern spirituality were making themselves felt in the south. The devotions in Egerton addressed the individual in a way that was unusual for manuscript prayerbooks during this period. The reader was no longer assumed to be static in his responses, or limited to the traditional attitudes of repentance, adoration, petition, and worship. If his devotions were to involve him, then there must be an individual present to engage and respond, and the unmistakable implication of the Egerton devotions is that the concept of the individual is not only recognized, it is understood to be at the heart of a program concerned with repentance, felt prayer, and emulation of saints. The spirituality present in Egerton is conditioned by the subject-reader's involvement with Christ's passion, which in turn links him to the larger Christian community through which that passion is shared. With its new orientation and expanded concerns the Egerton prayerbook may fairly be said to stand at the head of the tradition of affective prayer and meditation which, in subsequent centuries, moved cleric and lay person alike.

Yet for all of its importance in demonstrating the dissemination of monastic spirituality, Egerton's testimony is that of an effect, not a cause. It engages the individual Christian, whom it conceives of as an active subject confronting a not particularly sympathetic world. To him it offers the strength and recollection—but also the joy—of the psalter and the liturgy, and the mortification and exaltation of prayer. All of these states had their roots in Benedictine practice, but their organization into a portable manuscript designed for reading by an individual, even by an archbishop, suggests a somewhat altered spirituality. No longer must the subject relinquish his self in order to approach God; no longer are the circumstances in which he finds himself assumed to offer support to his spiritual life. He will now turn to prayer, like any devout monk, and yet like an embattled saint he must arm himself against the world. A powerful sense of the world and its wiles informs Archbishop Arnulf's prayerbook, which seeks to stir the reader, already disposed to prayer, to a lively consciousness of

[15] Chris Wickham, *Early Medieval Italy. Central Power and Local Society 400-1000* New Studies in Medieval History (Totowa, N.J. and London: Barnes & Noble Books and Macmillan Press, Ltd., 1981), especially pp. 188-91.

his spiritual state. But Egerton 3763 is the first fully developed example we have for this practice, the first time self-consciousness is presented as an integral part of private reflection. Earlier prayers were born of monastic devotion; Egerton's draw on the same sources, but with an altered sense of the subject. It is a small change which, repeated and emphasized, would become a large one. It is the thin edge of a wedge.

The circumstances of the Egerton prayerbook are at once familiar and unfamiliar. The prayer (and the hand), as Turner first noted, do indeed reach back to the Carolingian prayerbook.[16] Its Augustinian psalter, even in the abbreviated form present in Egerton, was not unknown to the ninth century, and certain of the prayers received new emphasis in the Frankish monastic revival. But beyond these influences, Egerton 3763 also shows the organization of prayers prefigured in the Sessorianus MS. Structure reflects use. Prayers follow the discipline of the psalter and direct the subject toward admired saints, but they also reflect something of the subject himself. He now begins his devotions with an acute awareness of his fallible and sinning state. The appeals for mercy and pity with which the Egerton prayerbook begins, familiar enough in earlier tradition, receive an emphasis and a focus which is new. The subject begins not with adoration but with repentance, and it is from this that his devotions rise. In time he will turn to the greatest of saints—Augustine, Ambrose, Gregory among them—and in acknowledging their powers he will seek to emulate a greater good.[17]

---

[16] Turner notes that the "revival of Benedictinism in Northern Italy may be related to the monastic origin of so many of the prayers in Egerton 3763...[which] is written in a Carolingian miniscule which looks more to the tenth than the eleventh century" (383).

[17] The illuminations contained in MS. Egerton 3763, which I have not discussed, are reproduced in color in Angelo Paredi, ed. *Vita e meriti di S. Ambrogio. Testo inedito del secolo nono illustrato con le miniature del salterio di Arnolfo.* Fontes Ambrosiani in lucem editi cura et studio Bibliothecae Ambrosianae XXXVII (Milan: Casa Editrice Ceschina, 1964), *passim.* Taken together, they work toward the awareness which is such an important part of the manuscript's devotional program. By presenting the image of the saint addressed they testify, among other things, to the previous but real existence of his body, and so encourage the devout reader to emulate and remember. They may have carried other connotations as well. To take but one example: whatever the connotations of the "Vexilla Regis" for contemporary papal policy, it stood as well for the battle the Christian must fight in the world, however exalted his station. As such, there was no surer sign of commitment to faith, and to the notion of individual commitment itself. But the attitudes represented in the Egerton illuminations are traditional and unlike those associated with prayer in such later texts as the

III.

Apart from the testimony of a few witnesses like Egerton 3763, evidence for the development of a new religious consciousness appears as well in the transmission of certain prayers, particularly those addressed to the Virgin, whose devotion seemed always to involve a greater measure of felt responsiveness than those addressed to Christ or to the Trinity or to the majority of saints—though by the twelfth century evidence of affective devotion can be discovered in many devotional texts.[18] I shall treat here only one prayer to the Blessed Virgin, the *Singularis Meriti*, and place its earliest version against those preserved in three eleventh-century English manuscripts and one late thirteenth-century Norman psalter, so as to show the kinds of responses, several indicating a movement toward affective prayer, which the prayer evoked. In doing so I have attached a marked degree of importance to individual variants—the changes which scribes and other writers introduced—which I do not believe to have been at all random, and which taken together show with some clarity the early history of affective devotion in England.

Singularis Meriti is a useful prayer for this purpose because of its relative popularity and because it is possible to observe limits to its circulation. By the twelfth century the primitive version I am concerned with here was replaced by a later and longer redaction, which indeed shows both variation and affective elements, but has not the illustrative interest of its early ancestor.

Early Version

Cited from: Henri Barré, *Prières anciennes de l' Occident à la mère du Sauveur, des origines à saint Anselme* (Paris: P. Bethielleux, 1963), pp. 75-76.

---

manual of prayer attributed to Peter the Chanter. See Richard C. Trexler, ed., *The Christian at Prayer. An Illustrated Prayer Manual Attributed to Peter the Chanter.* Medieval and Renaissance Texts and Studies, volume 44 (Binghamton, New York: SUNY Press, 1987).

[18] See Mary Clayton, *The Cult of the Virgin Mary in Anglo-Saxon England*, Cambridge Studies in Anglo-Saxon England 2 (Cambridge: Cambridge University Press, 1990), and Henri Barré, *Prières anciennes de l' occident à la Mère du Sauveur des origines à saint Anselme* (Paris: P. Lethiellevx, 1963) for accounts of early devotion to the Blessed Virgin; and for a searching theological examination see Ignace de la Potterie, S.J., *Mary in the Mystery of the Covenant*, trans. Bertrand Buby, S.M. (New York: Alba House, 1992). I am grateful to Edward Bodnar, S.J., to Msgr. Walter Edyvean and to the late A. N. Sherwin-White for helpful comment on this part of the chapter.

[Version 1]

OBSECRATIO AD SANCTAM DEI GENETRICEM

Singularis meriti sola sine exemplo mater et uirgo Maria, quam Dominus ita mente et corpore inuiolatam custodiuit ut digna existeres ex qua sibi nostrae redemptionis pretium Dei filius corpus aptaret, obsecro te, misericordissima, per quam totus saluatus est mundus, intercede pro me spurcissimo et cunctis iniquitatibus foedo, ut qui ex meis iniquitatibus nihil aliud dignus sum quam aeternum subire supplicium, tuis, uirgo splendidissima, saluatus meritis per[h]enne consequar regnum. Amen.

L=Liber Trecensis (9th cent.); B=Beauvais Psalter; F=Fleury Ms.; P=Paris Ms.; T=Tours, Troyes, 1742.

Obsecratio . . . genetricem] Oratio ad sanctam Mariam F, Oratio eiusdem ad sanctam Mariam L; 3 inuiolatam] *om.* L; existres] existris L; 5 misericordissima] *add.* Domina L; 6 foedo] fedo T, foedatissimo F, fetido P; nihil] nil FPL; 7 aeternum] aeternae damnationis F; 8 perhenne] perenne FTPL; Amen] *om.* L, Per Dominum F, per eundem P.

Translation

Virgin mother Mary, alone without parallel for your unique merit, whom the Lord so protected unsullied in mind and heart, that you were worthy of being the one from whom the Son of God fashioned for himself a body as the price of our redemption, I beg you, most merciful one, through whom the entire world has been saved, intercede for me, who am most vile and defiled by all iniquities, that I who am worthy because of my sins to undergo nothing other than eternal punishment, may obtain the everlasting kingdom, saved by your merits, most glorious virgin. Amen.

BL Cotton MS. Titus D XXVII, folio 82-82 verso

[Version 2]

Winchester, written for AElfwine the deacon, who became abbot in 1035. N. R. Ker, *Catalogue of Manuscripts Containing Anglo-Saxon* (Oxford: Clarendon Press, 1957, rpt. 1990), No. 202, pp. 264-66.[19]

[19] Ker reports "The manuscript was the personal property of AElfwine at the time when he was deacon of New Minster—he became abbot in 1035—as appears from obits in the calendar D.xxvii ff. 3-8v...and from an entry on D.xxvii f. 13... The drawing on D.xxvii f. 65v is inscribed 'Hec crux consignet AElfwinum corpore mente' " (p. 265). The manuscript has now been published (see note 9, above), and the prayer appears on p. 134.

Throughout this and subsequent texts I have modernized word division, but preserved capitalization and the ampersand, which may have functioned as guides to devotion. I have retained only the *punctus*, but have printed *punctus elevatus* as *punctus*. I have not recorded the cedilla. Page division is recorded by a double stroke, thus: //.

ORATIO DE S*AN*C*TA* MARIA
Singularis gratia sola sine exemplo mater & uirgo maria quam d*ominus* ita mente & corpore castam inuiolatamq*ue* custodiuit ut digna existeres ex qua sibi n*ost*re redemptionis precium d*e*i filius corpus aptauit. Obsecro te misericordissima p*er* cuius partum totus saluatus est mundus intercede pro me misero spurcissimo // cunctis iniquitatibus fedo ut qui ex meis actib*us* nihil aliud dignus sum quam eternum subire supplicium sed tuis uirgo splendidissima saluatus meritis & intercessionibus p*er*enne c*a*elorum consequar regnum. Annuente ih*es*u xpo filio tuo d*omi*no n*ostr*o qui cum d*omi*no co*a*eterno patre & sp*irit*u s*anct*o uiuit.

Bodleian Library MS. Douce 296, folio 125
(*Summary Catalogue* 21870) Arch. F.d.12
[Version 3]

ORATIO AD S*AN*C*T*AM MARIAM

SINGULARIS GRATIAE SOLA SINE EXEMplo mater & uirgo maria quam d*ominus* ita mente & corpore castam inuiolata*m*q*ue* custodiuit ut digna existeres ex qua sibi n*ost*rae redemptionis pr*a*ecium dei filius corpus aptaret. obsecro te misericordissima per cuius partum totus saluatus est mundus. intercede p*ro* me spurcissimo & cunctis iniquitatibus fedo. ut qui ex meis actibus nihil aliud dignus sum quam aeternum subire supplicium. tuis uirgo splendidissima saluata meritis & praecib*us* perhenne caelo*rum* consequar regnum. annuente filio tuo d*omi*no n*ost*ro qui cum deo coaeterno patre & sp*irit*u s*anct*o uiuit & regnat d*eus* p*er* om*n*ia s*ae*c*u*la s*ae*c*u*lo*rum* AM*EN*

BL Harley MS 863, folio 115 verso
[Version 4]

11th century (third quarter). N. R. Ker, *Catalogue of Manuscripts Containing Anglo-Saxon*, No. 232.

OR*ATIO* AD SANCTAM MARIAM
Singulari meriti solo sine exemplo mater uirgo S*AN*C*T*A MARIA. quam d*ominus* ita m*en*te & corp*o*re inuiolatam custodiuit. ut digna exis-

teres ex q*ua* sibi n*ostrae* redemptionis preciu*m* d*ei* filius aptaret. obsecro te mis*ericor*dissima domina p*er* quam totus saluatus e*st* mundus. intercede p*ro* me spurcissimo & cunctis iniquitatib*us* fedo ut qui meis ex iniquitatib*us* nichil aliud me*re*ar quam et*er*num subire supplicium. tuis uirgo splendidissima. & mater s*anct*issima saluat*us* meritis & precib*us* p*er*henne consequar regnum. Prestante d*omi*no n*ost*ro ih*es*u xpo cui est honor & gl*oria* in s*aecu*la s*aeculorum*. AMEN.

BL Arundel MS 60, folio 136
[Version 5]

11th century (fourth quarter) ca. 1099. N. R. Ker, *Catalogue of Manuscripts Containing Anglo-Saxon*, No. 134.[20]

OR*ATIO* DE S*ANCTAM* MARIA

SINGULARIS meriti sola sine exemplo mater & uirgo s*anct*a MARIA qua*m* d*ominus* ita mente & corpore custodiuit. ut digna ex qua sibi n*ostrae* redemptionis carne*m* dei filius aptar*et* obsecro te misericordissima p*er* qua*m* totus saluatus est mundus. intercede p*ro* me spurcissimo. & omniu*m* uitioru*m* pondere pregrauato. ut qui ex meritis meis nil aliud dignus su*m* qua*m* aeternum subire suppliciu*m* tuis uirgo splendissima saluatus meritis p*er*enne consequar regnu*m* p*er* xpm d*ominum* n*ostrum*.

BL Additional MS 16975, folio 260 verso
[Version 6]

Normandy. Psalter. Very late 13th or very early 14th century.

Or*atio* ad s*anct*am mariam.
Singularis meriti sola sine exemplo mater & uirgo maria templum d*omi*ni. sacrarium sp*iritus* sancti. q*ua*m d*ominus* ita mente & corpore inuiolatam custodiuit. Vt digna existeres. ex qua sibi n*ost*re rede*m*ptionis precium dei filius aptaret. Obsec*ro* te misericordissima d*omi*na p*er* q*ua*m totus mundus saluatus est. intercede pro me misero peccatore quia corpus meum obuolutum est iniquitatib*us* multis & pessimis & nichil aliud dignus sum. q*ua*m eternum subire supplicium. nisi tua michi succurrat pietas mater. pietatis. Dep*re*cor ergo te uirgo splendidissima. mi*sericordissima* mater. ut tuis meritis & int*er*cessionib*us* apud misericorde*m* filiu*m* tuum michi succurras. quatenus saluari & et*er*ne beatitudinis regnum. p*er* te s*anct*a maria uirgo p*er*petua consequi merear. Amen.

---

[20] On the religious orbit of this manuscript see Thomas H. Bestul, "St. Anselm and the Continuity of Anglo-Saxon Devotional Traditions," *Annuale Mediaevale*, 18 (1977), 39 ff. and *Ibid.*, "British Library MS. Arundel 60 and the Anselmian Apocrypha," *Manuscriptia*, 35 (1981), 271-275.

Between the first two versions there are a few significant changes which give evidence of a new hand at work on the text, drawing out some implications, adding others. Thus "meriti" has become "gratia" ("gratiae" in version three), and though this alteration did not last (perhaps because it was too close to the opening of an already familiar prayer), it already suggests something of the more intimate associations between the divine and the human which, as it developed, the prayer itself would show. But these associations were not developed simply by humanizing Mary. "Corpore inuiolatam" in version two became "corpore castam inuiolatam" in version three, and, as if to emphasize an even greater distance between the increasingly pure Virgin and the suppliant, the devout reader now asks intercession not "pro me spurcissimo" (version one) but "pro me misero spurcissimo" (version two). But if an increased sense of distance between Virgin and suppliant was a part of the prayer's eleventh-century history, so was an increased sense that Mary would bridge the gap. "Meis iniquitatibus" (version one) became "meis actibus" (version two)—so emphasizing the penitant's personal actions and thus his personal responsibility—and the final lines were changed from "tuis, uirgo splendissima, saluatus meritis perenne consequar regnum" (version one) to "sed tuis uirgo splendidissima saluatus meritis & intercessionibus perenne caelorum consequar regnum" (version two). The four words added in the new version—"sed, & intercessionibus, caelorum"—emphasize further the greater stature of the Virgin and the consequent distance from the devout Christian who addresses her, but insist too on the grace of line 1, and thus on the role of the Virgin as intercessor between God and humankind. Thus the added "sed" has the effect both of emphasizing the distance between divine and human affairs, but also of implying a connection: the distance is not absolute, any more than that the defilement of a sinner is his necessary final state. The " & intercessionibus" makes explicit what the text already implied, but the addition is important both because of the new distance which the earlier additions created, and because of the stamp of the Virgin's role which the words make clear. The final addition—the addition of "caelorum"—thus is slightly ambiguous, since it not only emphasizes Mary's abode, but also shows the destination of the devout reader, a destination which will bring him into appropriate association with the venerated woman whom he now addresses.

Thoughout, the earliest English versions show apparently opposing tendencies—they emphasize the purity and divine power of the Virgin, and the even more miserable condition of the person who addresses her, yet they insist on the connection between these two beings, on the role of the Virgin as intercessor, and, by implication, on her power and willingness to save the sinful. These are less theological reflections than devout attitudes built into a prayer written in one case for a deacon, AElfwine, who would become abbot at Winchester in 1035, in another case for the affluent owner of a particularly attractive psalter. Each manuscript addresses the attitudes and reflections of the Christian in prayer, and seeks to elicit a response appropriate to the occasion. The reader is left free, to be sure, to be moved or not by the words on the page, but the chance of deepening, of making the devotion more affective, has not been lost. The tendencies present in this early recension are indicative of later developments the prayer would undergo, and they speak to the earliest tradition of affective prayer.

But subsequent redactions of the *Singularis Meriti* made other important additions and alterations. The fourth and fifth versions return to the original opening—"meriti" not "gratiae"—but make other important changes too. "Maria" becomes "Sancta Maria" in both, thus again deepening the sacredness of the woman addressed, though both versions omit "castam inuiolatam" of the earlier versions, thus giving a more even balance to "mente & corpore." But the great addition of the fifth version follows the abject reference to the penitent, adding to "pro me spurcissimo," in place of "et cunctis iniquitatibus foedo ut qui ex meis actibus," the more personally imposing " & omnium uitiorum pondere pregrauto ut qui ex meritis meis." The additions have the effect of drawing even more sharply the distinctions imposed since the first version, and, particularly in the last addition, of focusing even more sharply the personal compunction of the reader.

The fourth version, however, somewhat moderates this astringency, and does so by laying slightly more emphasis on the person of Mary herself. She is indeed styled "Sancta Maria," but "inuiolatam" is restored, and "misericordissima" becomes for the first time "misericordissima domina," while shortly thereafter the formal "uirgo splendissima" adds " & mater sanctissima," while her "saluatus meritis" has added to them " & precibus." These clearly more humanizing elements of the fourth version give a good indication of what is to develop in the fifth and later versions. But whatever attributes are now added to the Virgin are attached to an image of almost Byzantine formality. What we observe is an accretion of detail which presents a new representation, but one in which elements of the earlier prayers remain like granite, influencing and informing the meaning.

The sixth and last version I have printed shows a final development, one in keeping with the eleventh-century alterations, but with a new direction as well. Mary now becomes the "templum domini sacrarium spiritus sancti," a later medieval recollection of the Annunciation, though "sacrarium" is also a place to keep holy oils, and the passage alludes to the anointing of the Holy Spirit. The devout reader now asks prayers "pro me misero peccatore quia corpus meum obuolutum est iniquitatibus multis & pessimis," an addition which directs attention away from the saving person of Mary, to a kind of repentance unknown in the earlier versions. Indeed the ending of this last version differs markedly from what has come before:

> "Therefor I beg you, most glorious virgin [and] most merciful mother, to rescue me by means of your merits and intercessions with your merciful son, to the extent that I may merit to be saved and to obtain the kingdom of everlasting happiness through you, holy Mary ever virgin."

The last major addition, however, returns to the nature of the relationship between the subject and Mary which the earlier addition obscured. He now prays fearing for his salvation " nisi tua michi succurrat pietas mater pietatis. Deprecor ergo te uirgo splendissima." Yet even this addition takes quite a new tone. The intimacy towards which the earlier versions reached—an intimacy achieved by setting the greatness of the person addressed against the sinfulness of the one speaking—has shifted to a more reasoned, even a more legalistic understanding, in which the Virgin's elect status, designated by the Holy Spirit, still stands against the sinning (more than the sinful) speaker, who fears for his salvation unless his entreaty be heard. What has changed is a matter partly of tone, but also of substance. The abject attitude of the reader is now assumed, not established, by the prayer, as is the effectiveness of Mary's mediation—it is almost as if she will act only if the words are said in the right order, the speaker having first assumed the right attitude and spirit. Much of the force of the earlier formality came from the bringing together of these rather separate states—but now their linking is all but taken for granted.

By the late thirteenth century affective prayer was well-developed, and this late version is hardly one of the more extreme examples of its kind. But in its eleventh-century English recension it is possible to see the development of certain devout attitudes which would, in time, transform the practice of Christian spirituality in the West.

These are matters which differed according to place and to practitioner, so that it is difficult to generalize, even when, as in the cases I have cited here, particular circumstances permit a measure of confidence. But by the end of the twelfth century such spirituality was well-advanced, springing from, but also contributing to, the evident development of Christian faith. But these shifts of meaning, these redefinitions of devotional patterns, took place against a complex intellectual background, which in later centuries can be seen to have had its roots both within and outside of the Western religious tradition, as we shall see in the next chapter.

CHAPTER TWO

BUDDHISM AND SPIRITUALITY IN MEDIEVAL ENGLAND

It is hardly possible to forget that many of the ideas and attitudes which fed the development of medieval spirituality had their origin outside of Western Europe. Christianity, in origin an Eastern religion, was from its inception influenced by the contexts within which it moved and gained significantly from all of its associations. In matters pertaining to its spirituality, at least, the image of a religion which plunges on, like a mad crusader, ignorant of and insensitive to all surrounding influences could not be further from the truth. But Western spirituality, unlike Eastern, rarely cultivates an image of exoticism. Rather it tends toward a mean, one in which mountains are leveled, and poles meet. The extraordinary efforts which these extraordinary feats require are rarely apparent, a fact which makes the religious attitudes which emerge a good deal more difficult to examine than they otherwise might be.

At least three important medieval English texts may reasonably be said to have retained traces of sources which seem, at first glance at least, somewhat exotic, but which on closer examination can be said to represent an identifiable tradition, one not apparent either to author or to audience. Such differences and such difficulties as the texts presented could be accounted for, by redactor and audience alike, by reaching into a Western tradition with which both were familiar, and which seemed to offer a reasonable explanation (or at least a way out) of a confusing episode or a difficult reading. There is nothing inescapable about the tradition I have sought to indicate, but it is real enough, and present, and there are important gains to be made by its examination.

Each of these three works, the long Middle English prose version of a work universally known as *Barlaam and Josaphat*, but spelled in Middle English *Barlam and Iosaphat*, the morality play *Everyman*, and Chaucer's *Pardoner's Tale*, derives from an identifiable Buddhist source, but one which has come under Manichaean influence, emphasizing some aspects, obscuring others. This tradition is thus a composite, but I shall be less concerned with the changes the Middle

English version reveals than with the tradition which it preserves. In other words, the changes are obvious: but what aspects of Eastern Buddhism actually reached the West?[1]

Barlam and Iosaphat not only originated in a life of Buddha, but also contains a number of apologues, one of which was the source for my second example, the morality play *Everyman.* The route it took West has been largely established. The Sanskrit original, perhaps a version of the *Buddhacarita* by the second century A.D. poet Aśvaghoṣa, probably passed into Chinese along the Silk Route before being translated, possibly in the sixth or seventh century, into Sogdian, though Sogdian translations direct from Sanskrit are not unknown. This Sogdian text, the first attested version of the work, is preserved only in a fragment, but its existence attests to the evident Manichaean influence in the work. Manichaean Sogdian scripts are distinctive, and so give good evidence of transmission, and Manichaeans were particularly drawn to texts like this one, which contain allegory of a recognizably dichotomous sort.[2]

The Sogdian version issued in a Phelavi, and that (to shorten things) in several Arabic versions, one of which was translated early in the eleventh century, into Georgian, and was almost certainly the first Christian version, which exists in both a short and a long version.

---

[1] My edition of *Barlam and Iosaphat. A Middle English Life of Buddha,* EETS OS 290 (1986) indeed cites eastern sources and analogues but does not engage the intellectual tradition I am going to treat here. For *Everyman* I cite the edition of A.C. Cawley, Old and Middle English Texts, ed. G.L. Brook (Manchester: Manchester University Press, 1961, rpt. 1970.) Separate editions of the *Pardoner's Tale* are not uncommon in Britain, where the work (perhaps surprisingly) has been set for schools. See the editions by Carleton Brown, ed. (Oxford: Clarendon Press, 1935); Nevill Coghill and Christopher Tolkien, eds. Harrap's English Classics (London: George G. Harrap & Co. Ltd., 1958); A.C. Spearing, ed. (Cambridge: Cambridge University Press, 1965); and N.R. Havely, ed. The London Medieval and Renaissance Series (London: University of London Press, 1975). Havely's edition also includes texts of the *Friar's Tale* and the *Summoner's Tale.*

[2] On the Manichaean influence see the Introduction to *Barlam and Iosaphat,* pp. xxiii-xxviii, and further Samuel N.C. Lieu, *Manichaeism in the Later Roman Empire and in Medieval China. A Historical Survey.* (Manchester: Manchester University Press, 1985, rpt. 1988), esp. 206-213 on Mani as "the Buddha of Light," and the fact that in a Manichaean liturgical text "sung at the end of meals we find a list of some of the principal deities of the Manichaean pantheon, including Jesus, being hailed as Buddhas" (p. 208). Some aesthetic connections which parallel the literary and religious one already noted are reported by A.M. Belenitskii and B.I. Marshak, "The Nature of the Cultural Relations of Sogdiana," in Guitty Azarpay et *al., Sogdian Painting. The Pictorial Epic in Oriental Art,* (Berkeley, Los Angeles and London: University of California Pres, 1981), pp. 26-34.

The longer version was, in the same century, translated into Greek, though the Greek version was restructured and rewritten. The following century saw this changed Greek version translated into Latin, and during the twelfth century, the second Latin version spread across Europe. Vernacular translation began in the thirteenth century, though in the fifteenth century there was a resurgence of interest in the work, and several vernacular translations date from that period.

But what was the text? I have called it a life of Buddha, recognizable from certain identifiable events which occur in the narration: the prediction at Iosaphat's birth, and his subsequent enclosure in a palace from which all pain and suffering are excluded; his encounter, as a young man, with an old man, a sick man, a corpse, and a mendicant—though these "four encounters" have been modified in *Barlam and Iosaphat*, much is preserved. The fourth encounter is in fact with Barlam, and it is he that Iosaphat goes to seek—they end in the desert, living a life of Christian asceticism, so distant from the teaching of Buddha, who finally rejected asceticism in discovering the "Middle Way" that was and is Buddhism. But events alone, even where they lie at the heart of a myth, are only part of the story. By themselves, they cannot determine the extent to which *Barlam and Iosaphat* may be said to be a Buddhist narrative. To answer that question I shall have to speak in general terms, but these are the terms of the text itself, and indeed *Barlam and Iosaphat* owes its longevity not only to a certain elasticity in its teaching, but also to the conviction of depth and warrant which it imparts.[3]

The basic teaching of Buddha is contained in The Four Noble Truths: the first of these is that life is *dukkha*, it is unsatisfactory: but the finally untranslatable word also implies suffering, emptiness, unsubstantiality, imperfection. Buddhism does not deny happiness, but sees it as passing, passing on to old age, sickness, death. It is not a

[3] Introductions to Buddhist thought are legion, but differ in quality. One of the best I have found is that of Walpola Sri Rahula, *What the Buddha Taught*, 2nd edn. (London: Gordon Fraser, 1967), though in my own short account I am indebted to the same author's "Fundamentals of Buddhism," a 27 May 1956 address reprinted in *Zen and the Taming of the Bull. Towards the Definition of Buddhist Thought* (London: Gordon Fraser, 1978), pp. 37-48, and have been influenced by "Buddhism in the Western World" in the same volume, pp. 25-36. I am grateful to Dr. Grace Burford for useful discussion of this section of the paper.

pessimistic teaching Buddha brought, but is, in the extended (but not Western theological) meaning of the word, satisfactory.

The Second Noble Truth is that the origin of this suffering or imperfection is in craving or in desire, which arises from a double misconception: first, that objects are themselves eternal, and second, that there is something eternal within each of us, which we call a soul. Each individual person actually consists of five ever-changing aggregates: matter, feelings, perceptions, mental formations, and consciousness, which, taken together, we ignorantly call our self. For this so-called self, we desire to get and to hold on to things; but because of the ever-changing nature of the aggregates, our desire, our craving, is bound to lead to disappointment. Just as our ignorance of the impermanence of things and of the non-reality of our self leads to desire, so desire, based on a misapprehension of reality as it is, leads in turn to disappointment.

The Third Noble Truth is that there is a cessation of suffering, called *Nirvana*, a super-mundane category of absolute truth that can't really be explained. The medieval Western tradition refers to a *summum bonum*, and if I must say something about it I suppose I might say it is something remotely like that.[4]

The Fourth Noble Truth is that there is a Way leading to the cessation, and that is the middle way of Buddhism, "middle" because it rejects the extremes of sensual pleasure and of extreme asceticism. This is also called the Eightfold Noble Path, and is composed of Eight Parts: Right Understanding, Right Thought, Right Speech, Right Action, Right Livelihood, Right Effort, Right Mindfulness, and Right Concentration. What underlies these categories is a fundamental concern for Ethical Conduct (*sila*) and Mental Discipline (*samadhi*), which lead in turn to Wisdom (*pañña*).

The ethical conduct required by this path involves compassion and love, and these are important in Buddhism—Iosaphat's compassion for a Princess sent to tempt him, regarded with horror by the Christian redactor, would have received more understanding from some Buddhists. Ethical Conduct involves right speech, right action, and right livelihood, the last of these meaning that one should refrain from a profession which brings harm to others, like trading in arms,

---

[4] For a more searching definition of Nirvana see Francis H. Cook, "Nirvana," in *Buddhism. A Modern Perspective*, ed. Charles S. Prebish (University Park and London: Pennsylvania State Univ. Press, 1975), pp. 133-136.

or in alcoholic drink, or in poisons, or butchering animals. These are prerequisites for mental discipline which will go on to wisdom, but I will not press these points since they do not figure in the Westward transmission.

But even with this rather compressed introduction I think it may be possible to suggest that some Eastern texts do carry into the West certain great themes present in their origins. Of the Four Noble Truths, it is not too much to say that the first three—well, and a trace of the fourth—are present in the texts I have mentioned. In my Introduction to *Barlam and Iosaphat* I noted the astringent asceticism which the text presents—but it is possible to go further and believe that there is an emphasis on imperfection, and on suffering, on desire as being the source of that state, and on there being a way to gain release from it.

These themes are hardly unknown in the West, and the fact that *Barlam and Iosaphat* was taken up as it was shows that it was regarded as orthodox by various Christian redactors. But what we actually see is that it was viewed as *almost*, or as nearly, orthodox. What the Western reception in fact shows is that, with a few necessary changes, the text could stand. The First Noble Truth seemed, at first glance, to have monastic overtones, to sound the right sort of *contemptus mundi*—but on second thought it seemed to do so with a little too much emphasis. The self, and with that the soul, so important to the Western Christian, are to the Buddhist a misconception. In some ways this is a more important distinction than the one usually cited—that in Buddhism there is no personal, omnipotent God, as there is in Christianity. Buddha himself made no claim to divinity; indeed his enlightenment was predicated on the assumption that he was himself a man.

But to many Western minds the self is the center of action—and of thought. So far from being a misconception, it constitutes what is essential—and that is one reason that some readers felt a little uneasy with too profound a contempt for things of this world. Even the idea that desire is at the root of the imperfection we experience needs, from this point of view, a little clarification. After all, there are different kinds of desire. If by desire you mean cupidity, and if you want to add that it is the root of all evil, all well and good. But, if by desire you simply mean desire, and if you want to insist that it is at the root of everything, then you will meet objections. For St. Augustine, after all, we define ourselves morally by what we love, an act which involves the will, and which is predicated on the self. Though the definition is not an absolute one, we move to God *non ambulando, sed amando*: not by walking, but by loving, in his famous turn of phrase (*De Trinitate* 8). Thus even an author not temperamentally unsympathetic to the sort of dichotomous distinction Manichaean teaching imposed on Buddhist texts might be inclined to modify an apparent East/West harmony.

But in spite of Western alteration, there are strains in *Barlam and Iosaphat* which reach back to the earliest period of its coming together as a text. Some part of its *contemptus mundi* may reasonably be put down to Manichaean, and subsequently to Christian, emphasis. But it is possible to see beyond the text's apparent asceticism, to see its movement West less in terms of texts than of ideas. Iosaphat's quest is very different from the one numerous ascetics have undertaken in the desert—at least in its inception. It began, after all, as a search for enlightenment, not for personal salvation, though the distinction was lost *en route*, and Western redactors quickly ignored the sense of imperfection, of suffering, that burns still in the early stages of Iosaphat's narrative, and placed him instead where Western tradition directed he should go. But the larger perspective Buddhism affords makes it possible to understand Iosaphat's decision to relinquish his kingdom, leave his newly converted people behind him, and set out alone.[5] The larger realities of the Four Noble Truths are present in his renunciation, though articulated here in terms compatible with Western asceticism. The perception of the incompleteness of human happiness is central to Iosaphat's narrative, as is his rejection of the acquisition of success and power which his father urges on him. His end in the Middle English version is no "Middle Way," but it is still concerned with a renovation which despises the self, and so leads to a kind of enlightenment, albeit of a distinctly Western sort, attached firmly to personal salvation as it is. Traditional Western categories have indeed been absorbed into the narrative, but they have not completely obscured its hard Buddhist center. The same process, changes having been made, can be observed in certain of the allegori-

[5] *Barlam and Iosaphat*, p. 165 and n. to l. 6067, p. 193, for Iosaphat's Great Renunciation. Compare the renunciation reported in *The Buddhacarita. Or, Acts of the Buddha*, ed. and trans. E.H. Johnson, Punjab University Oriental publications No. 32 (Lahore and Calcutta: Baptist Mission Press, 1936, rpt. New Delhi: Oriental Books Reprint Corporation, 1972), pp. 61-80, where Buddha's renunciation is linked to his rejection of sleeping women.

cal passages embedded in the text, including the one which issued in the Middle English morality play *Everyman.*

A good deal of commentary upon *Everyman* has pointed to the central theme of salvation, but its Buddhist origin (and Manichaean transmission) can supply a somewhat different perspective.[6] The character of Everyman is not altogether sympathetic, though it tends to become so as the drama develops. Certain productions I have seen rely on stage business—Everyman enters drunk, for example—to emphasize this from the start, but the text quickly creates sympathy for him, if only because Everyman is on a path which, in time, the audience must follow too. Beyond the identification of the protagonist, there is a problem posed by the agencies that save Everyman in the end, Grace and Confession to be sure, but also, and more important, Good Deeds. The Christian concept of good deeds which lead to reward is different from the Buddhist concept of Merit, or *puñña*, the "spiritual energy which results from good moral actions (*karma*) and which brings happiness in this or in a future life." [7] Buddhism, however, unlike medieval Christianity, does not treat meritorious activities as guarantees of other worldly reward, but as the opportunity for further perfection. They are indeed a means to an end, but the end is spiritual, *Nirvana*, not physical, personal, or compensatory. In transmission this Eastern teaching did accord with more dichotomous (especially Augustinian) thinking, particularly since it had its roots in the Buddhist concept of rebirth, which implied a relativising continuum, as birth followed death, and avoided any notion of the individual salvation of a "soul"—though Buddhism did teach that by acquiring *puñña* one could come to face death without fear.

It was possible, of course, to combine these traditions, to claim, as Mani did,[8] that rebirth would lead to redemption, thus linking rebirth

---

[6] On the Augustinian reading, Lawrence V. Ryan, "Doctrine and Dramatic Structure in *Everyman,*" *Speculum,* 32 (1957), 722-735 and John Conley, "The Doctrine of Friendship in *Everyman,*" *Ibid.* 44 (1969), 374-382. On the connection to *Barlam and Iosaphat,* V.A. Kolve, "Everyman and the Parable of the Talents," in *The Medieval Drama,* papers of the third annual conference of the Center for Medieval and Renaissance Studies, 1965 (New York, 1972), pp. 69-98.

[7] Roy C. Amore, *The Abingdon Dictionary of Living Religions* (Nashville, Tenn.: Abingdon, 1981), *s.v. Puñña*; the entry derived from Amore's "The Concept and Practice of Doing Merit in Early Theravada Buddhism," Columbia University dissertation, 1970.

[8] " ... those previous souls that in their own religion have not accomplished the works, will come to my religion (*i.e.,* through metempsychosis), which will certainly be the door of redemption for them." Jes P. Asmussen, ed. and trans. *Manichaean*

with the Christian concept of salvation. As syncretic a religion as Manichaeism thus could relativise both Buddhist and Christian concepts by setting one against the other in an allegorical framework, like the one *Everyman* supplies, and the resulting narrative would then require a Christian redactor to supply a mediating agency, such as the one Grace and Confession offer, to alter the outcome.

In this case it is the action of the principal, not his faith, which is at issue, but Everyman's actions are linked, in the teaching of the play, to his salvation, and so to the resolution of the fears which have moved him. In a certain way the movement of the drama is away from, not toward, the importance of the self, and certainly not toward its perpetuation after death. This feature of the narrative is largely obscured by the characters and the scenes the Western dramatist has interpolated into the narrative—the scenes with Grace and Confession, for example—which do indeed reformulate the direction of the text. But the terms in which Everyman has understood and defined his self: friends, family, goods, even his appearance, all fail him, all prove in the end impermanent. Only Good Deeds—or, strictly speaking, the merit acquired as a result of good deeds—proves lasting. The teaching of the drama *Everyman* is indeed both Western and Christian. But the frame of reference, and certain of the features of the quest, retain certain unmistakably Buddhist features.

An even more complex example is Chaucer's *Pardoner's Tale*, where the source can be identified with even greater confidence than in the case of *Barlam and Iosaphat*. Yet here too the theme, as it emerges in the tale, is by no means exclusively Eastern, for the uselessness of riches when confronted, unexpectedly, with death, is a

Literature. Representative Texts Chiefly from Middle Persian and Parthian Writings, Persian Heritage Series No. 22, UNESCO Collection of Representative Works (Delmar, N.Y.: Scholars' Facsimiles & Reprints, 1975), p. 12. "Some Manichaean concepts were also given Buddhist equivalents. The Manichaean concept of Metempsychosis ... for instance, approximates closely to Buddhist samsara ('rebirth and redeath') and in Manichaean Parthian and Chinese Texts the respective terms of *zadmurd* and *sheng-ssu* (birth-death) used to translate the Manichaean concept both call to mind the Buddhist equivalent ... . Several Manichaean deities also took on the epithet of Buddha. This is particularly evident in Chinese Manichaean texts, as there is no convenient non-Buddhist Chinese word for translating the Iranian term *yazd* (god). Thus in a *gatha* to be sung at the end of meals we find a list of some of the principal deities of the Manichaean pantheon, including Jesus, being hailed as Buddhas." Lieu, *Manichaeism in the Later Roman Empire and in Medieval China*, p. 208. See further Julien Ries, "Jésus-Christ dans le religion de Mani," *Augustiniana*, 14 (1964), 437-454, and especially, "Jésus-Sauveur," 443-445.

theme found in many literatures, East and West. The sudden and dramatic realization of this contingency was embedded in the third of Buddha's Four Encounters.

Perhaps because of its central position in Buddha's own myth the theme emerged early in the Buddhist canon, and appears frequently, though in different forms, in the *Jātaka*, a collection of 550 (actually 547) *exempla* representing Buddha's former births, which is preserved in a Pali source of the early fifth century (430) A.D., itself descended from a lost Singhalese tradition, which in turn had derived (probably) from a collection made (perhaps) in the third or fourth century B.C., of previously existing stories. One of these tales, No. 48 in the canon, has since 1881 been recognized as the ultimate source for Chaucer's *Pardoner's Tale*, and though it has undergone marked changes in the course of its transmission, enough of the original remains to make a comparison instructive.[9]

The *Jātaka* version concerns the experiences of a young Bodhisattva, the pupil of a Brahmin, who with his master was captured by a band of 500 robbers and held for ransom. Dispatched to obtain the money—while his master was held hostage—the prescient pupil warned his master not under any circumstances to cut short the time of his uncomfortable captivity by reciting a charm which, because of the annual conjunction of the planets, would bring down a shower of riches. But once his pupil had left the Brahmin did so, thus obtaining his release. Shortly thereafter the first band of robbers was apprehended by a second, also 500 strong, who demanded their newly acquired treasure. The first band of robbers pointed out the Brahmin, who found himself unable to repeat his trick until a year had passed—too long for the impatient robbers. As a result of his inability to produce a second shower of riches, first he and then the first band of robbers were quickly killed. The second band fell out among themselves and continued the slaughter until only two were left, one of whom went off for food while the second stood guard. But when

[9] *The Jātaka or Stories of the Buddha's Former Births*, 7 vols, Gen. Ed. E.B. Cowell (Cambridge: Cambridge Univ. Press, 1895-1913), no. 48, I, vol. 1, trans. Robert Chambers, 121-24. The *Jātaka* was edited by Michael Viggo Fausböll of Copenhagen (*The Jātaka Atthavannana*, 1861), and briefly discussed in connection with Chaucer's tale by Richard Morris, "The Book of Birth-Stories," *The Contemporary Review*, 39 (1881), 728-749. The first English translation was by C.H. Tawney, "The Buddhist Original of Chaucer's *Pardoner's Tale*," *The Journal of Philology* (formerly *The Cambridge Journal of Philology*), 12 (1883), 202-208.

the food came it was poisoned—though the second robber killed the first before tasting it. When the Bodhisattva returned with the now-superfluous ransom he saw what had happened and reflected that "through not following my counsel my master in his self-will has been the means of destroying not himself only, but a thousand others also. Truly, they that seek their own gain by mistaken and misguided means shall reap ruin, even as my master." The treasure the Bodhisattva then carried to his own home, where he used it in almsgiving and in other acts productive of merit.

The story is reported to have been told by the Master (Buddha) to a "self-willed" follower: "Said the Master to that Brother, 'This is not the first time, Brother, that you have been self-willed; you were of just the same disposition in bygone times also; and therefore it was that, as you would not follow the advice of the wise and good, you came to be cut in two by a sharp sword and were flung on the highway; and you were the sole cause why a thousand men met their end'." [10]

The theme of the *Jātaka* is said to be "misguided effort," misguided not only because the recitation of the charm leads to the destruction of the Brahmin in question (who is both the center and the reason for the tale's being), but also because it causes the deaths of a thousand others—and the humane sympathy in the narrative, as in Buddhism itself, does not excuse the men's deaths simply because they were self-inflicted, or because they were by profession robbers.

The narrative that reached Chaucer—no doubt the transmission was largely oral—had changed even before it arrived. The thousand robbers had become three (or four, counting the corpse who opens the tale), and the theme of death emerges early—though it does in the *Jātaka* too, if we include the introduction. Chaucer's Old Man who directs the robbers can now be seen to have a literary ancestor not only in the Brahmin who causes the shower of riches, but also in the wisdom of the pupil, who advises him to do no such thing. Apart from his admonitory function, the Bodhisattva has also the role of observer and teller—though his belief in reincarnation finds only a dim echo in the *Canterbury Tales.*

But there are other, perhaps more important correspondences which Chaucer's tale and the *Jātaka* have in common. The first of these is the theme of self-willed and misguided effort which achieves

[10] Chambers trans., I, 121.

the opposite of what is intended. The second is the admonitory nature of the narrative itself—it is intended to instruct, even to reform, those to whom it is directed. The third is the somewhat complicated point of view from which it is told. Within this framework other elements remain, even when they change in form. Thus, for example, the element of the fantastic present in the charm which delivers the shower of riches in the *Jātaka* becomes in Chaucer the miraculously discovered eight bushels of gold ("as hem thoughte"), a number divisible by two, but not by three.

Apart from these similarities, there are two important elements in Chaucer's tales which have no exact correspondence in the *Jātaka*: the not so much self-willed as self-consumed Pardoner, and the discussion of sin which he at once introduces and exemplifies. These important additions have directed, or at least influenced, the reading of the tale to such an extent that they seem to me to have all but buried it. That this is so is perhaps not surprising: the treatment of sin after all comes first, so that by the time the tale begins—after about 330 lines if we count the *Prologue*—we are disposed to interpret it, or reduce it, to the Pardoner's own example. With such a beginning it is no wonder that for some readers the phrase radix *malorum est cupiditas* says it all, while for others the Old Man, viewed in newfound theological terms, is the fulcrum around which the narrative moves.

Both of these elements, however, echo some aspect of the *Jātaka* tale. As we have seen, the remarks of the Bodhisattva when he returns to find his master dead—"They that seek their own gain by mistaken and misguided means shall reap ruin, even as my master" [11]—recalls the *radix malorum* theme, while the self-willed master may be a kind of literary ancestor both to the Old Man and to the Revellors.

But the larger emphasis which the additions supply shifts the focus away from an astringent analysis of human behavior—balanced by a humane attitude toward the lot of all—to a more simple, if rhetorically complex analysis of personal wrongdoing, and consequent guilt and punishment. The distinction is important for understanding exactly how the presentation of the Pardoner works on the logic of the tale—though shift is present too in some of the analogues, and prop-

---

[11] *Ibid.* I, 123-24.

erly represents a Western, as well as a Chaucerian, reaction to the narrative.

The refashioning of the tale worked in two directions, for the *Jātaka* contains two apparently contradictory emphases not present in Chaucer. On the one hand it presents an even starker view of the nature of human life—all men, not simply evil ones, are caught in a most imperfect of worlds, where happiness will finally elude them, and where secular attempts to seek gratification will bring only more and evident sorrow. On the other hand it shows wrongdoing, "misguided effort," with greater compassion, even with greater respect—though its failure is not disguised. Humans err, but are not consequently either despicable or damned, and even robbers, who have in the *Jātaka* collection as a whole something of an ambivalent status, are to be regarded with cautious respect. The resolution to this only apparent contradiction of course lies in the Bodhisattva, and in the conclusion, which anicipates the "Middle Way" of Buddhism. The *Jātaka* is entirely consistent with the Four Noble Truths of Buddhism, which together stress the imperfection of the world and consequent human suffering, the origin of this suffering in desire, and the cessation of both desire and suffering present in the Middle Way. The Eightfold Noble Path can no doubt be read into the narrative—though it is not really there—even if the thought-world from which it issues is.

Against the more humane if more violent *Jātaka*, Chaucer's tale stands out in vivid relief. Instead of the perception of imperfection and suffering, there is wrongdoing — the seven deadly sins, to be sure, but murder, real or intended, as well. Original sin may lurk in Chaucer's narrative, but it neither excuses nor, in terms of the narrative, explains the mad quest to kill Death on which his characters are engaged. Beyond these concerns, there is little enough compassion for the thieves, all of whom get what they have coming, and are damned into the bargain: and listener, if you don't want to join them, you had better give the Pardoner his alms.

This late medieval astringency, unyielding in its way, embraces for some readers not only the robbers and the Pardoner, but the Old Man who gives directions. How much of this damnation is in the eye of the beholder, how much in Chaucer's narrative, depends at least in part on the degree of interest the reader takes in the person of the Pardoner, a concern which in turn depends upon his view of the tale-teller relationships in the *Canterbury Tales* in general. But even in

Chaucer the tale still retains something of its origin, and some of the critical reaction (particularly on what is taken to be its theology) is certainly overheated.[12] Apart from the evident interest in sin, there is too a more impersonal but also more humane dimension which derives from the tale's ultimate source. The world is fallible and unfriendly; imperfection and suffering are the lot of all. That being so, too much emphasis on damnation is inappropriate. That there is in the world culpable wrongdoing both tale and *Jātaka* agree, and they agree too that desire, or *cupiditas*, is at the heart of it. But that said, the angles of vision diverge, though perhaps not as sharply as certain readings would imply. Chaucer's narrative stands in clear reproach not only to the person of the Pardoner, but also to his own interpretation of the tale with which he seeks his ends. The tale itself retains a measure of Buddhist understanding, sympathy, and detachment which has escaped its more Augustinian critics.

At the beginning of this inquiry I suggested that a Buddhist tradition in Middle English literature might become apparent, and, distinctions being observed, I believe it has. The texts I have been concerned with share not only an ultimately Buddhist-Manichaean background, but also certain motifs: the traveler who seeks a way which will help him understand his disquiet, the letting-go of past assumptions (or the failure to do so) which is a part of his reeducation, and the embracing of an attitude often described in the West as ascetic, but which is here more complex, a search that leaves nothing to chance, an understanding sprung as much from mind as from experience. These concerns seem to me relevant to editors of Western texts derived from Eastern sources, and interesting too because of the light they throw on a related matter.

It is not uncommon in common parlance to use the words *Western* and *Christian* as though they were inextricably linked, whether in a medieval or a modern context. A current concern of certain theologians, relevant to these matters, may help to correct the balance. Among a group of scholars concerned with the extent to which Chris-

---

[12] Important new readings in their day, the interpretations relied upon a tale-teller relationship of unusual closeness, commonly accepted then, now the subject of debate. Alfred L. Kellogg, "An Augustinian Interpretation of Chaucer's Pardoner," *Speculum*, 26 (1951), 465-481, and Robert Miller, "Chaucer's Pardoner, the Scriptural Eunuch and the *Pardoner's Tale*," *Speculum*, 30 (1955), 180-199. See also Kellogg's "St. Augustine and the *Parson's Tale*," *Traditio*, 8 (1952), 424-430.

tianity may have relevance in non-Semitic Asia, there is study already well-advanced seeking to determine the interpenetrations possible between Western cultures, and those imbued with Sino-Indian religiousness.[13] Identifying Graeco-Roman models of inculturation which have succeeded in Europe but which fail in Asia—like the Patristic rejection of non-Christian religions, the separation of religion from culture and both from philosophy—the founder of the Tulana Center in Sri Lanka, Aloysius Pieris, S.J., has argued for the creation of an "indigenous ecclesiastical identity from within the soteriological perspective of Asian religions ... wherein our cosmic involvement with the Present is tempered by a metacosmic orientation towards a future which constantly relativises the Here and Now."[14] Sensitive to both the Hindu concept of metempsychosis and the Buddhist of rebirth, Pieris also argues that, in political terms, Asian theology requires not instrumentalising non-Christian orientations (that is, objectifying for Christian use; a practice of which these texts give repeated evidence) but assimilating them. The process Pieris is concerned with is a complex one, but even in outline it casts an interesting perspective on the process of examining the works I have been concerned with. These texts represent, after all, a cultural redefinition of certain central Buddhist teachings, yet they retain important features of their source. These features were unobserved not only by the redactors who transmitted them, but by students of a Western intellectual tradition which still privileges (and often identifies) authorial intention and thematic unity, even though both concepts have only limited relevance to works of this complexity, since they specifically obliterate the larger patterns to which the texts respond, and the associations and correspondences between and among cultures which they repeatedly hold out. For example, each of the three texts I have been alluding to

---

[13] I refer in particular to the work of Aloysius Pieris, S.J., "Western Christianity and Eastern Religions (A Theological Reading of Historical Encounters)," *Cistercian Studies*, 1 (1980), 50-66 and 2 (1982), 150-171. Certain of Pieris' essays have been collected in *An Asian Theology of Liberation* Faith Meets Faith Series (Edinburgh and Maryknoll, N.Y.: T. & T. Clark and Orbis Books, 1988). See particularly chapters 5 and 6, "Western Models of Inculturation: Applicable in Asia?" and "Speaking of the Son of God in Non-Christian Cultures," pp. 51-65.

[14] Pieris, "Interculturation in non-Semitic Asia," *The Month*, N.S. 19 (1986), 83-87, quote from p. 85. See also Pieris, *An Asian Theology of Liberation*, p. 51 ff. I am grateful to James Reddington, S.J., for useful discussion of Pieris' work, and for further comment upon this chapter.

contains a more or less obvious tension between consciousness and what came to be called the self, which crosses another between time and what the Western redactor designated salvation, and these tensions became central as the Eastern narratives entered into Western categories.

On the one hand the entry confirmed an attitude toward the so-called self which was, in the narrative's inception, only a misconception, but on the other the alteration, begun under Manichaean influence, maintained the original sense of the suffering of life, and of the way in which suffering can be alleviated only by understanding and adaptation.

Such considerations move unremittingly away from a soteriology based more or less exclusively on the perpetuation of some form of the self, to one which resides in cognition and in ethical conduct arising from (and leading to) that cognition.

If Everyman's quest led him only to understand that the self he has so carefully nourished in this world can, with a few modifications, be perpetuated into the next, he has not come very far. If the kingdom Iosaphat attains after death is simply better in degree than the one he has relinquished, it is only his cunning we must praise. If Chaucer's Revellors only need to turn to *caritas* to speed well who cares how they end up? Or what the Old Man stands for? Or what the Pardoner thinks?

But Iosaphat's concern for his subjects, like Buddha's for his followers, is an integral part of the change of attitude which is a part of his conversion. The rejection Everyman experiences from those to whom he is closest contributes importantly to his understanding that it is the terms in which he has conceived of his experience which are mistaken. The revellors' quest for Death leads inescapably to their discovery of gold, from which, however, the reader should take only regret, not pleasure.

In leaving his kingdom, more than when he dies, Iosaphat quite deliberately steps out of time, as (less deliberately) do Everyman and Chaucer's Old Man. Iosaphat's concern for his father, like his longing for Barlam, is based upon a misconception, as is Everyman's for his self, as is the felt need for money and for action, which move Chaucer's revellors.

These are examined lives, and the Eight-Fold Path has not misled its followers. Iosaphat begins by questioning the reason for being, and for pain. Everyman, who thought he knew, learns otherwise.

The Revellors never learn and fall away from the initial confusion which could have taught them. However shaped by Western dress, by Augustinian dichotomies and scholastic forms, the rock from which these texts were hewn will not be hidden. It still influences, still informs their meaning, and can thus help to remake the questions we pose, the processes we follow, the reason we follow the path we do.

CHAPTER THREE

THE GODS APPEAR: REPRESENTING THE DIVINE IN QUEST NARRATIVES

Sir Gawain and the Green Knight, Havelok, Lay le Freine

I.

Although recent scholarship on late medieval literary texts has evinced a pronounced interest in aesthetic, moral and social considerations, it has been a good deal less concerned with religious ones. Indeed, it has sometimes seemed a matter of irritation to some medievalists that there is an aspect of the Christian devotional tradition which esteems humility more than letters, and which privileges faith as the central motivating force in the lives of many persons. Related to this disinterest is an inclination to rate religious faith and the behavior which it occasions according to a kind of scale. Indeed some contemporary writers seem almost to argue that mystics (for example) should be assigned a grade, and Morton Bloomfield no doubt spoke for many when he remarked of Julian of Norwich that "at present her mystical experience is somewhat overrated." [1] It is difficult to escape the impression that, in expressing this reservation, Bloomfield was writing with what he believed to be understatement.

Yet it must be admitted that this somewhat tiresome disinclination to engage religious attitudes sometimes has had reason behind it. It cannot be said that such investigations were always innocent of partisan considerations which now seem quite removed from the more disinterested procedures of modern scholarship, though equally what has presented itself as scholarly objectivity has sometimes set its face against any concern for religious attitudes at all.[2] But as scholarship

[1] *Speculum* 55 (1980), 548, in a review of Edmund Colledge, O.S.A. and James Walsh, S.J., eds. *A Book of Showings to the Anchoress Julian of Norwich* Studies and Texts 35 (Toronto: Pontifical Institute of Medieval Studies, 1978). One difficulty with this learned edition is the extent and nature of its annotation, and the impression it leaves that Julian's spirituality is largely the product of literary sources. But a less learned spirituality is not necessarily inferior, and Bloomfield's objection seems focused more on the mystic than on the edition.

[2] For an interesting example see David Knowles, *Cardinal Gasquet as an Historian*, originally published as the Creighton Lecture (London: Athlone Press, 1957), re-

has itself become more engaged, admitting new questions of gender, race, and class into discourse, a certain broadening of critical attitude has become apparent.[3] The result has been that certain hitherto marginalized topics have been accorded a new degree of respect, and the range of discourse surrounding them has considerably broadened.

In the course of these developments interest in religious texts, unpublished ones in particular, has increased, and with it a welcome inclination to take seriously texts hitherto regarded as "minor," though the manuscripts in which such texts are preserved are often approached for their codicological interest, rather than for any intrinsic interest the works they contain may reveal. Perhaps as a result, there has been a tendency to treat certain concepts categorically, even ones like "mysticism," which continue to mean different things to different scholars.[4]

But the fixing of a definition can have a complicated effect on any attempt to discern the actual significance of a given religious phenomenon. Many medieval authors, for example, have represented the intersection of divine and human worlds with a sense of disparity, but not always of disquiet. Thus although the realization of supernatural presence can cause even fictional characters to reform goals, attitudes, and objectives, it equally can confirm them in a course al-

---

printed in *The Historian and Character and Other Essays* (Cambridge: Cambridge University Press, 1963), pp. 240-263. There are of course other examples: G. G. Coulton's position is particularly important, since his attitudes have had wide circulation, and sometimes even now impair the temper and extent of the discourse among those working in the area. On Knowles' own attitudes see Dom Adrian Morey, *David Knowles. A Memoir* (London: Darton, Longman & Todd, 1979), responded to in Christopher Brook, Roger Lovatt, David Luscombe and Aelred Sillem, *David Knowles Remembered* (Cambridge: Cambridge University Press, 1991), see particularly Sillem, pp. 27-46.

[3] The bibliography is now far too extensive to list here, but see for example two recent anthologies of medieval feminist criticism both published by the University of Georgia Press: *Women and Power in the Middle Ages*, eds. Mary Erler and Maryanne Kowaleski (1988), and especially *Medieval Women and the Sources of Medieval History*, ed. Joel T. Rosenthal (1990), both of which contain relevant methodological contributions. More traditional studies have also shown a greater interest in gender: two volumes edited by John A. Nichols and Lillian Thomas Shank deserve special mention, *Medieval Religious Women*, Volume I *Distant Echoes*, and Volume II *Peace Weavers*, Nos. 71 and 72 of the Cistercian Studies Series (Kalamazoo, MI.: Cistercian Publications, Inc., 1984 and 1987).

[4] Or even different things to the same scholar. Late in life Hope Emily Allen revised many of her attitudes and opinions, though her language remained (in many cases) the same. See my *Hope Emily Allen. Medieval Scholarship and Feminism* (Norman, Oklahoma: Pilgrim Books, 1988), pp. 146-152.

ready chosen, and I propose here that the treatment of behavior and motivation in the face of supernatural religious phenomena in certain literary texts bears a relationship to the more direct encounters of the mystic. From one point of view, after all, mysticism represents only one aspect of a religious attitude within which the relationship between a devout person and a transcendent absolute becomes manifest. And although poet and mystic both agree that God may respond directly to prayer, or even speak uninvited, both equally understand that mysticism does not undermine more traditional forms of spirituality, rather it supports them, and indeed from one point of view constitutes their foundation.[5] The connections between mysticism, spirituality, and literature are thus complex, but they are real and lasting, and they find expression in a complex of attitudes toward religion present in the period.

Concern with the supernatural was more general in literary texts of the period than it is sometimes understood to have been, and several late medieval works give good evidence of contemporary attitudes. But the evidence they offer is complicated by their narrative setting and literary form. Imagery, for example, often plays a crucial role, conveying meaning less by argument than by wonder, a trait poet and mystic both share. Likewise, a concern with gender can have a religious as well as a narrative effect, and further define the circumstances within which the supernatural is represented.

But for the poet, narrative circumstance is hardly less important than the supernatural presence itself, and can sometimes limit the depth to which the poet or translator is able to explore its significance. In spite of these (and other) difficulties, however, the appearances of religious attitudes in literary works are important, both because of the resonances they reveal in texts directed toward a lay audience, and because of the openings they offer for understanding the religious attitudes of the period.

---

[5] Eastern religions in particular often allow for the continuing influence of mystical experience. See Frits Staal, *Exploring Mysticism. A Methodological Essay* (Berkeley, Los Angeles and London: University of California Press, 1975), pp. 92-101, though for Staal mysticism " need not necessarily be regarded as a part of religion" (p. 4; *cf.* 190-99). Compare Andrew Louth, *The Origins of the Christian Mystical Tradition. From Plato to Denys* (Oxford: Clarendon Press, 1981), especially "The Monastic Contribution," pp. 98-131, and John Bowker, *The Sense of God. Sociological, Anthropological and Psychological Approaches to the Origin of the Sense of God* (Oxford: Clarendon Press, 1973), *passim.*

II.

There is a scene in *Sir Gawain and the Green Knight* in which the protagonist, riding in prayer through the cold countryside, between forest and swamp, beseeches Christ and his mother "of sum herber" [some lodging] (755) so that he might attend Christmas mass and matins the following morning; he prays, crosses himself several times, and proceeds on his way.

In *Havelok* there is another scene where its protagonist, a child and under the power of his enemies, lies bound hand and foot, awaiting the time when he will be drowned in the sea. But when the wife of his would-be murderer and future protector arises at midnight to blow up the fire, she sees a light so bright that, about the boy at least, it seems to be day already. It is as if a "sunne-bem" [sun beam] (593) was being emitted from Havelok's mouth, making the room so bright that it seems as though wax candles were burning in it. "Ris up, Grim," she calls out to her husband, "and loke wat [see what] it menes!" (598).

Finally, there is a scene in the Middle English *Lay le Freine* in which the maid-midwife sets out in the cold, clear night to abandon the yet unnamed child who will shortly be baptized as "Frein" [ash tree] (235). Passing through heath, field, and wood under a bright cold moon, she pauses exhausted when, from the cocks crowing and the dogs barking, she realizes that she is near a settlement. Finding houses and a church (but neither street nor town) she understands she is near a house of religion, a convent as it transpires. She goes to the church door where she finds growing a well-branched ash tree, within whose trunk she places the child "for cold," wrapped in a "pel" [robe]. She then blesses it, and "[w]ith that it gan to dawe [dawn] light" (180). The woman turns, and makes her way home again.[6]

Each of these scenes is a preparation for more important events to come: Gawain's encounter at the castle, Havelok's voyages, Frein's

[6] I cite *Sir Gawain and the Green Knight*, eds. J.R.R. Tolkien and E.V. Gordon, 2nd ed. by Norman Davis (Oxford: Oxford University Press, 1967 rpt. 1972); *Havelok*, ed. G.V. Smithers (Oxford: Clarendon Press, 1987), and *Lai le Freine*, ed. Margaret Wattie, *Smith College Studies in Modern Languages* 10:2 (Northampton, Massachusetts and Paris: Smith College and Librairie E. Champion, 1928), except that I have preferred to write *lay* for *lai* following the practice of the Middle English scribe in lines 22 and 24.

discovery and subsequent adventures. If, as I am going to argue, each of these scenes in some sense displays the presence of the supernatural, each also indicates that it is often at the boundaries of experience that the supernatural presents itself. Each scene is also intimately associated with certain aspects of nature: all three are associated with the cold, and two with the winter and night. What is interesting about the cold in these scenes, however, is the way in which it suggests its opposite, and the way the associated appearance of light further identifies the authorial attitude which informs the event in question. The order to which the passages speak is not social, but neither is it impersonal. All three come at crucial moments of a passage, at a time when there is no turning back, yet when what is to come is not at all clear, and when the next event may well determine the course of things. In such moments events take on a life of their own and seem to direct not only the protagonist but also the audience to consider the significance of what is to unfold, and to do so against an imagistic background which reveals much.

In *Gawain*, the bare branches and cold birds of the deep forest seem to find an echo in the midnight bedroom (*cleue* 558, 597) in which Havelok lies, and those in turn in the cold night in which Freine is abandoned. But in each case the image does not exist in isolation, and the cold is set against the phenomenon which, whether known to the protagonist or not, is about to occur: the refuge for which Gawain prays appears; the light from Havelok's mouth transforms Grim's task; Freine is discovered and protected. In the last two cases, though significantly not in Gawain's, the events are linked to an associated image, that of light. In the case of Havelok, that light is described as being like a sunbeam, but then in an important extension, like that of wax candles (*cerges* 594, *cf.* 2126), suggesting a religious, even a liturgical association, and in any case disarming a simply magical one. There is a humorous echo of this image later in the romance when the boy Havelok is hired as kitchen help, to swill dishes and fetch water, but he also volunteers that he can kindle a fire and make it burn bright (915-16). Later, when Havelok's bride finds herself lamenting her marriage and the light appears again, it is described as fair and bright and is said to burn like a blaze of fire (1254); subsequently, and at another crucial moment, it returns once again (2122-23), this time preserving not his life but his crown.

The same association of light and heat which stand against cold appears in the *Lay le Freine*, where however the link is made even more explicit. After her prayer, the maid places the child in the tree trunk "for cold" (177), wrapped in the important "pel" (178), where she blesses it "with al hir might" (179). "With that" the poem somewhat ambiguously continues, "it gan to dawe light" (180). The birds pipe up, not for cold this time, farmers go their way and the maid heads home, just before the porter from the abbey appears to spot the pel and make his discovery, thanking "Iesu Cristes sond" [ordinance] (198) as he does so. Against the cold stands the subsequent protection of another woman, the porter's daughter, who warms the child and "Gaf [gave] it souke [suck] opon hir barm, / & seththen [then] laid it to slepe warm" (207-08). The association of day and light with protection from the cold carries with it an assurance of divine protection which, as I have argued elsewhere,[7] was one of the chief new concerns of the Middle English translator, who realized providential and religious themes not present in his courtly source.

Neither of these associations of heat and light against cold is present with Gawain at his key moment, and their absence suggests that the poet regards the condition in which he finds himself as conditional and ambiguous, in spite of the apparently miraculous appearance of the castle. His prayer, like the maid's, may anticipate events which are about to unfold and invite the consideration that they are connected, but the crucial moment quickly becomes ambiguous, as, once inside the castle, the wine climbs to Gawain's head, and an old woman passes before his eyes.

But the scene before Gawain reaches the castle is interesting too because it has its mirror in the even more problematic scene at the beginning of the fourth fit, when Gawain awakens on a dark and cold morning to hear the cock crow and see a light burning in his room. This scene has only a chill echo of the supernatural in it, and the sense of expectation it contains is conditioned by the green girdle, and by the short ride Gawain soon must take. His earlier prayers had offered him no safe "herber" (755, *cf.* 812). He had still to rely upon his "trawthe" [integrity] and his wits, and the result was always in doubt.[8] This scene, though equally contingent, has no such uncer-

---

[7] See my "Providential Concern in the 'Lay le Freine'," *Notes and Queries*, n.s. 16 (1969), 85-86.

[8] On Gawain's "trawthe" see Ross G. Arthur, *Medieval Sign Theory and Sir Gawain and the Green Knight* (Toronto: University of Toronto Press, 1987), pp. 90-94 for an interesting reading of it as "contingent." But it exists too in a series of less personal associations which help to define its propositional character. John A. Burrow's

tainty. The die has been cast, and it remains only to see what if anything Gawain's new protector, the green girdle, will do. Night changes to day, but the cold remains, and except for the brief respite which the mass brings, there seems to be nothing supernatural in the air, no hint of divine presence—again, the light and the cock crow apart—in the course he has chosen.

In the history of *Gawain* criticism, the main focus has been on the knight himself, on his putative "sin" in accepting the gift and not returning it, and on the moral complexities for the individual his actions reveal. But another aspect of the romance is at once more and less personal. The entry of the divine contextualizes these events, and suggests a different way of understanding what transpires. It is no longer Morgan le Fay who determines the course of things, but a providential and supernatural engagement which manifests itself not only at one key moment, but also in the course of the action, and which allows Gawain the freedom to determine his own course of action, while reducing the manipulative powers of even the most apparently powerful actors to a game. From this point of view it is not simply his bad choice which Gawain regrets, but his momentary blindness to the ideal world in which his deepest values, both sacred and secular, reside. He understands at the end of his quest that he no longer has anything to fear at the Green Chapel, and in the end the unknowing court will restore the balance and welcome him back into the human community which it is his fate to share. The religious attitudes in the romance finally define its context in less individual, and so less modern, terms than the brilliant if paradigmatic narrative has suggested, and in so doing it has placed Gawain's actions in the context of Christian salvational history, and restored hope to its ending.

In what I have said so far I have made certain assumptions about imagery it would be well for me to make explicit. I have been concerned with how images work together, and by implied association, to inform a given, and particularly a transitional, scene. Even when one

---

influential reading in *A Reading of Sir Gawain and the Green Knight* (London, Henley and Boston: Routledge & Kegan Paul, 1967, rpt. 1977) focuses on the concept of sin, of which the green belt becomes "a reminder" (151). But the religious attitudes I have been addressing suggest a somewhat more important role for the supernatural order within which the action is cast.

powerful image, like that of the cold, dominates a scene, it will sometimes trigger a series of associated images which serve to define its implication and effect. This complex pattern, I believe, can sometimes be accounted for by reference to a larger cultural setting, and in this case I believe a religious association, to which it responds. The linking of heat and light with prayer has associations which will be apparent, for example, to any student of English mysticism,[9] though to these have been added one other imagistic pattern, that of passage or voyage. This particular *topos* is of course so familiar that its effect is sometimes lost, but in each of the cases I have been examining it is contextualized in such a way as to bring it vividly into being.[10] The hero's journey is either begun (Havelok), interrupted (Gawain), or ended (Freine) by the manifestation, so that it is as if, for a moment, all of the possibilities of life are renewed, and its goals and meaning are present to the reader.

In her penetrating study of Romanesque church facades in Aquitaine, Linda Seidel alludes to "a new vocabulary of images" (13) which emerges from a complex pattern of influences "political, liturgical, militaristic and poetic" (16), to transform the figurative art of the period.[11] Her approach differs from more traditional treatments, illuminating in their way, like Ilene Forsyth's of the Romanesque *sedes sapientiae* in France, which document a series of statues without contextualizing them, and thus without addressing the complex cultural problems which figural images can reveal.[12] But in treating the

---

[9] See Wolfgang Riehle, *The Middle English Mystics*, trans. Bernard Standring (London, Boston and Henley: Routledge & Kegan Paul, 1981), especially chapter VI "Metaphors for Speaking about God in English Mysticism," pp. 76-88.

[10] On the *topos* see Gerhart B. Ladner, " *Homo Viator*: Medieval Ideas on Alianation and Order," *Speculum*, 42 (1967), 233-259, best read against the same author's "Medieval and Modern Understanding of Symbolism: A Comparison," *Ibid.* 54 (1979), 223-256.

[11] Linda Seidel, *Songs of Glory. The Romanesque Facades of Aquitaine* (Chicago and London: The University of Chicago Press, 1981, rpt. 1987). Localized traditional examinations do not engage such questions, see for example Arthur Gardner, *Medieval Sculpture in France* (Cambridge: Cambridge University Press, 1931), pp. 129-148 on sculpture in Romanesque Aquitaine, or Marcel Aubert, *La sculpture française au moyen-age* (Paris: Flammarion, 1947) pp. 127-134.

[12] Ilene H. Forsyth, *The Throne of Wisdom. Wood Sculptures of the Madonna in Romanesque France* (Princeton, N.J.: Princeton University Press, 1972); a recent general history tries to strike a balance: see Georges Duby, Xavier Barral i Altet and Sophie Guillot de Suduiraut, *Sculpture. The Great Art of the Middle Ages from the Fifth Century to the Fifteenth Century* (New York: Skira/Rizzoli, 1990), in particular "Sculpture and New Devotions," pp. 181-191.

attitudes which images in literary texts both inscribe and reflect it is important to remain attentive to context. Figural sculpture, whether on or within a church, places the human actions within a larger setting, and so causes them to partake of resonances which appear in literary texts as well. But in literary texts the role of imagery in encoding meaning is, if anything, even more powerful. Narrative, meaning, and attitude are all involved in the passages I have been examining and seem, like the sculptures in Aquitaine, to be in some sense a new development, a response to the larger religious influences of the period, a movement which involved individual encounters of an even more direct kind.

But there is one other aspect of these passages which I should like to indicate. In each case the conjunction of light and heat with cold is further conditioned by an association with women. It is Grim's wife who calls her husband's attention to the supernatural phenomenon taking place in their room; Gawain, alone and friendless, prays to our Lord and also to Mary, whom he calls upon as "myldest moder so dere" (754), a description which stands in direct contrast to his own present condition; the association of women in the *Lay le Freine* is pervasive: mother, maid, daughter, and girl all conspire, each in her way, to create the scene in question, but I should note that in this case the prayer the maid offers is to Christ, though he is called upon to act for the love of Mary, his mother, an appropriate appeal given the nature of the events, and reminiscent of Gawain's prayer, which concludes with a "pater and aue and crede" (758).

Thus the presence of women at once deepens the significance of the event and provides an appropriate witness to the sacred moment. Gender functions here to focus, to recall from abstract association the images I have indicated, and to locate them in the lives of the men and women concerned. Gender does not simply restate the terms for sacredness which the texts inscribe, but it is deeply involved with the very terms through which that definition is attempted, and perhaps more importantly with the ways in which those terms function in the visible world.[13]

---

[13] See Caroline Walker Bynum, "...And Women His Humanity": Female Imagery in the Religious Writing of the Later Middle Ages," in *Gender and Religion. On the Complexity of Symbols,* eds. Caroline Walker Bynum, Stevan Harrell and Paula Richman (Boston: Beacon Press, 1986), pp. 257-288, and also Bynum's *Holy Feast and Holy Fast* (Berkeley, Los Angeles and London: University of California Press, 1986), chapter 10 "Women's Symbols," pp. 277-296.

Against the larger pattern I have been concerned with, the explicit association of women with the supernatural is important, though in each case what is being appealed to is less doctrine than spirituality. I understand that the conditions in *Havelok* are different in theological terms from those which obtain in *Gawain* and in the *Lay le Freine*, but imagistically I propose that they are not dissimilar, and that the effect in each case is to establish a sense of the supernatural which springs from a meeting of narrative event, cultural association and the individual religious inclination—the faith—of the Middle English author. The narrative requirement was of course what indicated the presence of women in these passages, but in each case the requirement triggered a series of other associations which find deeper resonances outside of the romance tradition, and which inscribe meaning in significant ways. The process in which they take part informs the more compelling issues these texts evoke, issues which engage questions less of theme than of authorial attitude and finally of belief. One of these issues too concerns the depth of the religious attitudes which the texts present, another, the nature of their religiousness, and the extent to which it encodes both religious attitudes and some aspects of visionary spirituality.

III.

Yet even within this interplay, what is it possible to say about the connections, not readily apparent but unmistakably present, between these manifestations and the more powerful ones of which the mystics give evidence? In the medieval period as now, revealed religion had many voices, and any encounter with the supernatural was likely to provoke more than one interpretation. But it is still to the mystics that we must look to ascertain what the parameters of encounter were, how a sense of divine presence was received, and what attitudes subsequently developed. The presence which appeared—not always to those concerned, but finally to the audience—often came suddenly and usually changed things. Sometimes a sense of reassurance accompanied it, as the one involved contended with adversity, and the reader at least became able to perceive the nature of the assistance now available. But the encounter had too the effect of placing action in a broader context, at once deepening and rendering newly intelligible the behavior and motivation of those concerned.

It is these qualities rather than any more definite ones which are at the heart of the matter. Because we are here dealing with a finally human responsiveness rather than with a particular representation of it, it will not do simply to catalogue the images associated with the manifestation of the supernatural as a way of inspecting the event, or ascertaining when, in fact, a manifestation has occurred. Thus, although certain images recur in the texts I have been examining, I cannot say too strongly that it is the context of these images, as much as the images themselves, which encodes meaning. Heat and light, even when cited in a religious passage, do not universally point to a divine presence, nor even to any less specific sense of the supernatural. It is not difficult to find such images as these in a Christian context outside the tradition of Western mysticism upon which, I believe, medieval English texts like the ones I have been examining often depend. Images of light and heat figure, for example, in Origin, where they represent Platonic rather than mystical attitudes,[14] but that is why context is as important as it is, and why it is in the problematic area of human responsiveness that meaning resides. What events lead up to the particular moment? How is the moment itself represented, but also, and not less important, what is its aftermath and effect? How does it tell on those involved, or on the reader? What does the poet's attitude toward the event seem to be? The answers to these questions, I submit, do not admit of a common denominator, but in their aggregate, particularly when questions of literary form are also engaged, they seem to me to reveal much.

In another place I have argued that late medieval England produced a number of religious practices which formed a kind of border area between mysticism and other kinds of devotion.[15] What emerges in these texts is related, for they too reveal a sense of presence rather than of encounter. There is no overwhelming awareness

---

[14] See John Dillon, "Looking on the Light: Some Remarks on the Imagery of Light in the First Chapter of the *Peri Archon*," in *Origin of Alexandria. His World and His Legacy*, eds. Charles Kannengiesser and William L. Petersen, Christianity and Judaism in Antiquity, volume 1 (Notre Dame, Indiana: University of Notre Dame Press, 1988), pp. 215-230, and compare Riehle *supra* n. 9, chapter VIII "The Experience of God as a Spiritual Sense Perception," pp. 104-128, for a treatment of the frequent use of sensual terms in English mysticism, a practice "which indeed goes back to Origin" (p. 104).

[15] See my *The Revelations of Margery Kempe, Paramystical Practices in Late Medieval England*, Medieval and Renaissance Authors, vol. 10 (Leiden and New York: E.J. Brill, 1989), pp. 19, 90-91.

of discovery, no sense at all of union. The supernatural appears, makes itself known or at least felt, and events proceed again. But the presence unmistakably informs the action into which it has intruded. Whether it comes in response to a petition or simply at a moment of danger, it changes the course of things, and protects some at least of those concerned from harm.

Thus, access to the divine is a complicated matter. As Gawain and Freine's maid both recall, in one way—through prayer—everyone has it, though the form and character of a sought-for response need not conform to human expectations, even when it encompasses them. Thus there is often an element of the unknown in such manifestations, an x in the equation, so that such moments often seem related not so much to the moment of mystical encounter as to its aftermath.[16] The event itself, however important, rushes by, but the entry of the supernatural into human affairs has its effect and takes its toll. Human agency is neither superceded nor commanded, but it is engaged, and it does not fail to alter course, sometimes in the interests of others. Often the moment has too an organizing effect, appearing to be both a part of a continuing influence, and yet influential itself in providing for future action. However suddenly, however unexpectedly these manifestations occur, they do so in the context of an encounter, and become the single most important link in a chain which seemed to indicate a very different conclusion.

I noted at the beginning of this chapter that religious attitudes are not often examined, and I have suggested that they sometimes become intelligible when poetic topics are evoked to examine literary forms and narrative moments which inscribe meaning. What emerges in this kind of examination, I believe, is not a simple affirmation of either traditional beliefs or devout practices, but rather an integration of those assumptions which reader and protagonist share, particularly those which, at important moments, record the ways in

---

[16] I am thinking here of the fourth of the still valuable criteria for determining religious experience which Joachim Wach has identified, that "it issue in action. It involves an imperative; it is the most powerful source of motivation and action." *The Comparative Study of Religions*, ed. Joseph M. Kitagawa. Lectures on the History of Religions Sponsored by the American Council of Learned Societies, New Series, Number Four (New York and London: Columbia University Press, 1958, rpt. 1961), p. 36. See also chapter four, "The Expression of Religious Experience in Action," pp. 97-120. I have discussed one possible application of Wach's criteria in "The Experience of God: A New Classification of Certain Late Medieval Affective Texts," *Chaucer Review*, 11 (1976), 11-21.

which the sacred and the secular interact. Of the three texts I have been concerned with, it is of course *Sir Gawain and the Green Knight* which realizes these concerns most fully, and which offers, in its fusion of imagery and narrative, a redefinition of the ways in which meaning emerges in secular and devout, courtly and religious, discourse. Gawain's prayer in the wilderness hangs over the events which follow: the cold and the dark prepare for the light and the fire to come. The linking of religious attitudes and imagery associated with mystical encounter has a complex effect in a text like this one, which formulates significance less in theological than in heuristic patterns, and which examines both courtly experience and religious implication in light of their mutual interaction. But in the end attitudes and images together attest to a larger context within which the characters move and from which they take their bearings. The context serves to complete, rather than to diminish, the individual persons who take part, but equally it strips them, as Gawain learns to his cost, of the assurance that their fortunes lie entirely in their own hands, a truth they had long understood but seldom acknowledged. As the mystics knew, the encounters of passage are only a shadow and an echo of those to come.

Imagistic and religious patterns associated with mystical encounter and with faith have a complex effect when they appear in literary texts. In their context, organization, and positioning, but also in their religious association, they encode both meaning and significance, and in doing so they reveal important dimensions both within the texts in which they appear and within the minds which created them. Their recognition thus reveals an often unrecognized source of energy and power, and helps the student to speak with some confidence about the often unsuspected interplay of image, attitude, gender, symbol, and meaning.

CHAPTER FOUR

IS THE *BOOK OF MARGERY KEMPE* A FEMINIST TEXT?

If spirituality was both developed and transmitted by persons, the fact that there are two genders is not a detail. Nor was gender passed over in silence by many of those who were concerned with spirituality's growth. But the role of gender was complex and took many forms. In this chapter I am going to address a particularly interesting text, now universally known as the *Book of Margery Kempe*, which addresses, among many other things, the relationship between gender and spirituality.

In an earlier account of the *Book* I suggested that the relationship between the subject of the work, Margery Kempe, and the scribe who wrote it was associative, and that the responsibility of authorship was shared.[1] I am now going to explore the nature of that relationship by examining certain competing attitudes which I believe Margery and her scribe entertained, by considering the nature of their interchange, and by suggesting a larger literary pattern into which their interchange falls. Two different attitudes toward spirituality emerge from the text, Margery's and the scribe's, but the scribe's are largely reactive to Margery's own.

There is such a wealth of spiritual allusion in the *Book of Margery Kempe* that it is necessary to be selective. But three specific devotional attitudes which Margery articulates, toward the Blessed Virgin, toward the Trinity, and toward Margery's spiritual marriage with Christ, each reveals a different aspect of the *Book*, and I am going to

[1] John C. Hirsh, "Author and Scribe in the *Book of Margery Kempe,*" *Medium AEvum,* 44 (1975), 145-150; the idea has been much discussed: see, for example, Sandra J. McEntire, ed. *Margery Kempe. A Book of Essays* Garland Medieval Casebooks 4 (New York and London: Garland Publishing, Inc., 1992), and my review in *Medium AEvum,* 63 (1994), 142-44. See too Denise L. Despres, "The Meditative Art of Scriptural Interpolation in *The Book of Margery Kempe,*" *Downside Review,* 106 (1988), 253-63. Although it does not address the scribe's role, there are important distinctions relevant to the matter of the scribe's role concerning the three kinds of confessor-penitent dialogues present in the *Book* in Elizabeth Alvilda Petroff in *Body and Soul. Essays on Medieval Woman and Mysticism* (New York and Oxford: Oxford University Press, 1994), pp. 152-56.

focus on them in order to examine some aspects of the work's spirituality, and its feminism, whether actual, putative, or proto. The first of these seems to me the most personal and perhaps the most important of the three, and the one in which the scribe's influence is most difficult to discern. Repeatedly in the *Book* the protagonist is represented as being the handmaiden of the Blessed Virgin at the time of Christ's infancy.[2] Initially, the *Book* reports that the image came to Margery while she was in a meditation which Christ had enjoined, her mind a blank, "nowt knowyng what sche mygth best thynke" (18/11). She appealed to Christ for direction, and he "answeryd to hir mende" (18/13), indicating that she should "thynke on my Modyr, for sche is cause of alle the grace that thou hast" (18/14-15). At this point the *Book* reports that Margery saw (but I believe it means she saw in her meditation), "Seynt Anne gret wyth chyld," whom she prays to serve as maid and servant. Anne was an ambiguous saint, associated both with the family and with living a chaste life, but markedly popular as the century advanced, particularly with members of the urban middle classes.[3] But Margery's petition apparently is granted, and when the Blessed Virgin is born Margery is appointed to look after her with good food and drink, dressing her in white, until she is twelve years old. This she does, and then a conversation takes place in which Margery tells the child Mary that she "schal be the Modyr of God" (18/21-22), whereupon Mary replies ' "I wod I

---

[2] The theme was first identified by Hope Emily Allen in her notes to *The Book of Margery Kempe*, eds. Sanford Brown Meech and Hope Emily Allen, EETS OS 212 (London: Oxford University Press, 1940), Vol. I, p. 265, note to 18/31, and subsequent allusions. The role may be associated with the white clothes in which Margery Kempe dressed. See Hope Emily Allen's notes for 32/17, 34/13 and especially 124/13, which moots the possibility that the dress was associated with the Flagellants. But it was also associated with the Bianchi, persons who dressed in white and attended to religious duties and devotions from the Alps to Rome. See Daniel E. Bornstein, *The Bianchi of 1399. Popular Devotion in Late Medieval Italy* (Ithaca and London: Cornell University Press, 1993), 61-161, and Mary C. Erler, "Margery Kempe's White Clothes," *Medium AEvum*, 62 (1993), 78-83.

[3] Ton Brandenbarg, "St. Anne and her family. The veneration of St. Anne in connection with concepts of marriage and the family in the early-modern period," in *Saints and She-Devils. Images of Women in the 15th and 16th centuries.* Trans. from the Dutch by C.M.H. Sion. (London: The Rubicon Press, 1987), pp. 101-127, and *Interpreting Cultural Symbols. Saint Anne in Late Medieval Society*, eds. Kathleen Ashley and Pamela Sheingorn (Athens, Georgia and London: The University of Georgia Press, 1990), *passim*, but especially Pamela Sheingorn, "Appropriating the Holy Kinship," pp. 169-198.

wer worthy to be the handmayden of hir that shuld conseive the Sone of God" ' (18/23-24), to which Margery replies, ' "I pray yow [you], Lady, yyf [if] grace falle yow forsake not my seruyse" ' (18/25-26). The text here is revealing. Mary speaks with seemly humility, but the voice is obviously Margery's own. The theme of willing submission by becoming a servant occurs three times in this somewhat problematic meditation: when Margery offers herself as a maid to St. Ann, when Mary declares herself to be unworthy to be, in effect, her own maid, and when Margery seeks that office for herself.

Once established, it is a role (and a theme) which Margery embraces. Subsequently, Mary speaks to Margery (or is envisioned to be doing so), directing her as " 'thy modyr, thi lady, and thy maystres' " (50/9-10), who will teach her " 'in al wyse how thu schalt plese God best' " (50/10-11). When Margery later, at the direction of "the good preste hir confessowr" (85/33-34), acts as a maid to an old and poor woman in Rome, the *Book* records that she did so "as sche wolde a don owyr Lady" (85/37). Subsequently she envisions herself with Mary, still as her servant, at the time of Christ's passion (190/12-14), and after Christ's death it is in her office as servant that Margery seeks to comfort her mistress (195/11-12), only to be told, in a late-medieval devotional commonplace, that there is no sorrow like her sorrow, since no woman ever had a better son than Christ, or one who was "mekar to hys modyr" (195/16). The image Margery evokes of herself is repeated, and forms one of the themes which connects the sometimes disjointed structure of the *Book*.

The image is interesting for several reasons. For one thing, it stands against the sometimes enthusiastic, sometimes abrasive representation of Margery which the *Book* often evokes, and yet represents a clearly important aspect of her spirituality. It is by no means the most self-abnegating image of Margery in the *Book*, but it is, to a marked degree, deferential, and poses interesting questions about her spirituality and her feminism.

Yet most feminists would have little trouble in accounting for the particular devotional attitude I have been describing.[4] Under the

---

[4] Three recent studies of the *Book* treat different aspects of its authority: Karma Lochrie, "The *Book of Margery Kempe*: The Marginal Woman's Quest for Literary Authority," *Journal of Medieval and Renaissance Studies*, 16 (1986), 33-55; Janel M. Mueller, "Autobiography of a New 'Creatur': Female Spirituality, Selfhood, and Authorship in 'The Book of Margery Kempe'," in *The Female Autograph. Theory and Practice of Autobiography from the Tenth to the Twentieth Century*, ed. Domna C. Stanton (Chicago

patriarchy, women are required to assume a subordinate and passive attitude, and if they can be made to internalize their oppression, so much the better. But what was—or what is—the patriarchy? The concept is an important one for modern feminism, and though there are those who would replace or at least deemphasize it, the idea remains one of the few central concepts upon which there is a measure of agreement among feminists.

Lisa Tuttle's *Encyclopedia of Feminism*[5] defines it as "the universal political structure which privileges men at the expense of women; the social system which feminism is determined to destroy" (p. 242, *s.v.* patriarchy). Tuttle indicates that the word, among feminists, has various meanings, sometimes being used "as a synonym for male domination; sometimes to refer to a specific historical, social structure." Its origins are in anthropology, but, as Tuttle points out, many (she implies all) feminists believe "that *all* societies, whatever their economic, political or religious differences, are patriarchies. All known societies are ruled by men, who control and profit from women's reproductive capabilities. Under some systems women have more privileges, even token power, than in others, but everywhere men are dominant, and the basic principles defined by Kate Millett in *Sexual Politics* (1970) remain the same: 'male shall dominate female; elder male shall dominate younger.' "

Tuttle's book seems somewhat influenced by certain attitudes then

---

and London: University of Chicago Press, 1987), pp. 57-69; and Sidonie Smith, *A Poetics of Women' s Autobiography. Marginality and the Fictions of Self-Representation* (Bloomington and Indianapolis: Indiana University Press, 1987), Chapter 4, " *The Book of Margery Kempe*: This Creature's Unsealed Life," pp. 64-83.

[5] London: Arrow Books, 1987. There are those who would deny the use of the term in this context, and indeed insist that, strictly speaking, the defeat of the patriarchy was an important aspect of medieval canon law, particularly in the twelfth-century decretal of Pope Alexander III (based on Peter Lombard) concerning the importance of the free agreement of a couple for the sacrament of marriage to be valid. See David Herlihy, *Medieval Households*, Studies in Cultural History (Cambridge, Mass.: Harvard University Press, 1985), pp. 80-82, and James A Brundage, *Law, Sex and Christian Society in Medieval Europe* (Chicago: University of Chicago Press, 1987), pp. 331-341. But legal definitions are rarely working ones. See also Gerda Lerner, *The Creation of Patriarchy*, Women and History, vol. 1 (New York: Oxford University Press, 1986), which stresses the difficulties of treating all patriarchy as oppression, and suggests subordination as an alternative, pp. 231-243. See also Cheris Kramarae and Paula A. Treichler, *A Feminist Dictionary* (Boston, London and Henley: Pandora Press, 1985), *s.v.* patriarchy, authority and autonomy, which points out that it was during the 1970's that attention was paid to "the relationship between language and authority" p. 62.

current among certain American feminists, and carries through the universalizing tendencies implicit in some of its sources. The definition of rape in the same book is concerned with political, not legal issues, and begins "An act of political terrorism, used systematically by all men to intimidate and oppress all women" (p. 269). But on the whole it avoids treating conceptual terms (patriarchy is an exception), and two terms particularly useful in discussing medieval feminism, *authority* and *autonomy*, have no entries.

The idea of patriarchy, however, is indeed useful in discussing the *Book of Margery Kempe.* As Tuttle represents the concept it is most easily applicable to post-industrial society, where social and political structures are entirely secular and usually identifiable, and where the notion of what constitutes a woman's "sphere," however fraudulent, is at least apparent. The medieval patriarchy resembled the modern, but in many ways was even more intractable. For one thing, the secular institutions, particularly those directed toward war and so toward wealth, were almost invariably ruled by men, whose power reached out, through more local structures, to touch each subject. But the patriarchy had an ecclesiastical as well as a secular aspect: the Pope, the Cardinals, the hierarchy, were, like the priestly group which supplied their members, entirely male. For them, this was the proper state of things. There were correspondences between the secular and the ecclesiastical orders, and a human male deity was placed above all: but that was not how Margery Kempe saw things.

Repeatedly, her *Book* gives evidence of her challenging, but with different emphasis and different motives, both ecclesiastical and secular institutions, particularly when they threatened to limit her freedom of action. Her persistence in causing her husband to go through the considerable difficulties involved in disavowing what were thought to be his marital rights, her sense of what she could require, on pilgrimage, of her fellow pilgrims, her social sense of what was fitting for a mayor's daughter,[6] all testify to her engagement on a theoretical as well as on a practical level, of the power of the patriarchy. Addressing the ecclesiastical order her reactions differed, though not perhaps

[6] On Margery Kempe's social position see Anthony Goodman, "The Piety of John Burnham's Daughter, of Lynn," in *Medieval Women. Dedicated and Presented to Professor Roaslind M. T. Hill*, ed. Derek Baker, Studies in Church History, Subsidia I (Oxford: Published for the Ecclesiastical History Society by Basil Blackwell, 1978), pp. 347-358.

in kind. She was direct in dealing with what she took to be hypocrisy or sham, whether against clerics who were not acting worthy of their calling, or ones who expected of her a difference she was not disposed to accord them. But in other cases, she could be a good deal more circumspect. The protection she needed to carry on the life she had chosen, and to express and record her religious awareness, required sympathetic and sustained support, and these she seems to have acquired with relatively little trouble.

But in spite of her keen sense of how these two hierarchies could inhibit her freedom, Margery Kempe was disinclined to apply to what she clearly regarded as the sacred sphere the same responses she regularly employed on the other two. I understand that the meditative image of a handmaiden to Mary at the time of Christ's infancy is not at variance with the social persona Margery presents, and I accept too that it would be possible to address this devotion in more narrowly psychological terms,[7] but I think it is important to notice the distinction Margery observes, if only to avoid the suggestion that her evident theological moderation was either uncritical, or that she succumbed privately to the requirements of the patriarchy. In the context of the *Book* it is clear that she did neither, and that she differentiated sharply between sacred and secular orders, and put the ecclesiastical somewhere between the two. The connections between and among these orders was not an analogy and not a metaphor. The image of the handmaiden to Mary serves to indicate an important term of reference, in which Margery represents the divine in language which is responsive to her gender. Her lord is a woman: first St. Ann, then more importantly and more lastingly, Mary. Christ she apprehends as feminized, both in his infancy and in his passion, physically helpless and at his mother's disposal in either case.

But this image of Margery as handmaiden is mediated through her scribe's pen, and no doubt through his mind as well. Two different spiritualities, Margery's and her scribe's, emerge from the *Book* as competing though not conflicting. The priest-scribe of Margery's *Book* took no exception to the identification of St. Ann and the

---

[7] See Michael P. Carroll, *The Cult of the Virgin Mary. Psychological Origins* (Princeton: Princeton University Press, 1986), pp. 49-74, but see also Caroline Walker Bynum, "The Mysticism and Asceticism of Medieval Women: Some Comments on Max Weber and Ernst Troeltsch," in *Fragmentation and Redemption* (New York: Zone Books, 1991), pp. 53-78.

Blessed Virgin as objects of veneration, but that may have been because he did not fully grasp the implications of the devotion. It has been reasonably argued that religious men, not women, were the chief votaries of the Blessed Virgin during the late medieval period, and her identification in a devotional context would have provided no difficulties.[8] Similarly, both Margery's service to a poor woman in Rome, a duty placed on her by her confessor, and the continuing image of Margery as servant, are in a context which disarms them of any heterodox implication.

But it is in the terms of her apprehension that it is possible to observe a difference between Margery's spirituality and that of her scribe. On the one hand, Margery places herself under the direction of a woman, not under that of a man, and in so doing retains a degree of autonomy in her freely given service, which contributes to the authority she assumes in the process of composition. True enough, she is corrected by the Blessed Virgin when she offers consolation too easily, but this only serves to increase her subsequent authority when she presents her *Book.* What was to the scribe a devotional commonplace was to Margery Kempe the core of her spirituality.

Other aspects seem to me somewhat problematic. For example, it is not easy to estimate the effect of the references to St. Bridget in the text.[9] Do they show a conscious manipulation of audience by implied identification? And if so, by whom was the link made? It is sometimes implied that it was done so by Margery herself, though Saint Bridget's maid remarked that she was "goodly & meke to euery creatur" (95/17), while the "good man" (95/18) where Margery was stay-

---

[8] Caroline Walker Bynum, *Jesus as Mother,* pp. 136-137 and 162. Elsewhere Bynum emphasizes the "manipulation and maneuvering" which she takes to be "the pattern of Margery [Kempe]'s life," "Women's Stories, Women's Symbols: A Critique of Victor Turner's Theory of Liminality," in *Fragmentation and Redemption,* pp. 27-51, quote from p. 41. While it is true that these played a part in Margery's life, it is equally true that she was to an extraordinary degree open and candid in her attitudes and speech, and it was the candid, and usually quite orthodox, quality of her spirituality which first impressed, and led to her being believed as often as she was.

[9] Clarissa W. Atkinson, *Mystic and Pilgrim, The Book and the World of Margery Kempe* (Ithaca, N.Y.: Cornell University Press, 1983), pp. 174-179. But it is worth remembering that what seems to us the most telling parallels between Margery and St. Bridget—their marriages and their children, for example — go unremarked in Margery's *Book.* It was probably Bridget's spirituality as much as, if not more than, her life which Margery found attractive. See further Nancy Partner, " 'And Most of All for Inordinate Love': Desire and Denial in *The Book of Margery Kempe,*" *Thought,* 64 (1989), 254-67.

ing (who also had known the saint) "wend lityl" (95/20) that she had been as holy a woman as she was "for sche was euyr homly & goodly to alle creaturys that woldyn spekyn wyth hir" (95/21-22). But these are not the attributes which first come to mind when thinking of Margery Kempe. Even the description of Christ saying that he will prophesy (an earthquake, in this case) to Margery "rygth as I spak to Seynt Bryde" (47/32) sounds as much as anything like a literary allusion, one for which the scribe, not Margery, may have been responsible. Indeed there is at least as much evidence that the identification of Margery and St. Bridget, if it exists at all, is the scribe's doing, and Margery was simply concerned to act in cooperation with a cult which she admired.

A sharper contrast appears in the larger attitudes which exist between Margery and her society, or more broadly between religion and culture. For it is not clear that it is Margery who sees religion as a bulwark against the sexism of the culture in which she moves, so much as it is her scribe who does so. Margery tends rather to reinvent that culture, to use it, to inform it, so as to alter the conditions of her own and others' lives. The *Book's* interest in the extent to which Margery is confirmed by ecclesiastical authority was probably shared by both, though for Margery the point seems linked to the authority which her revelations have given her. In this as in other matters, it may have been the scribe's questions—and so the scribe's concerns—which drew her out, and though in speaking her mind she often gave the answer expected of her, there is a sense in which the *Book* is shaped by a dialogue: by Margery's mind on one hand, by the scribe's shaping influence and questions, on the other.

I do not wish to overstate the division between Margery and the scribe, whose attitudes seem to me congruent—but differ they did. For the scribe, the established order of things—the patriarchy, the rule of church law—was still in place, and Margery's contribution was to give effective witness, not finally to challenge or subvert. To this Margery would have agreed, at least in part. She was (as she proved often enough) no Lollard, and moved with relative ease in ecclesiastical circles, with which she had a marked degree of sympathy, as long as its members remained true to what they professed. But if she did not address these circles combatively or defensively, neither did she capitulate to them. Instead she found a convenient middle ground, in which she was able to respond to evident differences between the secular and ecclesiastical patriarchies, and in which she was able to commit herself to a sacred order which she confused with neither of the other two. Her scribe, as far as he was able, sympathized with, and partly understood, her inclinations and respected, if imperfectly, her intention. But what was that intention? A consideration of the two other spiritual practices with which I began this essay will help to clarify this particular matter further. One of these concerns is the Trinity, the other Margery's mystical marriage to Christ.

The Trinity figures importantly in Margery's thought, as indeed it does in Western definitions of God. It is difficult to imagine a more complex or powerful Western evocation of the *numinous* than this one, which nonetheless appears often in the popular idiom, whether in vernacular lyrics, valedictions, and devotions, or in marginal manuscript illuminations, like those in the Luttrell Psalter. In Margery's case, the devotion to the Trinity had a personal history, since she is probably to be identified with the "Margeria Kempe" who was admitted to the Trinity Guild of Lynn (cp. 9/3), and a 1415 Norwich civil document begins with an invocation to the Trinity in a way that identifies the devotion with Norwich itself (compare 169/11 and 221/3). It is probably too much to say that the devotion was by itself a sign of orthodoxy, though it is not one which commended itself to the Lollards, who, however, seem to have attacked it only infrequently.[10] In the *Book of Margery Kempe* it figures regularly, whether as a repeated but passing reference (20/11, 25/16, 39/19, 60/35, 82/21, 87/10, 89/6, 102/25), or more substantively, as when Margery Kempe "was howselyd al in white" on "Trinite Sunday" (104/23), or when members of the Trinity Guild to which she probably belonged maintained six chaplains at St. Margaret's church in Lynn. The references to the Trinity in the *Book of Margery Kempe* bob in and out, and sound for all the world like repeated assurances of orthodoxy. In fact, the assurance seems to have been largely unnecessary. The fact of its presence, and the repeated emphasis it receives, seem to be one of those instances where protagonist and scribe were acting together, offering a testimony to theological conservatism which would seem to curb any more centrifugal force emanating from the *Book*'s more enthusiastic practices.

---

[10] Anne Hudson, *The Premature Reformation*, reports one instance of "rare comments ... that express obscurely doubts about orthodox teaching on the Trinity" (p. 384), but suggests that this particular attack was uncommon.

But in the 'Spiritual Marriage' between Margery and Christ it is possible to sense two different minds at work. The event may have been anticipated in the account of Margery's discovery of a lost ring which she had been directed to have made when she was in England (78/12),[11] but the marriage is said to have taken place when she was in Rome, at the church of St. John Lateran, on the feast day of the Church, December 6 (cap. 35). But the whole sequence is curious: the initial words of God the Father: "Dowtyr, I am well plesyd wyth the in-as-meche as thu beleuyst in alle the Sacramentys of Holy Chirche & in al feyth that longith therto, & specialy for that thu beleuyst in manhode of my Sone & for the gret compassyon that thou hast of hys bittyr Passyon" (86/11-15). It is quite probable that much of this has come under the scribe's correcting influence. The theologically appropriate "in-as-mech as thu beleuyst in alle the Sacramentys of Holy Chirche & in al the feyth that longith therto" is aimed fairly clearly at Lollard teaching. The emphasis on Christ's human nature, which follows, and on Margery's devotion to Christ's passion (which in fact was only one of many devotions which she practiced), act as a kind of apology for Margery's spirituality: the suggestion is that she nourishes profoundly *one* aspect of Christ's nature, the one which appeared most often in passion meditations. A few lines farther on, God the Father remarks that he will show to Margery "my preuyteys & my cownselys" (86/17-18) in language which is fairly clearly influenced by the priest-scribe. The actual marriage ceremony itself, on the other hand, may well have been Margery's own creation. She stands silent—but weeping—when asked if she consents to the wedding, but Christ asks his Father to excuse her silence "for sche is yet but yong [young] & not fully lernyd how sche shulde answeryn" (87/12-13). When the Father takes Margery by the hand to wed her He speaks the traditional promise, and both requires obedience of her and promises in turn that "ther was neuyr childe so buxom [obedient] to the modyr as I shal be to the bothe in wel & in wo,—to help the and confort the. And therto I make the suyrte" (87/21-23).

It is often difficult to be certain where the scribe intervenes and where Margery speaks, but in the passage in question the theologically radical promise of God to be obedient is disarmed by the almost

[11] As Hope Allen believed. Compare her note to the incident of the ring, *Book of Margery Kempe*, 78/12, p. 297.

explanatory note which immediately follows: "By obedient I mean that I shall help and comfort you." Margery's spirituality was less concerned with such distinction, though her sense of an approachable divinity which still stood apart from the conditions of society meant that she could equally command the obedience of God the Father and submit herself to His Son's mother as well.

This relationship between Margery and her scribe was far from unique. Among the other works where a similar relationship can be discerned I would list three: the Middle English version of Margaret Porete's *Mirror of Simple Souls*, St. Bridget of Sweden's *Revelations*, and the long version of the *Showings* of Julian of Norwich. I am not going to discuss the additions to the Middle English *Mirror of Simple Souls* which are relatively clear—the anonymous commentator "M.N." adds comments to clarify apparently heterodox opinions and to place in an appropriate theological context a work he admires—but I would point out that these broad similarities link the work to the others I have named, though in this case, exceptionally, the additions are separated from the text they seek to elucidate.[12] In the case of St. Bridget of Sweden's *Revelations*, the case is less clear. Presented in seven books, the work is preserved in two versions, one in Latin and one in Old Swedish, neither the saint's autograph. These versions apart, there are two fragments in Old Swedish known to be in St. Bridget's hand. The relationships between and among these versions is still subject to debate, but a recent study has argued again that the Old Swedish text is earlier than the Latin, but that the Latin was based not upon St. Bridget's autograph, which was preserved at the very monastery where the Latin version was executed, but upon the later Old Swedish version.[13] The reason may have been prudence, since the Latin

[12] Margaret (otherwise Marguerite) Porete, "'The Mirror of Simple Souls,' A Middle English Translation edited by Marilyn Doiron, with an Appendix, The Glosses by 'M.N.' and Richard Methley to 'The Mirror of Simple Souls' by Edmund Colledge and Romana Guarnieri," *Archivo Italiano per la storia della pietà*, 5 (1968), 241-382. The glosses here provide important information abouit one kind of late medieval spirituality which I have discussed in *The Revelations of Margery Kempe*, pp. 35-43. There are some revealing comments on the editorial decisions behind the Pontifical Institute edition *A Book of Showings to the Anchoress Julian of Norwich* (1978), edited by Edmund Colledge, O.S.A., and James Walsh, S.J., in Colledge's "Editing Julian of Norwich's *Revelations*: A Progress Report," *Medieval Studies*, 38 (1976), 404-427.

[13] Hans Aili, "St. Brigitta and the Text of the *Revelations*: A Survey of Some Influences Traceable to Translators and Editors," in *The Editing of Theological and Philosophical Texts from the Middle Ages*, Acts of the Conference arranged by the Department of Classical Languages, University of Stockholm, 29-31 August 1984, ed. Monika

version, prepared to assist in the process of canonization, presents a more polished account of St. Bridget's attack upon a number of abuses within the Church, but it also offers testimony to the role St. Bridget's friend and scribe, Alphonso of Jaen, played in editing the text of the *Revelations.* It was probably Alphonso, it has been argued, "... who arranged the huge mass of Revelations, as yet only sporadically collected into coherent units, into seven books. He also excluded passages or even entire Revelations that he judged to be unsuitable in view of his expectations that Brigitta's Revelations were to be used as evidence in the process for her canonization. He was probably also responsible for formulating the rubrics given to various Revelations; this he did while editing the text of the seven Books of Revelations" (p. 83).

In Julian of Norwich's *Showings*, I submit, something of the same pattern may be observed. The Long Version, written some twenty years after the Short, shows a number of departures, and these are usually understood to have been introduced by Julian herself, as some of them clearly were.[14] Two long added sections, for example, the dream-parable of the Lord and his servant in chapter 51 and the extended treatment of the motherhood of God in chapters 59-65, show Julian authorship, though even within these chapters it is possible to observe a second presence intervening, for example, in the treatment of Adam in the first of these passages (II, 532-34). But whether or not such theological elaboration within the passages is authentically Julian, there are other passages which appear in the Long version which seem to me to suggest, more or less obviously, the presence of a second voice, which is being addressed, responded to, and otherwise accommodated.[15]

For one thing, certain cancellations and shorter additions claim a new function for the work, that of instruction, not only of witness.

Asztalos, Acta Universitatis Stockholmiensis, Studia Latina Stockholmiensia XXX (Stockholm: Almqvist & Wiksell International, 1986), pp. 75-91.

[14] Colledge and Walsh, eds. *A Book of Showings to the Anchoress Julian of Norwich.* Citations are by volume and page number; the editors discuss "Relations between the Short and Long Texts," I, 18-25, and *seriatim* in the notes.

[15] On the allusions to Franciscan spirituality see Colledge and Walsh, *passim.* On the presence of Franciscans in Norwich see Norman P. Tanner, *The Church in Late Medieval Norwich, 1370-1532*, Studies and Texts 66 (Toronto: Pontifical Institute of Medieval Studies, 1984). There are elements of Julian's spirituality which accord well with Franciscan teaching, though it will be difficult to prove the matter beyond doubt.

Thus the degree of self-abnegation is lessened—"wrechid worm" becomes "wrech," for example (I, 219.5 and II, 320.36, but compare I, 226.2 and II 632.14 for a parallel structure), and a long section (I, 222) in which Julian had disclaimed the role of the teacher is quietly cut. This new claim for a second voice is not gender-specific, nor is it a claim for joint authorship. But it does suggest a new and possibly shaping influence, and has certain obvious parallels with the other texts I have been discussing. These few details by themselves will not argue the case, but they could fairly easily be extended, but in any case would cause problems for the twenty-year revision theory now current. I should add though, that evidence for a second voice is not entirely restricted to the Long Version. Some of the theological elaboration has its roots in the Short, and I am myself inclined to believe traces of it may be present there, too. My sense in each case is that the questions to which Julian seems to me to be responding are sympathetic, of the sort associated with a supportive but critical spiritual advisor. I understand that this suggestion will not please all of Julian's commentators, but it seems to me that one who is as concerned with the well-being of her fellow Christians as she is would not have been reluctant to invite comment on her experiences, or to adopt an exclusive attitude toward authorship. There seems to me nothing intrinsically implausible about the suggestion, which would offer the beginnings of an explanation for the way (and the reasons) Julian's book came to be written down, and would of course conform to the pattern I have been observing.[16]

Each of these three cases presents us with a sympathetic commentator, identifiably male in two of the cases, but present, I believe in all three.[17] He sought to make known, and also to make orthodox, the text which had come under his hand. He did so believing that his theological learning could be of service to the woman visionary

[16] The most persuasive accounts are those of Barry A. Windeatt, "Julian of Norwich and her Audience," *Review of English Studies*, n.s. 28 (1977), 1-17, and "'Privytes to us': Knowing and Re-vision in Julian of Norwich," in *Chaucer to Shakespeare. Essays in Honour of Shinsuke Ando*, eds. Toshiyuki Takamiya and Richard Beadle (Cambridge: D.S. Brewer, 1992), pp. 87-98.

[17] Nicholas Watson has argued that Julian's Long Text "is constructed as a dialogue not so much between God and Julian as between Julian-the-inspired-visionary (who received the showings) and Julian-the-questing-believer (who struggles to understand them." Watson's paper is unpublished; I have quoted from Barbara Newman, *From Virile Woman to WomanChrist, Studies in Medieval Religion and Literature*, Middle Ages Series (Philadelphia: University of Pennsylvania Press, 1995), p. 131.

whose work he addresses, but his authority is moderated. It is not so much that he abandoned the patriarchy, as that he placed it at the disposal of the visionary, assuming, no doubt too easily, that it would prove unassailable, that its identification with the sacred was complete. But in Margery's worship of St. Ann and the Blessed Virgin, in Julian's sense of the Motherhood of Christ, this is exactly what is under review.

It is these considerations which indicate a new relationship between Margery Kempe and her anonymous scribe. Since the 1940 edition of the *Book* it has been customary to refer to the scribe as an "amanuensis," but on the face of it, this is a most unlikely description either of the man or of his activity. In my 1975 *Medium AEvum* article I cited Chapter 28 of the *Book* as one in which the collaboration can be observed, with its detailed description of Margery's movements which only she could have supplied, followed by a quotation from a contemporary meditation (70/22-71/15) almost certainly supplied by the scribe. But it is no easy matter to say precisely when or how the scribe effected his intervention. In the case I have just cited, it seems to me unlikely that he did so in Margery's presence, and I suspect the work we now call the *Book of Margery Kempe* is very much a second draft, produced by the scribe as an entire work, descended from the first draft upon which Margery had cooperated earlier. It is possible that the disparity in length between the first and the second book of the work may give some indication of the extent of the scribe's intervention, though the second also shows his influence, if not to the same extent. The impression that has been built up of the scribe virtually taking dictation from Margery is groundless; indeed the *Book* itself reports that the priest scribe received that first version, probably set down by Margery's son, which he agreed *both* to copy out " & wrytyn it betyr wyth good wylle" (4/20). The two activities are specified and separated, and though the scribe was indeed working from an indistinct exemplar, it is clear that he agreed to do a good deal more than simply to recopy the text. Margery trusted him with the task because of the "gret affeccyon" (4/12-13) she had for him, and, after a delay, copy he did. It is true that "he red it ouyr be-forn this creatur euery word, sche sum-tym helpyng where ony difficulte was" (5/10-12), but this was clearly the first version, the one almost certainly written by her son. Once he understood it he could then set about his task, producing the text we now have.[18]

I have labored this not overly complicated point because objections have been raised against it. The main objection is that any attempt to read another voice into the *Book* detracts from Margery's accomplishment, and it insists further that the idea implies that it is "only" because of the co-authorship that the work is effective.[19] But this position surely relies on a too narrow view of what constitutes individual accomplishment. Given the amount and quality of academic work which has been produced in the half-century since the *Book* was identified, it is no longer necessary to defend Margery against all comers, or to claim for her a distinctively modern sensibility.[20] The point is rather to see what she may have thought, and to discover what her *Book* actually represents.

I understand that there are other objections possible to the theory, which may remind some of the way "interpolating monks" used to be produced, rather like rabbits from a hat, in order to explain Christian passages in Old English texts. But it is worth recalling that an earlier generation of scholars used to refer to Margery as an "hysteric," and that the present characterization of her as a mystic is due largely to Hope Emily Allen's contributions to the 1940 EETS edition. In her

---

[18] Marion Glasscoe, who sees things differently, insists that it is important that the second scribe reports that his work was "trewly drawyn" (220/23-24) out of the earlier copy, though in the same sentence the scribe writes that since the first scribe "wrot not clerly ne opynly to owr maner of spekyng he [that is, the second scribe] in hys maner of wrytyng & spellyng mad trewe sentens" (220/20-21). His claim is that he caught the first scribe's—and presumably, so he thought, Margery's—meaning, not only in a different dialect ("spellyng") but also with different expression ("wrytyng"). He makes no claim for scribal accuracy, only that he caught the first scribe's meaning, and made "trewe sentens." Indeed he all but insists upon the changes he made. Marion Glasscoe, *English Medieval Mystics. Games of Faith*, Longman Medieval and Renaissance Library (London and New York: Longman, 1993), pp. 315-316.

[19] Susan Dickman, "Margery Kempe and the English Devotional Tradition," in *The Medieval Mystical Tradition in England*, Papers Read at the Exeter Symposium, July 1980. ed. Marion Glasscoe, Exeter Medieval English Texts and Studies (Exeter: University of Exeter Press, 1980), pp. 156-172, rejects the suggestion that the scribe assisted even with the development of the work's structure (p. 159).

[20] I have surveyed that scholarship since Hope Emily Allen's 1934 identification of the *Book* in my chapter on Margery Kempe in *Middle English Prose. A Critical Guide to Major Authors and Genres*, ed. A.S.G. Edwards (New Brunswick, N.J.: Rutgers University Press, 1984), pp. 109-119.

[21] Bonnie S. Anderson and Judith P. Zinsser, *A History of their Own. Women in Europe from Prehistory to the Present* Vol. 1 (New York: Harper and Row, 1988), and Shulamith Shahar, *The Fourth Estate. A History of Women in the Middle Ages* (London and New York: Methuen, 1983). But see too Lynn Staley, *Margery Kempe' s Dissenting Fictions* (University Park, Pennsylvania: The Pennsylvania State University Press, 1994) for a treatment of the *Book* as a fiction rooted in religious biography and devotional prose and my review in *Studies in the Age of Chaucer*, 18 (1996), forthcoming.

signed notes to that text, Hope Allen sought to fix Margery in the tradition of continental mysticism, though she equally came to regard her as having played an important part in what she was going to call "the 'Counter-Reformation' in fifteenth-century England" (p. 349, note to 245/31). Her reading of the *Book* was influenced by her earlier studies of Richard Rolle, and although in this case she thought that there was no question of authenticity, she still found herself constrained to articulate the kind of felt personal spirituality she associated with women's expression in medieval religion. But she was aware too of the restraints Margery encountered, and was going to address these in the volume she intended to produce, primarily by placing her in a context in which traditional and moderate English piety had become charged with continental utterance.

But Margery's own narrative runs in quite another direction. She is less concerned with fixing an identity than with establishing and attesting to a religious truth—indeed she would have been less concerned with the truth or falsehood of any patriarchy than with what it expressed—at least on the level of sacred revelation. She would indeed have laid claim to a degree of authority, but curiously might have been less concerned with the concept of autonomy than she is now supposed to have been—a concept which she often sets aside in the *Book* in favor of the demanding life of the spirit.

I insist that these perspectives address the nature of her feminism and her spirituality, and that they redefine, rather than limit, their properties. Margery's feminism (and her spirituality) was confrontational as need was, and disposed to confront the ecclesiastical patriarchy, particularly when she discovered its sham and hypocrisy. But it was conditioned too by a profound sense of the sacred, one which bound the present with the divine, and that association deeply informed her radical understanding of gender. Feminist discourse admits of different readings on most points, though as I have noted, there is general agreement on the importance of the patriarchy, though not perhaps on the role of gender in the operation of faith. It is now usual for some feminist discourse to proceed toward a theology which is free of the patriarchy, and either identified by gender or androgynous. But this was not the perspective that a number of medieval women writers assumed. For Margery, and for others like St. Bridget of Sweden and Julian of Norwich, gender was not an ultimate category of definition, but one of the most important which they encountered in the course of a complicated struggle, one which was at once spiritual and secular. The nature of the relationship between gender and faith is treated more often and more easily, it seems to me, in medieval texts than in modern. But the writer of medieval texts often was concerned to establish not only a theology, but also an epistemology when dealing with the relationship.

It is of course axiomatic that the history of women in the medieval, and most later, periods has not been fully examined, and that a good deal of work is going forward which seeks to establish basic facts, and to give place and voice to medieval women and to aspects of their lives, art, and spirituality, which have been all but hidden hitherto.[21] But the voices which thus become audible are not always as radical as the ones which call them forth. One important aspect of Margery's *Book* is the way in which Margery reaches out to, and seeks a common ground with, individual men whom she encounters—particularly those who do not assume an authority over her, and who are, in their way, following hers. In doing so, she does not at all surrender her integrity, but neither does she assume a precedence of motive or intention. Margery's faith is deeply invested in the world, but it does not at all neglect the sacred; indeed it is within the sacred that genders meet, that men and women cooperate, that peace abides. Part of the intention of the *Book* is to make known the nature of Margery's faith, and the fact that it was transmitted through men is not necessarily destructive to that intention, though it is complicating.

There is a related point which should be made. The *Book* gives ample evidence of the difficulties Margery confronted, and these are often taken to have arisen as a result of her gender. This insight is not wrong, but there is more to it than that. Margery was not simply a woman, she was a religious woman, though not in orders. (It is apparent that it is now necessary to insist upon this point.) She had faith. And it was her mixture of faith and gender which marginalized her, which put her at the boundaries of her culture and her time. In her mind, gender and spirituality were, as I have been arguing, intimately connected, but Margery Kempe was no separatist, no essentialist, and her attitude toward both religion and the ecclesiastical forms (though not always the ecclesiastical structures) was rarely to deprecate them. Indeed it was at the boundaries that her faith was frequently quickened and was most alive.

In their writings, aspirations, and visions, medieval religious women were keenly aware of and responsive to gender, together with the strengths and the limitations which social construction imposed. But rarely did they conceive of their faith as antagonistic to their gender, as many commentators now assume. There is, in these writings, far more concern for dialogue than for announcement, for shared insight than for separatist ideology. Above all there is the sense of an unknowable other which guides and directs, illuminates and reveals, advises and encourages, and brings all things to good.

CHAPTER FIVE

FEMINISM AND SPIRITUALITY IN CHAUCER
The *Second Nun's Tale*

Women were not the only ones aware of the relationship of gender and faith in the medieval period, and this chapter will argue that in one of the *Canterbury Tales* the fourteenth-century English poet Geoffrey Chaucer (d. 1400) provides good evidence that the role of gender in the transmission of spirituality appeared to others as well. Yet it is probably more a sign of Chaucer's realism than his irony that the only saint's life in the *Canterbury Tales* is not only one of the most religious, but also one of the most feminist texts in the collection. Further, it is a saint's life set, carefully and by choice, in the early days of Christianity, when persecution had indeed forced faith to the outer limits, to the boundaries of the culture within which it was taking root. Already in the *Man of Law's Tale*, the *Clerk's Tale*, and the *Prioress's Tale* Chaucer had indicated an interest in the felt concern of women for religion and had developed the theme at some length, but in the *Second Nun's Tale* he does something more. For this tale not only turns again to the linking of women and religion already sounded, it also develops questions of power, authority, and autonomy, and links these to religious faith, in order to establish its theme and to reveal and support its energetic and powerful protagonist.

I.

As a devout woman concerned to alter the world she finds about her, Cecilia comes into contact with standing authority, which is entirely in male hands.

One recent account of medieval society has indicated the difficulties in applying the word "patriarchy" uncritically to ecclesiastical matters, reasonably pointing out that, from the twelfth century on, ecclesiastical structures often stood against secular ones in resisting the absolute manipulation of women,[1] and a like consideration has led another scholar to insist that, even within a patriarchy, subordination rather than oppression was the operative mode.[2] But it is not difficult to believe that male structures could become oppressive, and to understand the workings of medieval patriarchy it is useful to retain a degree of skepticism, and to look carefully at the terms of the debate.[3]

In the Prologue to her tale, Alice of Bath pointedly remarks that "Men may devyne and glosen" [speculate and interpret] (26), and so declines to work "After thy text, ne after thy rubriche" (346), but her complaint does not end there:

> By God, if wommen hadde writen stories,
> As clerkes han [have] withinne hire oratories,
> They wolde [would] han writen of men moore [more] wikkednesse
> Than al the mark [image, gender] of Adam may redresse. (693-96)

The pen is powerful less for its derogatory properties than for its lasting effect, and the religious women narrators of the *Canterbury Tales* draw very explicitly not only upon devout texts, but also upon the spiritual context to which these works, a miracle of the Virgin and a saint's life, respond. That spirituality elicits, as we shall see, a direct powerful response to a sacred order which provides motivation for heroic and saintly action. These two tales have one other aspect which separates them from the great majority of the *Canterbury Tales*—they were both written, more or less obviously, for specific events which seem to have been unconnected with the collection of tales their author was making, and absorbed into it only after their composition.[4] The attitudes they present were thus conditioned by

---

[1] David Herlihy, *Medieval Households* (Cambridge, Mass.: Harvard University Press, 1985), p. 81. Throughout I cite the text of Chaucer from *The Riverside Chaucer*, third edition, ed. Larry D. Benson *et al.* (Boston: Houghton Mifflin, 1987).

[2] Gerda Lerner, *The Creation of Patriarchy*, p. 233; cp. Mary Erler and Maryanne Kowaleski, *Woman and Power in the Middle Ages* (Athens, Ga.: University of Georgia Press, 1988), pp. 1-17.

[3] Robert W. Hanning, " "From *Eva* and *Ave* to Eglentyne and Alisoun: Chaucer's Insight into the Roles Women Play," *Signs*, 2 (1977), 580-99; Robert S. Sturges, " *The Canterbury Tales*' Women Narrators: Three Traditions of Female Authority," *Modern Language Studies*, 13 (1983), 41-51; Charles R. Sleeth, "'My Dames Loore' in *The Canterbury Tales*," *Neuphilologische Mitteilungen*, 89 (1988), 174-184; Graham Landrum, "The Convent Crowd and the Feminist Nun," *Tennessee Philological Bulletin*, 13 (1976), 5-12; and Jeanmarie Luecke, O.S.B., "Three Faces of Cecilia: Chaucer's *Second Nun's Tale*," *American Benedictine Review*, 33 (1982). 335-48.

[4] Mary Griffin, *Studies on Chaucer and His Audience* (Quebec: Les éditions l'éclair, 1956), p. 29; John C. Hirsh "Reopening the *Prioress' Tale*," *Chaucer Review*, 10 (1975), 37-41, and *Ibid.*, "The Politics of Spirituality: The Second Nun and the Manciple," *Ibid.*, 12 (1977), 129-37.

events now only partly understood, but their larger concerns seem still to have been Chaucer's own, not simply those of their pilgrim narrators. And it is possible to believe that both tales, one associated with the celebration of the feast of the Holy Innocents and the cult of Young Hugh of Lincoln, the other with the entry of a "pro-Urban" English cardinal into the papal court, were intended originally to contribute to specific ecclesiastical events.

The power of the patriarchy which the Wife of Bath describes appears likewise in the Prioress's Tale, but there it is acceded to, even regarded as benevolent. It is the secular patriarchy which secures revenge for the murdered boy, the ecclesiastical patriarchy which attends to him at the end. In each case the action is effective (if in one case vicious), and the mother's role is made secondary to that of her son. In the case of the Second Nun, on the other hand, the question of the patriarchy emerges distinctly, and again it is both patriarchies, ecclesiastical and secular, which are addressed.

II.

Throughout her tale Cecilia supports the Christian church, which is repeatedly associated with a named and historical pope. The fact that she does so is important, and raises the question of the relationship of that (or any other) power to Cecilia's own spirituality. Early in the tale she sends Valerian to meet Pope Urban I (beheaded 230 A.D.) at a place outside the city, and there Valerian encounters not one man but two. The first "holy olde Urban" (185) is indeed there, but soon "ther gan appeere [appeared]/ An oold man, clad in white clothes cleere [shining],/ That hadde a book with lettre of gold in honde [hand]" (200-202). It is the nature of this second man in Chaucer that he not be specified further and that his entry be dramatic and unexpected. Coming as he does, he represents part of the *mysterium* which will lead to Valerian's conversion. But it is important too that the book he is carrying is open to these words:

> O [one] Lord, o feith, o God, withouten mo,
> O Cristendom, and Fader of alle also,
> Aboven [above] alle and over alle everywhere. (207-209)

The lines are a close translation of those which appear in Chaucer's sole source for this part of the tale, the *Legenda aurea*:

> Unus dominus, una fides, unum baptisma, unus deus, et pater omnium, qui est super omnes et per omnia et in omnibus nobis.[5]

The reference to "one Christendom" alludes in all probability to the Great Schism, just as the presence of Urban I probably sounds a note of support for the reigning pope, Urban VI, difficult and contentious man that he was.[6] But the passage is interesting too for its explicit affirmation of the role of God as Lord and as Father, and for its repeated emphasis on unity, on the one. This second theme effectively qualifies the first: the ecclesiastical patriarchy exists under a God who may be described as both lord and father, but whose concern is for all who meet in one faith, one in which gender should be no final category of definition.

The power which thus emerges to define the tale's spirituality is at once sacred, because of the old man and his book, and ecclesiastical, because of Pope Urban, who baptizes Valerian on the authority and with the power which the sacred text gives. Together, the volume and the scene establish part of the context within which Cecilia will define her own spirituality. But that context is revealed too by her words and her actions, and not by the authority which tradition attaches to male power, which she clearly does not require to validate her beliefs! It is important in this context that both Pope and old man are indeed old: their authority is based on revelation and wisdom, not on physical vigor, the traditional male resort, which in the tale as a whole is attached rather to Cecilia, almost at the expense of her virginity.[7] The figures of male authority which open the tale are further conditioned by the context of persecution which has effectively marginalized Pope and Christian alike. The words written in gold point to a finally genderless extension of God's authority "over alle" which effectively condition the references to "Lord" and "Fader." It is not quite right that the men in this scene have been feminized so much as they have been rendered free of the traditional associations of either gender. Their position, both in society and in their own bodies, is so weak in human terms that Cecilia's strength seems to spring from the woman herself,

---

[5] W. F. Bryan and Germaine Dempster, eds., *Sources and Analogues of Chaucer's Canterbury Tales* (New York: Humanities Press, 1941, rpt.1958), p. 672; see too Sherry Reames, "A Recent Discovery Concerning the Sources of Chaucer's 'Second Nun's Tale'," *Modern Philology*, 87 (1990), 337-361.

[6] Hirsh, "Politics," 130, ff.

[7] Lueck, "Three Faces," 341 ff.

which lends support to (rather than drawing it from) the old men whose sense of the sacred informs the tale's spirituality, and prevents her from seeming to act capriciously.

This last point is important to establish Cecilia's authority to act and to speak as she does, and also to show the degree of autonomy she exhibits throughout. But the words authority and autonomy are likewise significant in feminism,[8] and have important implications here. Authority in the context of the *Second Nun's Tale* comes not from the saint herself, but from the complex and symbolic event we have been examining, which, however, seems almost to be at the saint's disposal. She draws her authority not from the books which the Wife of Bath describes, but from the book written in gold and from the sense of the sacred which attends upon its appearance. She is thus concerned with its sacred character, and even the Pope, sure male representative of the ecclesiastical hierarchy that he is, draws his authority from the same sacred revelation Cecilia defends. Cecilia's authority is thus based upon a manifestation of divine power, not upon an Augustinian or scholastic tradition which placed authority in the hands of those trained in Latin and in law. Her authority is essentially that of the mystics, though she is not one herself: from a direct encounter with the sacred order she addresses the secular one, deriving her power from God. The fact that she acts in cooperation with men does not lessen her autonomy, since it is clear that they were initially motivated by her, and that they serve the same order, expressed in the "O Lord" [one Lord].

This complex working out of authority and autonomy is important because the medieval terms are very different from the modern ones, and it is easy to misunderstand the powerful spirituality the tale reveals. A useful and learned article concerning the development of St. Cecilia's legend in the Middle Ages insists that in Chaucer's tale the abbreviated treatment Valerian and Tibruce receive from their English poet implies that:

> the human soul is incapable of responding in knowledge and love to the divine initiative. Nor are human fruitfulness and continuity very real possibilities in a world where converts are seized directly by a higher power and set on the shortest road to martyrdom. Faithfulness

---

[8] See Cheris Kramarae and Paula A. Treichler, *A Feminist Dictionary* (Boston: Pandora Press, 1985), pp. 61-62.

> remains, of course, although its significance has been reduced to the extent that the saints have lost the option of being unfaithful ... . Augustine, who believed that grace restored the integrity and power of the human soul, renewing the divine image within each person, would not have approved.[9]

This treatment of the brothers leads to what is described as "the Second Nun's theological pessimism" (55), a pessimism which is thought to emerge from a shift in Chaucer where "the coherent Augustinian theology of the *Passio* gives way to a series of simpler—and ultimately more pessimistic—lessons about the relationship between God and man" (42). The reference to Augustinian theology is important, Augustine having acquired a certain academic respectability which, in Chaucerian circles among others, the study of spirituality has not yet attained, except it be attached to traditional questions of methodology. Reames is speaking no more than the simple truth when she refers to "the prevailing assumption that Chaucer knew Augustine well and purveyed his ideas consistently" (54), and whatever its relevance to the *Passio*, her long discussion of grace in Augustine seems to me altogether different from the spirituality revealed in Chaucer's tale. But Reames perceives in the tale a "theological pessimism" (55) which she thinks Chaucer created, and she believes that he has visualized grace "as abolishing nature, not raising and perfecting it" (57). This view of things indicates to her "a turning point in the *Canterbury Tales*, initiating a final sequence which calls into question everything that has gone before and prepares the way for the Parson" (55).

But however learned its examination of the tale's several ancestors, it is difficult to imagine a reading less responsive to the tale's evident spirituality than this one. Chaucer has indeed shifted his focus to Cecilia, but she is not alone in having attained autonomy, and to

---

[9] Sherry L. Reames, "The Cecilia Legend as Chaucer Inherited It and Retold It: The Disappearance of an Augustinian Ideal," *Speculum*, 55 (1980), 38-57, quote from p. 54. Augustine's role was important in fourteenth-century religious thought, though it is not quite right to characterize it as pessimistic. See Heiko Augustinus Oberman, *The Dawn of the Reformation. Essays in Late Medieval and Early Renaissance Thought*, (Edinburgh: T. & T. Clark, Ltd., 1986), "Fourteenth-Century Religious Thought: A Premature Profile," pp. 1-17, and particularly "The Augustinian Renaissance," pp. 8-12, and William J. Courtenay, "Between Despair and Love. Some Late Medieval Modifications of Augustine's Teaching on Fruition and Psychic States," in *Augustine, the Harvest and Theology (1300-1650). Essays Dedicated to Heiko Augustinus Oberman in Honor of his Sixtieth Birthday*, ed. Kenneth Hagen (Leiden and New York: E. J. Brill, 1990), pp. 5-20.

deprecate the depth of Valerian's and Tibruce's conversion simply because the text now limits their roles suggests a certain unwillingness to allow for the extraordinary power of the religious tradition within which Cecilia moves. An awakened soul, whether Valerian's, Tibruce's, or Cecilia's, has acquired its own force, and there is no final contradiction between its freedom and autonomy, and the being or the direction to which it responds. There are (and always have been) difficulties for women who practice their faith courageously whether within an ecclesiastical context which privileges male authority, or against male secular power, and it is around these problems that the St. Cecilia legend developed. They are also central concerns in Chaucer's tale.

III.

After Valerian's conversion the focus of the tale shifts: the angel which the young man had demanded to see appears and bestows his crowns of lilies and roses, chastity and martyrdom respectively as the colors "Snow white and rose reed" (254) make clear; Valerian's brother Tibruce is converted, and "Parfit [perfect] in his lernynge [learning], Goddes knight" (353), sees the angel "every day" (355). Whatever he asks of God he receives "ful soone" (357), perhaps because of sacraments he may have received from Pope Urban.[10] Arrested, the brothers are soon beheaded, but not before having converted Maximus, an officer of the Prefect, and having been encouraged by Cecilia: "Youre cours is doon [your course is done], youre feith han ye conserved [your faith you have preserved]" (387). Maximus' own martyrdom follows soon after; then it is Cecilia's turn.

Cecilia's martyrdom, however, is very different from those which have gone before, both in its development and in its effect.[11] As one who has come "of noble kynde" [from the nobility] (121) her religiousness suffers no inhibitions born of class, a familiar theme in Chaucer, and she brings too an autonomy of character and a pur-

[10] Cyril A. Reilly, "Chaucer's *Second Nun's Tale*: Tibruce's Visit to Pope Urban," *Modern Language Notes*, 69 (1954), 37-39.

[11] C. David Benson, *Chaucer's Drama of Style: Poetic Variety and Contrast in the Canterbury Tales* (Chapel Hill: University of North Carolina Press, 1986), p. 177, and Roger Ellis, *Patterns of Religious Narrative in the Canterbury Tales* (London: Crome Helm, 1986), p. 90.

poseful authority Chaucer often associates with religious women. Brought before Almachius, her judge, Cecilia counters his demand "What maner womman artow [are you]?" by reminding him that she is "a gentil [noble] womman born" (424-25), an assertion of power which gives emphasis to her subsequent discourse. Asked "Of thy religioun and of thy bileeve" [belief] (427), Cecilia objects that Almachius has begun "folily [foolishly] ... that wolden [would] two answeres conclude / In o [one] demande" (428-30), but unless he was working from a defective manuscript Chaucer has markedly changed his source. In this last section he has shifted to the *Passio* of Mombritus, but the "duas responsiones"[12] referred to there are simply the first two questions Almachius asks, which he thinks will conclude his investigation. By touching upon Almachius' perceived difference between religion and faith (for Christians these are one) Chaucer again emphasizes the independence and power of mind of his protagonist and designates the source of her authority to speak as she does. But Almachius' questions seek to fix Cecilia without any real reference to her religious attitudes, only to her religious practices. As a judge, he claims the right and the power to condemn Cecilia by an act of legal definition, a categorization which aims to describe her in terms of class and observable practice. But the focus of Cecilia's life, and the movement of her tale, go quite the other way, and aim at inclusion not isolation. Her husband, his brother, even the officer in charge of them have been drawn into the faith they share, the "o feith" [one faith] written in gold on the sacred book. The inclusion and integration which is at the heart of Cecilia's faith explains too why Chaucer lays such emphasis on her public exhortation and conversion. By responsive heart and informed spirituality, more than by definition and categories, Cecilia makes her world.

But her spirituality is a closed book to her stupid judge. He plunges on, demanding to know "Of whennes comth [where comes] thyn answeryng so rude?" (432), rude because it fails to take into account his position of apparent power. But Cecilia denies his categories, and so demolishes his position. Speaking from conscience and good faith (not from pride, as he thinks), she applies a "nedles poynt" [needle's point] to his boastful pretensions, which are "lyk a bladdre ful of wynd" (439-40). In so doing she reveals her authority and asserts her

---

[12] Bryan and Dempster, *Sources and Analogues*, p. 682; Reames, "Sources," 118 and 127, and "Recent Discovery," *passim.*

autonomy: here as nowhere else, the two appear in perfect coordination. Increasingly frustrated, Almachius reminds her that she can escape by submission, again appealing to his power, delegated to him by "oure myghty princes" (444). But the ordinances he appeals to, Cecilia explains to him, are in error: they seek to enforce a foolishly mistaken definition ("Ye make us gilty, and it is nat sooth [truth]" 451), and simply because she and her coreligionists bear a Christian name "Ye putte on us a cryme [crime] and eek [also] a blame" (455). The language of law is based on definition and designation, though the world it makes is a false one. Cecilia knows that the Christian name is "vertuous" (457), and the word still carries something of the sense of "male strength" present in its Latin root. As if to prove her point, her now frustrated judge insists that Cecilia "Chees oon of thise two" [choose one of these two (alternatives)] (458), do sacrifice or deny her faith, but now the saint can only laugh at him, asking him if he really means to advise her to become "a wikked wight" [a wicked person] (465).

Almachius' retort is important because its claim is effectively undercut in the tale's conclusion. He insists that he has "bothe power and auctoritee [authority]/ To maken folk to dyen [die] or to lyven [live]" (471-72), but Cecilia reminds him that he may "oonly lyf bireve" [only take life away] (482). Yet when he does order her to be led out to execution, it transpires that he lacks even this power: the three strokes which the executioner aims at her neck fail to sever it, and Chaucer has added a passage which explains (ironically) that "ther was that tyme an ordinaunce" (528) that three strokes was all that was permitted at an execution. The execution is thus curtailed by a legal definition such as the ones Almachius has been advancing throughout, but one that now shows his impotence, and defeats him by the very means through which he had thought to win the day.

But before this end the sacred order manifests its power once again. Scorned by the people who now "laugh at thy folye [foolishness]" (506), Almachius first orders Cecilia executed by shutting her in a bath under which a "greet fyr [fire]" (518) is built, but the simple rules of cause and effect he has been clinging to fail him, and Cecilia sits "al coold" (521). He then sends for a sword.

IV.

The problems posed by the *Second Nun's Tale* are thus complex, but have two important aspects, one concerned with its feminism, the other with its spirituality. They are of course related.

First, the tale engages deeply the issue of the patriarchy, a topic to which it offers a complex reaction. The ecclesiastical order, firmly in male hands, Cecilia addresses with a certain respect, commending her husband to it, even supporting it by her own actions, but never handing over her courage, dedication, or commanding personality. It is important in this respect that the appearance of Pope Urban and the old man, one of the few direct appearances of the sacred order in Chaucer, takes place away from the trappings of power, and is deliberately stripped of the usual associations of rank and gender. A modern gloss on this matter may be useful. I understand that the Apostolic Letter of Pope John Paul II, *Mulieris Dignitatem* (1988), with its emphasis on motherhood and virginity, its dismissal of the idea of women priests, and its concern that modern women will "deform and lose what constitutes their essential richness" (269), is not attractive to many feminists, but certain aspects of this markedly traditional document are relevant, and are so at least partly because of the context within which they appear.[13] Discussing "The Anthropomorphism of Biblical Language," the Letter remarks:

> This characteristic of biblical language—its anthropomorphic way of speaking about God—points indirectly to the mystery of the eternal "generating" which belongs to the inner life of God. Nevertheless, in itself this "generating" has neither "masculine" nor "feminine" qualities. It is by nature totally divine. It is spiritual in the most perfect way, since "God is spirit" (Jn. 4:24) and possesses no property typical of the body, neither "feminine" nor "masculine." Thus even "fatherhood" in God is completely divine and free of the "masculine" body characteristics proper to human fatherhood. (267)

It is no doubt possible to object that words cannot be stripped so easily of their psychological connotations and social implications, but the intention of the Letter points directly to the sense of the sacred which Pope Urban and his divine companion evoke. The same Letter

[13] Pope John Paul II, *Mulieris Dignitatem,* authorized English translation in *Origins,* vol. 18, No. 17 (October 6, 1988), 262-283, and *Letter to Women, Ibid.,* vol. 25, No. 9 (July 27, 1995), 137-143.

also dismisses the traditional sexist reading of the biblical statement "Your desire shall be for your husband, and he shall rule over you" (Gn. 3:16):

This statement ... implies a reference to the mutual relationship of men and women in marriage. It refers to the desire born in the atmosphere of spousal love whereby the woman's "sincere gift of self" is responded to and matched by a corresponding "gift" on the part of the husband. Only on the basis of this principle can both of them, and in particular the woman, "discover themselves" as a true "unity of the two" according to the dignity of the person. (269)

In spite of the difficult phrase "and in particular the woman" (perhaps intended to reflect the imbalance in the verse?) the passage usefully indicates the orthodox nature of the relationship between Cecilia and Valerian at the beginning of the tale, and records that domination ("maistrye" would have been Chaucer's word) is not an acceptable attitude in Christian marriage. The point, obvious though it has become over the centuries, is worth emphasizing since much scholarship stresses the often calculated aspects of medieval marriage. A daughter of the Paston household marrying a steward, for example, or Margery Kempe obtaining her husband's agreement to live a chaste life, are often treated as markedly atypical, even bizarre. But the ability of medieval women to contend with a religious system which embraced a variety of symbols and attitudes is important, and helps to explain one way they had of dealing with the larger secular patriarchy which stood about them. I understand that there will be those who will be disinclined to allow that a distinction between the two exists, and indeed they often run together. But the powerful psychological support religion has often supplied both genders cannot be set aside so easily, and it is worth noting too that often in Chaucer references to the Blessed Virgin supply an image of power and an example of excellence which guides Constance, Madame Eglentyne, and the Second Nun on their way. It is as if Chaucer perceives this image as standing near the center of a felt spirituality, a spirituality he associated with, but not only with, women.

Second, there is the whole question of Cecilia's—and the tale's—spiritual vision. Against the embracing, integrating and sacred view of life implied in the image and in the life of St. Cecilia, stands the rationalizing, descriptive, and categorizing world of secular action. It is not only a world in which Almachius sets the rules, but also one in which Pilgrims contend for a meal, attack, answer and rebut, prove and try again to establish an idea, an identity, an argument. It is a world concerned with balance, not with apostrophe, with order, not wonder, with power, not love. It is a world admirably suited to the discordant and contending voices of the Canterbury Pilgrimage, and to the circumstances of much academic discourse.

Against such empirical, self-centered egotism, stands Cecilia's example. Her thought-world is best defined in the Prologue to the tale where, after a warning against spiritual idleness which prepares for the heroine's energy and stands against the less searching religiousness of the Prioress[14] and even the Clerk, the two themes I have been concerned with emerge with clarity. So far from being "solemn and impersonal" [15] the Prologue is sure and energetic, and prepares for the tale's embracing spirituality and authoritative commitment. Its Invocation to Mary is clearly spoken by a woman, who lists among Mary's titles "doghter [daughter] of thy Sone" (36), acknowledging the sacred order, but claiming for herself male status: "I, unworthy sone [son] of Eve" (62), in a line generations of male scholars took to imply that the tale was originally written for a male teller!

Insisting that "feith is deed [dead] withouten werkis [works]" (64), that faith becomes the action in which it issues, the teller warms to her theme, now naming Mary as "Cristes mooder [mother], doghter deere of Anne" (70), sounding the mother-daughter theme and so insisting on the relevance of her own gender, while not relinquishing her authority and power. But she also invokes Mary as a woman who will preserve her from "erthely [earthly] lust and fals [false] affeccion" (74), which Cecilia also rejected. Power is not her only concern, and the power she assumes is rooted in the complex relationship between faith and belief. Her interests are not tied to her own advantage, but rather to steadfast virtue instead.

From the affirmation of women's spirituality implied in the "Invocacio," the Prologue turns to the etymology of Cecilia's name, a definition that is more of an exploration than a fixing, and one that supplies a rich variety of meanings: "hevenes lilie [lily]" (87), "the wey to blynde" (92), "hevene" and "Lia" (96), "Wantynge of blyndnesse" (100), "the hevene of peple [people]" (104). These meanings address

[14] Benson, *Chaucer's Drama of Style*, 131-46.
[15] Reames, "Legend," 55.

the inner, not the outer person, and their effect is less to express a single moral significance than to engage the whole issue of definition, of fixing persons by things external, as Almachius will attempt to do in the tale. But an epistemology like his is false and deceptive, and finally without power. The spiritual possibilities Cecilia maintains, on the other hand, cannot be identified with any single category of thought. But as her life unfolds it assumes a form which, though directed by her own autonomy and her own spirituality, conforms to a larger pattern of spiritual unity "above all and over all everywhere."

Chaucer's tale thus reveals a spirituality which emerges directly, but also by implication and inference. Throughout the tale Chaucer responds with evident insight to implications which his fiction held out, transmitting what he found in his sources, but not without developing the importance of gender in the role of spirituality. This concern was present in his sources, but latent more than expressed: Chaucer understood its centrality to the dynamic with which he was concerned, and that dynamic was essentially the power and effectiveness of faith, and its ability to confront the world's snares and change the lives of those who embraced it. As much as any other text I have written about, this one offers an unmistakable testimony to the presence of spirituality, to the transmission of faith. It does so from the time in which Christianity took hold, so that it is almost as though Cecilia, no less than Christ, is responsible for the thought world in which the pilgrimage to Canterbury is carried out.

When Cecilia first converts to Christianity and later encourages Valerian in this new faith, when she brilliantly counters Almachius, when she preaches her faith after her execution, she does so out of her own spiritual reserves, but against a larger sacred order which informs her beliefs and lends significance to her actions. Her connection to this order, which draws on her belief and her faith both, resists final definition, but reaches out finally to include the people of Rome, those on a pilgrimage to Canterbury, all who listen to her tale.

CHAPTER SIX

CHRIST' S BLOOD

There is a passage in the eighth-century English poem *The Dream of the Rood* in which the narrator reports that at the conclusion of his vision of Christ's cross he became "blithe mode" (122), having learned that the end of the courage and suffering he has witnessed is joy, not death.[1] Elsewhere in British medieval literature the effect of Christ's passion is equally complex, whether in Julian of Norwich's *Showings*, with its emphasis both upon physical detail and upon reassurance and community, or in a text like Chaucer's *Prioress' Tale*, with its sentimentalized but evidently devout recreation of the Passion in terms which reflect back not so much on the teller as on the artist.

The Passion contains numerous objects of devotion, but the two most sacred are the body of Christ and his sacred blood.[2] That there was blood associated with the Passion is attested in the gospels, though often by inference: Christ's description of the wine in the chalice he offers the apostles as "my blood of the new testament, which shall be shed for many unto the remission of sins" (Matt.

---

[1] Possibly as early as 731. Some variant verses from the 156 line poem appear on the Ruthwell Cross, which has been dated by Douglas MacLean to the eighth century, perhaps about 731: "The Date of the Ruthwell Cross," in *The Ruthwell Cross. Papers from the Colloquium Sponsored by the Index of Christian Art*, ed. Brendan Cassidy, Index of Christian Art Occasional Papers I (Princeton, N.J.: Princeton University Press, 1992), pp. 49-70. The unique text of the poem is preserved in the Vercelli Codex, which was written in the tenth century, and has been edited by Bruce Dickens and A.S.C. Ross, *The Dream of the Rood*, 4th edition, Methuen's Old English Library (London: Methuen, 1956, rpt. 1967). The phrase I have cited seems to me largely rhetorical, and, if affective at all, it is probably, like the poem itself, proto-affective, conditioned more by the requirements of significance than by those of audience.

[2] On Christ's body see Sarah Beckwith, *Christ' s Body. Identity, Culture and Society in Late Medieval Writings* (London and New York: Routledge, 1993), particularly chapter 3, "'Dyverse Imaginaciouns of Crystes Lyf,' Subjectivity, Embodyment and Crucifixion Piety," pp. 45-77, and Miri Rubin, *Corpus Christi. The Eucharist in Late Medieval Culture* (Cambridge: Cambridge University Press, 1991). Examples are legion, but late medieval crucifixes often emphasize the physicality of Christ's suffering, and their public display effectively establishes the importance of Christ's blood. See Giampiero Donnini, "Di due altri crocifissi lignei in area fabrianese," in *I Legni Dovoti*, ed. G. Donnini (Fabriano: Soprintendenza ai Beni Artistici e Storia della Marche, Comune di Fabriano, 1994), pp. 64-68.

26:28), was attached in Hebrews to "the blood of calves and goats" with which Moses "sprinkled both the book itself and all the people, Saying '*This is the blood of the testament, which God hath enjoined unto you*' . The tabernacle also and all the vessels of the ministry, in like manner he sprinkled with blood. And almost all things, according to the law, are cleansed with blood: and without the shedding of blood there is no remission" (Heb. 9:19-22), Paul concludes.[3] Interestingly, it was this passage in Hebrews, together with its echo of Matthew, which became central to the development of the *cultus* of the sacred blood in medieval thought, spirituality, and literature, and which came to inform other biblical texts, like Judas' saying ' "I have sinned in betraying innocent blood" ' (Matt 27:4), Pilate's "I am innocent of the blood of this just man" (Matt 27:24), and the reply which became one of the most notorious justifications for medieval anti-Semitism, "His blood be upon us and upon our children" (Matt 27:25).

Within the gospel narratives of the Passion itself, blood receives relatively little emphasis. Even when the crown of thorns is imposed, the imposition is not directly associated with blood, and it is only in John that we are told that, pursuant to Pilate's order and in fulfillment of the prophecy, after Christ's death "one of the soldiers with a spear opened his side, and immediately there came out blood and water" (Jn 19:35).

This biblical tradition serves to illustrate both the non-narrative context within which the devotion developed, and the way in which the sacred blood was from the first associated, both historically and allegorically, with the eucharist. Among many, Peter of Lombard would insist that, as the blood of animals which Moses employed prefigured the blood of Christ, the water was to remind us of baptism, and the difference between Christian and Jewish sacrifice was that under the old law what appeared was a sign, but that under the new the sacrifice both signified and sanctified (*PL* 192.473-76; 192.839). The kind of biblical influence present here is complex, and was aptly identified by Otto Kurz, a former librarian of the Warburg Institute, who replied to a correspondent asking which was the best book on Christian symbolism, with: "Dear Sir, the best book on Christian symbolism is The Bible." [4]

---

[3] The Douay versions of the vulgate for 1582 and 1609 (rpt. London: B. Herder, 1912) are cited throughout. See also note 4, below.

[4] Cited in E. H. Gombrich, "Archaeologists or Pharisees? Reflections on a Painting by Maarten van Heemskerck," *JWCI*, 54 (1991), 253-56, quote from p. 253.

The biblical reluctance to focus on the physical details of the Passion was repeated in certain late medieval texts, though in others it was simply set aside. The "Five Wounds of our Lord" was a theme which flourished in many contexts, from church bosses to romances, and provided a variety of openings for meditation and narrative alike.[5] In many of the play cycles, on the other hand, the devotion is not much developed, and when it is sounded at all, as for example in the Townley crucifixion play, it is the theological dimension which appears. Speaking of his death, Christ remarks "Thus by [buy] I adam blode" [6], but the action of the play rather plays down this aspect of his sacrifice. Evidence for religious attitudes involving Christ's blood is abundantly present however in the mystical writing,

---

[5] See Douglas Gray, "The Five Wounds of Our Lord," *Notes and Queries* 208 [n.s. 10] (1963), 50-51, 82-9, 127-34, 163-8, J.A.W. Bennett, *Poetry of the Passion. Studies in Twelve Centuries of English Verse* (Oxford: Clarendon Press, 1982), p. 59 ff., and Louis Charbonneau-Lassay, *Le Bestiaire du Christ* (Paris: Desclee, De Brouwer & Cie., 1940; rpt. Milan: Archè, 1980), pp. 99-102 on Christ's heart, which is further explored in Joseph de Galliffet, S.J. *De Cultu Sacrosancti Cordis Dei ac Domini Nostri Jesu Christi* (Rome: Joannem Mariam Salvioni, 1726), *passim*, one of the early important accounts of the cultus. On the wound in Christ's side see Vladmir Gurewich, "Observations on the Iconography of the Wound in Christ's Side, with Special Reference to its Position," *JWCI*, 20 (1957), 358-362, and "Rubens and the 'Wound in Christ's Side,' A Postscript," *JWCI*, 26 (1963), 358; see also A. A. Barb, "The 'Wound in Christ's Side'," *JWCI*, 34 (1971), 320-321, and "'Vidi Aquam ...' and the Wounded Christ," *Faith*, 5 no. 1 (1973), 20-21.

[6] *The Townley Plays*, eds. George England and Alfred W. Pollard. Early English Text Society, Extra Series 71, (London: K. Paul, Trench, Trubney and Co., 1897), p. 266, l. 279. There may, of course, have been practical and dramaturgical reasons for this reticence, but the same cannot be said for the *Northern Passion*, one of the sources for many of the plays, which sounds the theme almost reluctantly. Of the six manuscripts Frances Foster prints in her Early English Text Society editions (Original Series 145 and 147: 1913 and 1916) which record, in one line, the shedding of blood during the passion, only two invest it with some of the feeling evident elsewhere in the period. Thus Cambridge MS. Dd.1.1 simply reports "out of his bodi blod ran & out of his mouth also" (EETS, OS 145, l. 1635), MS. Gg.5.31 "Downe fro his heuyd the blude ran," and Bodleian MS. Rawlinson C. 86 notes " ffro his hede the Blode Rane Rownde" (l. 1635, EETS 147, p. 152); BL Additional MS. 31,042 omits the line altogether. Harlian MS. 4195 on the other hand captures some of the new interest in the devotion, albeit in conventional language: "the blude brast out both bla and rede" (EETS 145, l. 1639) the colors are those of lyrics like *Index of Middle English Verse* 3965 preserved in MS Bodley 57, and Bodleian MS. Rawlinson C. 655 reads the line "Hot blod of his bodie ran" (EETS 147, l. 1635). But I stress again that this is only one line out of the work in which blood features, and *The Northern Passion*, like the plays which it informed, does not identify the Passion with this particular cult, even though, like the plays, it flourished in the North, where devotion to the sacred blood also prospered. See John B. Friedman, *Northern English Books, Owners, and Makers in the Late Middle Ages* (New York: Syracuse University Press, 1995), pp. 148-202.

in the lyric poetry, and in devotions and devotional tracts. Among the mystics the *locus classicus* in English would almost certainly be a passage in the fourth of Julian of Norwich's *Showings*, which deals with the flagellation. The Short Version contains this detail:

> And this was schewyd me in the semes of scowrgynge, and this ranne so plenteuouslye to my syght that me thought, 3yf itt hadde bene so in kynde, for that tyme itt schulde hafe made the bedde all on blode and hafe passede onn abowte. (227.15-19)

The Long Version expands the revelation thus:

> And after this I saw beholdyng the body plentuous bledyng in semyng of the scoregyng, as thus. The feyer skynne was broken full depe in to the tendyr flessch, with sharpe smytynges all a bout the sweete body. The hote blode ranne out so plentuously that ther was neyther seen skynne ne wounde, but it were all blode. And when it cam wher it shuld haue falle downe, ther it vanysschyd. Not with standyng the bledyng contynued a whyle, tyll it myght be seen with avysement. And this was so plentuous to my syght that me thought if it had ben so in kynde and in substaunce, for that tyme it shulde haue made the bedde all on bloude, and haue passyde over all about. (342.3-343.12).

It is probably not necessary to stress the way Julian reports that the revelation came to her "in semyng" quite as much as her editors have, but there is the sense here that she understood the symbolic nature of the revelation, understood it to be both "real" and yet not physical, and grasped as well the way it stood for the salvific nature of Christ's Passion and death. Julian's powerful image has all of the properties of her most developed spirituality, and it is not particularly helpful, *pace* Colledge and Walsh, to order her revelations greater to less on the basis of the putative theological sophistication each displays: the point is that they exist together. The revelation of the sacred blood in this fourth revelation is a case in point: though without the immediate theological overtones of, for example, the dried blood in the second revelation, it still reveals not only the nature of the sacrifice involved in Christ's death, but also the connection it establishes with the devout Christian—the "fellow-Christian" for whom Julian was writing—the acts of writing and reading further emphasize the theological given that it is not only for Julian that Christ died.

The physicality of blood in these passages emerges clearly, and becomes a reminder of the effect of Christ's sacrifice, which need not be understood in allegorical or mystical terms alone. Another attitude, though related, was likewise present in Scripture, one which treated the kinds of sacrifice present in the Hebrew Scriptures, but which focused more on the physical reality of blood as a purifying agent which involves both suffering and rebirth.[7] It retained a sense of allegory, but did not stop there, and emphasized the importance of blood as the life-giving force, one which, shed by Christ, would lead to atonement. In Leviticus the rites of sacrifice are detailed, the blood of the sacrificed lamb, for example, being used to cleanse a leper (Lev. 14:13-14), in a way typological commentary would subsequently develop. But within Leviticus there is an explicit acknowledgment of the centrality of blood to life, as well as the way that the shedding of blood may constitute an atonement: "Because the life of the flesh is in the blood: and I have given it to you, that you may make atonement with it upon the altar for your souls, and the blood may be an expiation of the soul" (Lev. 17:11).

This sense of blood being the irreducibly human part of all persons appears often in modern art, sometimes with demonstrably religious, or ironic-religious, implications. But sometimes too it testifies more simply to human mortality. In Neil Jordan's film *The Crying Game* (1992), the appearance of blood along Sam's mouth when, bound and hooded, he is struck on the head with a gun, is a moving reminder of his mortality—and a warning of his imminent death. It is as though for a moment the inner man has been revealed physically, and the image begins the search for atonement which Fergus, his reluctant captor, must pursue, an atonement which is realized ironically in the murder at the film's end, one in which the motif of blood is repeated from the earlier scene, one of the many revelations and recriminations which the film contains. The life of the flesh is in the blood indeed.

---

[7] Dennis J. McCarthy, S.J., "The Symbolism of Blood and Sacrifice," *Journal of Biblical Literature*, 88 (1969), 166-176 for a study of the significance of blood in pre-Christian traditions, particularly Hebrew and, to a lesser degree, Greek. Recently Ewa Kuryluk has remarked "what a bloody book the Bible is. In the New Testament the word 'blood' occurs around 100 times and refers mostly to the redemptive blood of Jesus which cleans, nourishes and assures immortality." See *Veronica and Her Cloth. History, Symbolism, and Structure of a "True" Image* (Oxford: Basil Blackwell, 1991), p. 130. But many of the allusions are in "Revelation," and one interesting aspect of the Passion is how infrequently blood is insisted upon. On the attitudes toward blood in the later mystics, particularly in Hildegard of Bingen and Mechthild of Magdeburg, see pp. 132-139.

Although the passages in Leviticus had less direct influence on the devotion to Christ's blood than the ones in Hebrews, they are important for understanding the adorational aspect of the *cultus*, the way in which alluding to Christ's blood could represent the veneration of an objective otherness which the subject in prayer viewed as apart from, not a part of, his mental apprehension of the divinity, and which evoked an awareness of Christ's sacrifice as historical and objective. Of course in the end this second more reasoned and human understanding of Christ's blood had to give way to the more theological interpretation, since theological discourse has a way of subsuming and preempting all others. But as the cult grew it is not difficult to observe two strains which developed, each with its roots in Scripture, but with different emphases and effects. Though connected to Christ's mission, the adorational tradition viewed Christ's sacrifice less as an event which took place outside of time than as one which happened within it, and which represented Christ's own human suffering more than his finally transcendent power or even his soteriological mission. It is by now a commonplace that it was Christ's suffering, rather than his power, which had to many late-medieval Christians most significance, but the image of Christ suffering is usually viewed in stylistic art historical terms, and sometimes it is assumed that it is part of what has been called the secularization of early modern England.[8] What I wish to do here, however, is to examine the religious attitudes which attended upon it, particularly, but not exclusively, in late medieval Britain. It is attitudes then, not any putative development, which are going to concern me.

Reference to Christ's blood which treat it as "the life of the flesh" and which focus on the physical, rather than the symbolic or allegorical, nature of his sacrifice are plentiful. As Margaret Aston remarked, "Popular belief attached itself to the concrete and the seen, not be-

---

[8] On this topic see C. John Sommerville, *The Secularization of Early Modern England. From Religious Culture to Religious Faith* (New York and Oxford: Oxford University Press, 1992), pp. 82-97, though in another form it is also the subject of a growing and lively debate sparked by Christopher Haigh and others. See Christopher Haigh, ed. *The English Reformation Revised* (Cambridge: Cambridge University Press, 1987) and his *English Reformations. Religion, Politics and Society Under the Tudors* (Oxford: Clarendon Press, 1993); and among other studies, Susan Brigden, *London and the Reformation* (Oxford: Clarendon Press, 1989); Ronald Hutton, *The Rise and Fall of Merry England. The Ritual Year 1400-1700* (Oxford: Clarendon Press, 1994); and Andrew D. Brown, *Popular Piety in Late Medieval England. The Diocese of Salisbury 1250-1550* Oxford Historical Monographs (Oxford: Clarendon Press, 1995).

cause the faith of the people was materialistic, but because for them matter was an expression of spiritual forces."[9] Among the seven sheddings of Christ's blood one of the most dramatic was the flagellation, an event which took on a special significance by the fifteenth century. In the Low Countries, ubiquitous passion tracts treated the scene in detail, drawing on the Hebrew Scriptures for details, which were itemized and treated allegorically, the two tormentors representing, for example, the gentiles and the Jews, each of which contributed to his suffering.[10] Even the number of wounds Christ suffered at the flagellation was well-known, though not agreed. The Middle English *Charters of Christ* put the number at 5,460, and in 1935 R. L. Greene declared that to be correct,[11] though he may simply have adopted the *Charters* number as convenient, since it matched one in certain of the carols he was editing. In any event, other popular numbers were 5,490, 5,115, and 5,466, though a number which was at least as well-known as any of these was 5,475[12]. This number appears, among many other places, in a popular devotional preface contained in several manuscripts, including Robert Reynes' commonplace book, MS. Tanner 407, the sort of late medieval text which Eamon Duffy has characterized as "a curious amalgam of pietism, presumption and insecurity."[13]

The version preserved in Tanner 407 recounts how "[A] woman solatarie and recluse" was told by Christ " 'Sey euery day be an hooll yeer .xv. Pater noster and xv Aue marie. And at the yeeres ende thow schalt hau wurcheped euery wounde and fulfylled the noumbre of the

---

[9] Margaret Aston, *Faith and Fire. Popular and Unpopular Religion, 1350-1600* (London and Rio Grande, Ohio: The Hambledon Press, 1993), p. 4. The same volume contains (p. 301) an unusual sixteenth-century woodcut of the miraculous blood of Wilsnack, in which, following a devestating church fire in 1383, three consecrated hosts were found unharmed in the tabernacle, though now sprinkled with blood.

[10] James H. Marrow, *Passion Iconography in Northern European Art of the Late Middle Ages and Early Renaissance, A Study of the Transformation of Sacred Metaphor into Narrative Description*, Ars Neerlandica, Volume I (Brussels: Ministerie van Nederlandse Cultuur, 1979), pp. 135-141.

[11] In *The Early English Carols*, ed. R.L. Greene (Oxford: Clarendon Press, 1935), p. 401. See Mary Caroline Spalding, ed. *The Middle English Charters of Christ*, Bryn Mawr Monographs, 15 (Bryn Mawr: Bryn Mawr College, 1914), p. 26 where the number 5,460 is cited.

[12] See Dom Louis Gougaud, *Devotional and Ascetic Practices in the Middle Ages*, trans. G.C. Bateman (London: Burns, Oates and Washbourne, 1927), p. 116 n.14.

[13] Eamon Duffy, *The Stripping of the Altars. Traditional Religion in England 1400-1580* (New Haven: Yale University Press, 1992), p. 255.

same'." [14] This linking of the number of prayers the subject was expected to say was one of the uses to which the numbers were put, though it is not clear that the numbers were fixed with this practice in mind: the version of one short prayer in MS. Douce 54 (*SC* 21628) adds the words "Swete Iesu Amen," to the end of the verses to bring the number of words in the poem up to 33, the number required for the symbolic commentary following, which is said among other things to be "mystecally representyng" the 33 years Christ lived.[15]

A more important connection, but one which is equally insecure, may be to the extraordinary number of years of indulgence which is present in certain manuscripts. The number of years indicated rose markedly at some point, probably early in the fifteenth century. The preface in MS. Tanner 407, for example, includes in the version preserved in Bodleian Library MS. Lyell 30 a promise of "playn remission" (f. 51v), together with Christ's promise of "xl daies of pardon that I schall graunt hy*m*" (f. 43). But compare that with the indulgence contained in Bodleian Library MS Gough liturg. 7 (*SC* 18340): "To all them that before this ymage of pyte deuotly say .v. Pater nostres .v. Aues & a Crede . pytously beholdyng these armes of cristes passion are grau*n*ted .xxxii. M .vii. hondred .lv. yeres of pardon" (f.59v). The "ymage" with which the indulgence is associated is a Gregory Mass, with its associated devotion of the *arma Christi*, and the *arma* indulgences are only now, I am told, being studied.[16] But the contrast between 40 days (in MS. Lyell 30) and 32,755 years (in MS. Gough liturg. 7) is not untypical of the period, and either reflects, or is reflected by, the jump from a relatively simple number of wounds—the five wounds, the seven sheddings of blood—to the number associated with the flagellation—say for the sake of convenience, 5,475—to the number of drops of blood Christ shed during the Passion as a whole—revealed to have been 28,430, though another tradition put the number at 547,500[17]—though later in the century the

[14] Printed in Cameron Louis, ed. *The Commonplace Book of Robert Reynes of Acle*, Garland Medieval Texts I (New York: Garland Press, 1980), p. 264.

[15] Published by me in "A Fifteenth-Century Commentary on 'Ihesu for thy Holy Name'," *N&Q*, n.s. 17 (1970), 44-45. See too J. T. Rhodes, "Syon Abbey and its Religious Publications in the Sixteenth Century," *Journal of Ecclesiastical History*, 44 (1993), 11-25, and for further discussion of the prayer-poem, pp. 12-14.

[16] By Dr. Flora Lewis. I owe this information to Dr. J.T. Rhodes, who read and commented on an early draft of this chapter, and kindly suggested a number of references to me.

[17] Gougaud, p. 116 n. 14, and for the larger number Thomas W. Ross, "Five

drops of blood would cause a theological division of no small proportions. But the geometric progression present in these representations of Christ's wounds and blood, to which scribes sometimes responded freely, may have followed a roughly chronological progression, and indulgences may have been caught up in that movement as well.

Not only quantity but also size figured in some devotions: the length of the nails used at the crucifixion is indicated (by a "scale" drawing) in MS. Tanner 407 (fol. 51), and in a prayer roll once owned by the young Henry VIII, now preserved at Usshaw College.[18] Bodleian Library MS. Latin misc. C. 66 (fol. 129v), also known as the Humphrey Newton MS. or the Capesthorne MS, preserves not only a Middle English note on the number of wounds Christ suffered (5,475), but also a colored drawing of Christ's heart which shows the "mesure" of the wound the spear made in it, together with those of the four nails.[19]

It was the smaller number of wounds which figured most frequently in literary works, though references to some at least of the larger ones are not hard to find, particularly in the lyrics. The seven sheddings of Christ's blood took place at the Circumcision, on Mount Olivet before the Passion, at the Flagellation, at the Crowning with thorns, at the Nailing of first the hands, then the feet, and finally at the soldier's spear thrust into his heart, a wound which took on a special significance. Allusions to the sacred blood appear in a large number of lyrics, and those with any pretention to meditational interest are likely to have a reference to the devotion somewhere. The treatment could be quite sophisticated. The seven sheddings of blood were frequently linked to the seven deadly sins and sometimes as well to the seven works of mercy, corporal or spiritual. In a lyric twice preserved in MS. Rawlinson liturg. g. 2 (*SC* 15834) one version of

---

Fifteenth-Century 'Emblem' Verses from Brit. Mus. Addit. 37049," *Speculum*, 32 (1957), 275, n. 9.

[18] Both have been published in Eamon Duffy, *The Stripping of the Altars*, plates 111 (facing p. 245) and 112 (facing p. 340).

[19] The page also contains a cartouche with a Middle English verse concerning Christ's blood: "For all the blod/I sched for the / bot hertely luffe / I aske to me": *Supplement to the Index of Middle English Verse*, no. 813.5. The colored heart has obvious meditational uses. This is true of many other manuscripts, like British Library Additional MS. 37049, which has figured in several literary studies. See for example Rosemary Woolf, *The Middle English Religious Lyric* (Oxford: Clarendon Press, 1966), p. 204.

which was printed in Smithers' revision of Brown's *Religious Lyrics of the XIVth Century*, No. 123, and a later version, *Index* 780, is printed in Brown's fifteenth-century volume, No. 62. Among the several lyrics of its type this one has special significance because of its extraordinary repetition in the Rawlinson manuscript, and because the repeated version (originally assigned its own number in the *Index of Middle English Verse*), varied the stanzas so as to give a different order to the Seven Deadly Sins with which the sheddings of Blood were associated. The order moved from Lechery, Wrath, Gluttony, Pride, Covetousness, Sloth, and Envy to Pride, Envy, Covetousness, Sloth, Gluttony, Lechery, and Wrath, thus emphasizing sins more likely to be addressed by a religious or at any rate by a devout Christian, and that fact, together with the religious nature of the Rawlinson manuscript within which the revision appears (itself a composite MS of three books of hours) suggests again the way in which this apparently ecstatic and powerful devotion could be pressed into the service of doctrinal orthodoxy.[20] The list could of course be lengthened, but these texts may stand for others which similarly represented a less affective tradition, but one which retained a measure of informed veneration of a finally unknowable but awesome phenomena, a sense that the life of Christ's flesh is in his blood, and an awareness that this blood was somehow bound up with the role of Holy Church and with doctrinal orthodoxy.

---

[20] Orthodox too was John Audelay's use of the devotion in a poem about the Eucharist:

Then aske thi sacrements per charyte,
And when thou resseyust that sacrament
Beleue in hert truly
that he is that Lord omnipotent
And Cristis god-son verament
that with His blod the dere hath boght,
that schal the Saue at His iugement.
Haue this in mynde, foregete hit noght.
ll. 287-94.

Audelay's linking of Christ's blood with the Eucharist and with redemption is graceful and conventional, insisting upon the salvational nature of the Passion, as well as the biblical linking of sacrifice and salvation. See *The Poems of John Audelay*, ed. Ella Keats Whiting, Early English Text Society, Original Series 184 (London: Oxford University Press for the Early English Text Society, 1931). More usual was lyrics like the one uniquely preserved in MS. Harley 4012, with its conventional but inescapable "The blod from thy hert fast gan ran downe" (l. 15), and its anti-Semitism, also and sadly a part of the tradition, biblical in origin: "Hit was our wynnyng and ther [the Jews'] grete losse / What tyme thy body with blod was so red" (ll. 116-117).

But what exactly was doctrinal orthodoxy, at least where Christ's blood was concerned? In the fifteenth century that was not an academic question. Towards the middle of that century, primarily in Rome, there developed an increasingly acrimonious discourse between Franciscan and Dominican theologians concerning the fate and the properties of Christ's blood, particularly during the three days between his death and his resurrection. In brief, the Dominicans held that during the days in question Christ's blood, whether spilled during his sufferings or remaining in his body after it, remained united with his divinity, so that at his resurrection he possessed all his blood in his body. Since relics of the blood were finally said to have been divinely supplied, the Dominican position (perhaps paradoxically) supported the *cultus* of the sacred blood which was observed in various places in Europe, including one particularly important place in England, as we shall see shortly. In contrast, the Franciscans specifically denied that any of the blood spilled during the passion partook of Christ's divinity; it was his death, not his blood, they not unreasonably argued, which brought about human salvation. In 1462 Pope Pius II issued a *Coram Papam*, which effectively took the matter out of discussion and enjoined members of both orders to refrain from attacking each other, now that the issue was being decided in Rome. In 1464 he issued a papal bull, which effectively resolved the matter in favor of the Dominicans, but which also insisted that the position of the Franciscans not be called heretical.[21] One result of this leniency may be the impression which is still heard that the issue was never finally resolved, but in fact the Dominicans seem to have carried the day. Certainly the bull allowed the *cultus* to

---

[21] P[ater] Natale Da Terrinca, O.F.M. Cap., *La Devozione al Prez. Mo Sangue di nostro Signore Gesu Cristo*, 2 edn. (Rome: Albano Laziale, 1987), p. 148. Earlier, Joseph Henry Rohling, C.PP.S., *The Blood of Christ in Christian Latin Literature before the Year 1000* (Washington, D.C.: Catholic University of America Press, 1932), and more recently Roberto Capuzzo, "Note sulla tradizione e sul culto del sangue di Cristo nella Mantova medievale," *Storia e arte religiosa a Mantova* (Mantova: Casa del Mantegna, 1991), pp. 61-72.

[22] It also had the effect of defining the theological limits of a potentially volatile devotion: in 1467 Francesco della Rovere completed his *De Sanguine Christi*, published in Rome in 1472, which took the Franciscan position, and insisted that humankind had been saved by Christ's death, not his blood, and that "The expiations of the Old Testament, effected through the blood of slaughtered animals, prefigure the expiation of the sins of mankind by the blood of Christ through His Death and Passion. That this is so becomes apparent to those reading the glosses to the ninth chapter of St.

continue unchecked, as (more or less) it had been doing, and attached papal approval to its doing so.[22]

This late fifteenth-century dialectic reached Britain early in the next century, and in 1521 Wynkyn de Worde published Andrew Chertsey's tract *The Passioun of Our Lorde* (*STC* 14558), translated from the French, a markedly orthodox theological treatment of the Passion, to which Chertsey had himself added this "Exposition": "And what shall I say to the blode of our lorde / whyder it taryed on the erthe or nay: I beleue that all the blode whyche was of the interyte and perfeccyon of nature humayne was receyued in the resurreccyon / but another ma*n*nes blode might haue taryed here with vs upon the erthe. As now dothe men say the holy blode of Hayles and of Bruges" (Pt. xxiii, sig. i viii).[23]

What is interesting about this passage is not only that it shows the way in which really very sophisticated theological debates could appear in devotional literature of a country as apparently remote as Britain, but also the empirical candor which the disagreement evoked. If all the blood was indeed subsumed into Christ's body at the resurrection, as the Dominicans taught, how could relics of it exist? Nor were these questions confined to Britain. In the church of Sant' Andre in Mantua there is preserved today a relic of the holy blood said to have been brought by St. Longinus, the Roman soldier alluded to in John's gospel, who is credited with having brought Christianity to the city. The relic was said to have been rediscovered in 1048, and was recognized as authentic by Pope Leo IX in 1053,

---

Paul's Epistle to the Hebrews." Quoted from L.D. Ettlinger, *The Sistene Chapel Before Michelangelo, Religious Imagery and Papal Primacy*, Oxford-Warburg Studies (Oxford: Clarendon Press, 1965), p. 84.

[23] *STC* 14558. STC Films 81. Tanner 193 (6). Signature i viii; xxiii pt of the text of the gospel. See J. [T.] Rhodes, "Private Devotion on the Eve of the Reformation," University of Durham Ph.D. Thesis, 1974, II, 248-249, n. 567, where the "rather ambiguous" passage is quoted. See also I, 432-434 for a further discussion of other devotions associated with Christ's Blood. The relic of the sacred blood at Bruges came from Thierry of Alsace who had been given the relic while on the second crusade by his cousin Baldwin, King of Jerusalem. The traditional date of its reception into Bruges is 7 April 1150; the Bruge procession began in 1303, to celebrate the French defeat of the previous year. Hayles was founded in 1246 by Richard, Earl of Cornwall the brother of King Henry III, as a result of a vow he made following his escape from a shipwreck. It was consecrated in 1251 with much ceremony, but by 1270 was in decline, though in that year its fortunes were restored when the founder's son, Edmund, presented the abbey with its soon-to-be-famous relic.

[24] *Catholic Encyclopadia* (1910), *s.v.* Mantua, IX, 612, and Giuseppe Coniglio, *Mantova, la storia* 3 vols. (Mantua: Istituto Carlo D'Arco, 1958-63). "Mantova nel periodo

the same year he was captured by the Normans after the defeat of the papal armies at Civitate.[24] The relic was both identified and approved during the Eucharistic controversy surrounding the teaching of Berengarius of Tours (d. 1086), who had argued for a symbolic, rather than an actual, change in the consecrated bread and wine, and the considerable controversy his position generated (which included a tract by Lanfranc) contributed to the development of the doctrine of transubstantiation, which was fully articulated only in the thirteenth century.[25] But the opportune appearance of the relic was no doubt connected to the theological circumstances surrounding it, as happened early in the fourteenth century, near Orvieto, in the Miracle of Bolsena, in which a host is said to have dripped blood onto a corporal during the consecration of the Mass, helping to determine Pope Clement VI to approve the feast of Corpus Christi. The detail that the priest concerned had begun to doubt the doctrine of transubstantiation was probably a later addition, perhaps carried over from similar miracles of bleeding hosts, of an earlier or later date.[26] But because of the establishment of Corpus Christi, the Miracle at Bolsena was particularly well-known, and as at Mantua, the relic of the blood is preserved in the Duomo at Orvieto to this day.

The result of the papal accommodation was, as I have indicated, to formalize a practice which was already widespread, and to apply to it a theological approbation which brought it within the orbit of orthodoxy and sanctioned its continued practice. In England, this approbation had particular relevance because of the presence both of the Lollard critique of the Eucharist and because of Hayles Abbey in Gloucestershire, at which a relic of the Holy Blood was widely believed to have been preserved. The cult came into Britain in the thirteenth century, following the sack of Constantinople, and in 1247

---

feudale," I, 71-115. On the history of Sant' Andrea see too *L' Archivo del Monastero di S. Andrea di Mantova* Series I, Monumenta, Vol. IV (Mantova: Accademia Virgiliana di Mantova, 1959), pp. 2-6.

[25] For Lanfranc's *De corpore et sanguine domini* see *PL* 150. 407-442, and further C.E. Sheedy, *The Eucharistic Controversy of the Eleventh Century* (Washington, D.C.: Catholic University Press, 1947), *passim.*, and Thomas Aquinas, *Summa Theologica* 3a, 75.4 for the fully developed position.

[26] See Miri Rubin, *Corpus Christi*, p. 176 ff. for the role of the miracle, which, like other commentators, she believes not to have been particularly influential in the establishment of Corpus Christi; for the connections between Orvieto and Bolsano during the period see *Codice Diplimatico della Citta D' Orvieto e la Carta del Popolo* (Firenze: Presso G. P. Vieusseux, 1881), vol. I, *passim.*

Henry III placed a relic of the Holy Blood at Westminster Abbey; Prince Edward did the same in 1267, and relics were placed at Ashridge Monastery in Hertfordshire, and in 1270 by Edmund, son of Richard Earl of Cornwall, at Hayles Abbey in Gloucestershire.[27] The relic seems to have rescued the fortunes of the recently founded abbey which, in spite of royal patronage, had fallen on hard times and found the influx of pilgrims most welcome. But whatever its attractions, the relic seems not to have had the immediate theological implications of its Italian counterparts, but rather to have been a part of the economic and social development of the Avon valley during this period, a development in which religious ostentation played a part.[28]

But among many pilgrims who came to Hayles Abbey was Margery Kempe, who "was schrevyn & had lowde cryes & boystows wepyngys" (EETS 212, 110.34-35), further evidence, if any was needed, of her essential orthodoxy and of that of the Blood. The extent of Hayles' popularity in the late medieval period is the subject of debate, but there are contemporary references to its popularity (Latimer, in a 1533 letter, reports that people "came by flocks" [29]), and there is a passing reference to it in Chaucer, in association with Christ's heart and the crucifixion nails, when the Pardoner's swears ' "By Goddes precious herte,' and 'By his nayles,' / And 'By the blode of Crist that is in Hayles" ' (C VI 651-52), which may suggest that the devotion was well known, if not much respected, by the intelligentsia at court.

---

[27] On Henry III's connections with Westminster Abbey see Antonia Gransden, "The Continuations of the *Flores Historiarum* from 1265 to 1327," *Medieval Studies* 36 (1974), 472-92, reprinted (with addition) in Gransden's *Legends, Traditions and History in Medieval England* (London and Rio Grande: The Hambledon Press, 1992), pp. 245-265 and 332-33. The traditional treatment is in H. Maynard Smith, *Pre-Reformation England* (London: Macmillan & Co. Ltd., 1938 rpt. 1963), pp. 183-186 but see Miri Rubin, *Corpus Christi*, p. 314. Smith suggests that the proverb "As sure as God is in Gloucestershire" is a reference to the relic (p. 184 n.2).

[28] See D. J. Keene, "Surburban Growth," in *The Medieval Town, A Reader in English Urban History 1200-1540*, eds. Richard Holt and Gervase Rosser, Readers in Urban History (London and New York: Longman, 1990), pp. 97-119, and figure 1, p. 101.

[29] Smith, p. 184: the letter was addressed to Morice, and went on to warn that sight of the relic "certified them that they be of clean life, and in state of salvation without spot of sin, which doth bolden them to many things." Later, printers would adapt their workbenches to contend with the new order: see J.C.T. Oates, "Richard Pynson and the Holy Blood of Hayles," *The Library*, Fifth Series, 13 (1958), 269-277.

That it was a reasonably well-appointed shrine is evident not only by the correspondence which passed between the last abbot, Stephen Segar, and Cromwell,[30] but also by a series of documents preserved in the Public Record Office in London, PRO SP 5/5/10-18, which are among the suppression documents associated with Henry VIII. The Hayles documents, however, record a series of depositions taken in 1541 by a royal commission concerning spoils taken from Hayles by persons not licensed to do so. They record an unusually large amount of glass and "painted bourdes from the autor wher the blode stode" (f. 14)—apparently there actually was a market for such things—along with the almost incidental pillaging of the lead from the roofs and the locks from the doors. The evidence which the commission took was largely hearsay, and it contains a reported conversation in which "oon Joahn" a servant to one John Harres "did say to the wiff of this deponent that she did se oon cum by nyght to t'housse of the seid Thomas Herres with certain Lockes from Hailis in bagges & parte of them were gret & substanciall. And then the seid Joahn said to her maister[: ']Fie[,] alas[,] why do yow ressaiff thus this stuff[?']. And then the seid Thomas said to her[: ']Hold thy peax for it is ther now[,] catch that may catch[,'] & then caused them to be hid in the stabeles of hey ..." (fol. 13).

There is of course a danger in making too much of an incident even as vivid as this one, but it is difficult to escape the impression that the servant's disapproval of John Harres' appropriation of the locks belonging to the abbey was brought about less by the recollection that he was stealing crown property than by a sense of blasphemy, a continuing regard for Hayles and its shrine. It was an important enough shrine for the crown to appoint a special commission, of which Latimer was an important member, which met to examine the famous relic and to disassemble it, on October 4, 1538, and which found within an unctuous colored gum which, seen through the glass, appeared red, but they uncovered no evidence of tampering, which the cooperative Abbot had himself repeatedly denied.

Still, the destruction and discrediting of the relic seems to have been thought important among later reformers in changing attitudes toward the Eucharist, and may help to account for a story Bishop

[30] Discussed in Smith, *Pre-Reformation England*, pp. 184-185.

Hilsey told in a sermon in February, 1538, at St. Paul's Cross, when he reported that twenty years before, at Oxford, he heard the confession of a miller's wife who told him of her relations with the Abbot of Hayles, and of the jewels he had given her, but when he offered her one which she knew had hung close to the Holy Blood she refused, whereupon he had said, "Tush, thou art a fool. It is but duck's blood." If the Commission's examination proved anything, it at least disproved Hilsey's story, which however continued to circulate in one form or another for years to come.[31] In a theological sense, it was to the eucharist that the Holy Blood led, though the late medieval and early modern devotions had other resonances as well, ones which were more apparent than they have since become. In general, the more learned the text, the more likely it was to involve the eucharist, but the adorational tradition was never far away, and proved at least as resilient. Powerful and even ecstatic as the devotion first appears, and as it is often represented in art, it emerged in the end as a compelling and complex embodiment not only of Christ's Passion, but of that Passion as it was understood by Holy Church. The more gruesome the representation the more noble the suffering displayed, and in certain circumstances that suffering seems to have had a resonance in human suffering as well.

This last point is hard to establish, but is readily apparent in certain modern instances, including one of particular interest:[32] the use which the image of Christ's blood has had in recent Mexican, Cuban, and Chicano art in North America. As the recent exhibition *El Corazon Sangrante/ The Bleeding Heart*, organized in 1991 by the Institute of Contemporary Art in Boston makes clear, the tradition in Mexico is an old one, with directly medieval roots, often filtered through slightly later examples. It is usual to cite Spanish or Spanish-American

---

[31] The story is cited in Smith, p. 184, which also quotes the 1552 account of "that imaginative Welshman" William Thomas, who, in his *Il Pellegrino Inglese*, asks: "And what blood, trow you, was this? These monks (for there were two especially and secretly appointed to this office) every Saturday killed a duck and revived therewith this consecrated blood as they themselves confessed, not only in secret, but also openly and before an approved audience" (pp. 185-186).

[32] But for early modern examples see now J.T. Rhodes, "The body of Christ in English Eucharistic Devotion, *c.* 1500-*c.* 1620," in *New Science out of Old Books, Studies in Manuscripts and Early Printed Books in Honour of A.I. Doyle*, edd. Richard Beadle and A.J. Piper (Aldershot: Scolar Press, 1995), pp. 388-419. The most famous reference from this period is Marlowe's "See, see where Christ's blood streams in the firmament," *Doctor Faustus*, V, ii, 143.

sources for such art, though given the circulation of modern art books it is possible to cite any of a number of sources, medieval and modern both. But what emerges on many canvases is not the transcendence of Christ's blood or any association with the eucharist, but the place of blood in human suffering, a quality which also resonates in the medieval devotions. In many of the works in the exhibition the viewer is never allowed to forget that in an age, among other things, of AIDS, blood remains a central fact of human life, a symbol of the suffering and the mystery which are somehow at its center.

What is interesting too about the exhibition of Latin American art is the way in which the human body, and often the bodies of women, figure, sometimes grotesquely, in the images.[33] But many of the modern artists attest to less restorative, but no less powerful images, like Frida Kahlo's "Self Portrait with Thorn Necklace and Hummingbird" (1940), which use Passion imagery to reveal the personal suffering which, cast in the light of the feminist interpretation of Kahlo's work, particularly the insight that what is private is also political, takes on a more broadly social significance. John Valadez's "Bus Stop Stabbing" (1984) employs imagery connected with the deposition, together with blood, to reveal a modern crucifixion, albeit one with an ironically religious resonance. David Avalos's "Hubcap Milagro—Junipero Serra's Next Miracle: Turning Blood into Thunderbird Wine" (1989) reveals a powerful image derived directly from religious

---

[33] There are, of course, medieval sources for this aspect of the cult, and the catalogue rehearses the story, from Thomas of Cantimpre, of Lutgarde d'Aywieres, whose vision of Christ in 1206 invited her to drink from the wound in Christ's side "a sweetness so powerful that she was from that time stronger and more alert in the service of God." Olivier Debroise, "Heart Attacks: on a Culture of Missed Encounters and Misunderstandings," in Olivier Debroise, Elisabeth Sussman and Matthew Teitelbaum, eds. *El Corazon Sangrante/ The Bleeding Heart* (Boston: Institute of Contemporary Art, 1991), p. 15. For other examples of the connections between Latin American and medieval devotions see Gloria Fraser Giffords, *et al.*, *The Art of Private Devotion. Retablo Painting of Mexico* (Fort Worth and Dallas, Texas: Intercultura and SMU, 1991), in particular Yvonne Lange, "The Impact of European Prints on the Devotional Tin Paintings of Mexico: A Transferral Hypothesis," pp. 64-72, and Virginia Armella de Aspe and Mercedes Meade, "An Introduction: The Context of the Mexican Retablo," pp. 73-80.
There are instructive parallels in Gertrud Schiller, *Iconography of Christian Art. Volume 2: The Passion of Christ,* trans. Janet Seligman (Greenwich, Connecticut: New York Graphic Society, Ltd, 1972), plates 667, 744, 810-11, and in Henk van Os, *et al.*, *The Art of Devotion in the Late Middle Ages in Europe, 1300-1500,* trans. Michael Hoyle. (Amsterdam and London: Rijksmuseum Amsterdam in Association with Merrell Holberton, 1994), plates 41, 59.

iconography, perhaps ultimately the images associated with the five wounds, though that of the hand of Christ also figures. The image is that of suffering and power carried, by Bingo and Thunderbird wine, to an ironic postmodernist adoration. In each of these works of art the centrality of the human body, as derived from the medieval sources we have been examining, emerges as a secular restatement, though often one not entirely severed from its roots, to evoke a resonant but postmodern sense of popular culture in which neither gender nor religion remains absolute.

The modern school of art is a particularly instructive analogue, at least in part because it reveals to an extraordinary depth the ways in which the image of blood can reflect human pain and suffering. Many of the artists in the Latin American school are homosexual, and the complications that presents within their culture, a culture within which the Catholic church and its teaching figure prominently, are not absent from their work. But this quality of suffering is exactly the one which is difficult to demonstrate, even when inescapably present, in the medieval representations.

The second, adorational tradition is neither passive or mechanical, and even though I believe it to be orthodox, and apart from the radical tradition which (for example) Lollardry represented, it seems to have had extraordinary range and significance. Those who responded to it, by which I mean those who spoke the words and responded to the visual representations which figured in its dissemination, found in it both awe and power, a quality which is difficult to recapture from the distance of five hundred years, but which viewed through the eyes of our own contemporaries is hard to escape.

I understand that the religious attitudes I am discussing are ones which popular accounts of "Medieval Religion" usually address with abandon, but which more scientific ones usually omit. But I am not convinced that they are ones which should be avoided. In 1909 Gilbert Murray remarked in his inaugural lecture as Regius Professor of Greek Literature at Oxford University, that "in dealing with Greek literature, as with every other, in order to understand we must also feel." More than half a century later another Oxford Regius professor quoted Murray's remark in his own inaugural lecture, but asked whether it was not "owing to that attitude that much of [Murray's] work has now become unfashionable." Hugh Lloyd-Jones also suggested that the reason questions of culture, motivation, and sentiment are as carefully avoided as they are is because, although "[i]t is easy enough to see where one's predecessors have failed by importing modern ideas and preconceptions, it is never possible to be sure one is not committing the same offence oneself." The study of attitudes, Lloyd-Jones reckoned, "can seldom hope to escape modification," but it was still possible, he believed, to "understand ancient thought, at least in some degree, without importing modern prejudices." [34] One way of doing so was suggested by the professor who held the chair between Murray and Lloyd-Jones. Professor E.R. Dodds took up the issue in his study "The Religion of the Ordinary Man in Ancient Greece," asking, though finally not answering the question, What did these ritual acts *mean* to those who took part in them? "Viewed from within," Dodds wrote, "religion is a state of mind, a complex of beliefs and feelings about the forces which govern man's life and situate it in the world. Such states of mind are personal and infinitely various ... . [T]he Classical age has left us no counterparts of Augustine or of Kierkegaard. In this sense the 'inner side' of Greek religion escapes us; we can study it only in its external, collective aspect, as a social phenomenon. And even about beliefs inspired in collective acts it is hard to speak with any confidence." [35]

The question of what religious texts and ritual actions mean to those who used them retains its interest, perhaps particularly in a period which seems sometimes to have produced a hundred Augustines if only a handful of Kierkegaards, and the method Dodds uses for the more limited question he is willing to address is interesting: he notes current, twentieth-century practices, in the Greek and Turkish countryside, of ritual practices preserved in classical texts.[36] These parallels allow him to consider attitudes which are not strictly present in classical texts, but which are clearly indicated by the circumstances of the ritual actions which are preserved.[37] And that is one of the

---

[34] Hugh Lloyd-Jones, *Greek Studies in Modern Oxford. An Inaugural Lecture.* (Oxford: Clarendon Press, 1961), pp. 11-12 and 23.

[35] E. R. Dodds, "The Religion of the Ordinary Man in Classical Greece," in *The Ancient Concept of Progress*, pp. 140-155, quote from p. 141.

[36] He takes up too the difference between religion and magic, remarking that "simple country people are commonly unaware of any distinction in principle between religion and magic; the magical act becomes religious when it is incorporated into an order of divine service and interpreted as a symbolic aid to prayer" (p. 148). On the importance of Augustine in this period see further Oberman, *The Dawn of the Reformation*, pp. 8-12, 277-82.

[37] For example, of feeding the dead he writes "This custom has gone on since Neolithic times and still goes on today. It is not 'ancestor worship'; it is simply a way

problems which confronts the student of medieval religious attitudes as well.

These concerns for personal motive and individual attitude have been present in many serious examinations of religious practice, which classical scholars, not less often than medievalists, have taken up. The questions which emerge from such studies usually involve not only motivation and personal significance, but also a web of historical, cultural, and literary structures which at once draw upon and yet also speak to these attitudes. In some things, at least, social constructions figure as importantly as religious ones. Attitudes of mystical awareness, of adoration, of simple prayer lie behind a devotion like the one associated with the Christ's Blood, made powerful by the stark death associated with it. But although it was a death freely accepted, it was also a death brought about by human action, so that observing, and yet remaining apart from that death, the devout Christian saw what was at the heart of his or her religion, an event he or she could grasp as a mystery, and which in some way reflected a complicated response to the pain and suffering which this devotion often contains. This quality emerges too in Latin American and Chicano paintings, even as it does in the medieval texts which have fed them, and taken together they reveal another dimension of a spirituality in which suffering and adoration, transcendence and mystical union, human love and divine mystery all have a place.

---

of feeling that the dead are not quite dead, they still need our care. They are fed in fact for much the same reasons that cause a little girl to feed her doll, but the fantasy is taken seriously because it is psychologically useful—it eases the pain of bereavement. In Classical times the family dead lived on *choai*, a mixture of oil, honey and water, which was poured on the grave or even into a feeding tube placed in the dead man's mouth. Such tubes can still be seen in cemeteries in Turkey and parts of the Balkans; fantasy can be very literal-minded. This sort of behavior was unaffected by the Homeric belief that the dead are in Hades, just as it is unaffected today by the belief that they are in Heaven" (p. 152). Dodds' own somewhat high church view of religion emerges even more clearly in his identification of the small altar present in most Greek homes during the Classical period as "the humble successor of the Minoan palace shrines; its own successor today is the holy ikon which is to be seen in every Greek cottage" (pp. 149-150).

CHAPTER SEVEN

THE LIBERATION OF MYSTICISM
A REFLECTION ON RICHARD ROLLE

> "As to your last suggestion that I make it appear that Our Lord was inferior to 'the really tip-top mystics' I do feel it rather difficult to write coolly."
> Evelyn Underhill to J. A. Herbert, 30 March 1913.

> "There is no question that the mystics are the ones who have kept Christianity going, if anyone has."
> Thomas Merton, 3 May 1963, referring to Marguerite Porete, burned in Paris as a lapsed heretic, 1 June 1310.

In two earlier chapters I have argued that a large number of late medieval texts which concerned women addressed the patriarchy, and considered how women could maintain identity, while at the same time entering into dialogue with an interlocutor who at once challenged and yet also esteemed their faith. In this chapter I am going to turn to the other side of that dialogue, and see in what ways faith reached out to men and women, and the spokesperson I have chosen is the mystic, but in living as much as in writing. The general tendency of mystical writing is to move toward union, a union from which others, indeed from which all creation, are excluded. But one hallmark of mysticism is speech, not silence. The mystic speaks or writes, and in doing so addresses others. For Joachim Wach, a true religious experience must "issue in action." [1] The question is why?

---

[1] Joachim Wach, *The Comparative Study of Religions*, ed. Joseph M. Kitagawa, Lectures on the History of Religions Sponsored by the American Council of Learned Societies, New Series, No. 4 (New York: Columbia University Press, 1958), p. 36. The fourth of four criteria for defining religious experience, the others are: "a response to what is experienced as Ultimate Reality" (30); "a total response of the total being to Ultimate Reality" (32); "intensity" (35). For a critique of the personalizing aspects of Wach's thought, see Ninian Smart, *The Science of Religion and the Sociology of Knowledge. Some Methodological Questions* (Princeton, N.J.: Princeton University Press, 1973), p. 64 ff. See too William P. Alston, *Perceiving God. The Epistemology of Religious Experience* (Ithaca and New York: Cornell University Press, 1991), especially "Can the Christian Mystical Perceptual Doxastic Practic Be shown to Be Unreliable?," pp. 226-254. See too Dupré, "Christian Experience of Mystical Union," 5-7, and Yves Congar, "The Holy Spirit in the Prayer of the Western Church During the Middle Ages," in *I Believe in the Holy Spirit*. Volume I, *The Holy Spirit in the 'Economy.' Revelation and Expe-*

This chapter proposes an answer. In doing so, it compares certain aspects of the life and public address of the fourteenth-century English mystic Richard Rolle (d. 1349) and the Brazilian theologian Leonardo Boff (b. 1938), formerly a Franciscan and a priest. There are evident differences between the two men. Of Rolle, we know with certainty only the year of his death, and a number of works which, with differing degrees of certainty, can be attributed to his pen. His commentaries on the Psalter, his important *Form of Living*—a text I shall be concerned with here—and his meditations on the Passion are supplemented by others—his tract on the Ten Commandments and the gifts of the Holy Ghost—all of which were directed toward followers, many well-known to him.

But Rolle is interesting too because of his life: he went to Oxford and perhaps to Paris for his education; on his return he decided on his new mode of life and called his apparently younger sister to him in the countryside, bidding her to bring two gowns, one white, one gray. She did so, and he put both on (suggesting that he was slight of stature?) having first removed the arms of the grey one to make a kind of scapular. When his suitably astonished sister cried "My brother is mad!" he urged silence on her—perhaps with threats—and then ran away so as to avoid an ignominious return home. Parental authority was more absolute in the fourteenth century than it has since become, but even so, the well-attested story has something of the Boys' Book in it, a touch of innocence that rings true in spite of its source, a document intended, years after the event, to promote Rolle's canonization. According to the same work, Rolle subsequently was protected by one John Dalton, who heard him preach in church, and this protection was evidently useful not only in warding off any attempt of his family to bring him home, but also in assuring him a place in society. The presence of friends is a continuing motif in his life. I should add that little is known about the role that this John Dalton (or any subsequent patron) actually played in his life. Then as now, lay persons rarely preach in church, and that fact has been used to argue that Rolle was ordained in Paris before his return

---

rience of the Spirit, trans. David Smith. (New York: The Seabury Press and London: Geoffrey Chapman, 1983), pp. 104-114.

I am very grateful to my colleague Thomas Schubeck, S.J., of the Woodstock Theological Center at Georgetown for helpful comment on the present chapter, but any faults or eccentricities within it are mine, not his.

to Yorkshire.[2] But one other aspect of his early years has not received much emphasis. For it is apparent that Rolle's spirituality communicated itself readily and that his followers, both early and late, understood that communication as well as meditation, fellowship, and solitude were at the core of his achievement. In later years Rolle would look back on his younger self with amusement and recall how he had argued, more against authorities like St. Anselm than against any immediate threat, that the life of the solitary was better than that of a monk, but not because it was undertaken alone.[3]

The extraordinary thing about Rolle is that he regularly and conscientiously directed the spiritual life of his followers, many of them women, and that he wrote about the process, if indirectly. Recent scholarly emphasis on establishing, editing, and commenting upon his texts has distracted attention from this practice, or has left the impression that it was subordinate, rather like a well-known scholar who also dabbles in politics. But in Rolle's case (and not only in his case) the influence runs the other way. His writing sprang from his spirituality and was a part of that, and if his spirituality emerges only indirectly and by inference that is no reason to put the cart before the horse. From what little is known about his biography, Rolle seems to have attended most carefully to his spiritual life—but it was a life he shared with others. They may not have been the reason for its being, but they were a part of the means by which it proceeded, and if they were sometimes a distraction, they were also a sustaining influence. No doubt they gave as good as they got.

Things were not less difficult in subsequent periods for those who, like Rolle, sought for points of contact between the life of the spirit and the way things are. In early May 1985, the Congregation for the Doctrine of the Faith (formerly the Holy Office) ordered the Brazilian

---

[2] Dom Maurice Noetinger, O.S.B., "The Biography of Richard Rolle," *The Month*, 147 (1926), 22-33, and *contra* Hope Emily Allen, *Writings Ascribed to Richard Rolle, Hermit of Hampole, and Materials for His Biography*, The Modern Language Association of America, Monograph Series III (New York: D. C. Heath and Co., and London: Oxford University Press, 1927), pp. 490-500, which contains information on Rolle's life cited above. For a useful survey of recent scholarship see John A. Alford, "Richard Rolle and Related Works," in *Middle English Prose* (New Brunswick, New Jersey: Rutgers University Press, 1984), pp. 35-60. The best recent study is Nicholas Watson, *Richard Rolle and the Invention of Authority*, Cambridge Studies in Medieval Literature 1 (Cambridge: Cambridge University Press, 1991).

[3] On Rolle's reconsideration of his younger attitudes see E.J.F. Arnould, "Richard Rolle and a Bishop: A Vindication," *Bulletin of the John Rylands Library*, 21 (1937), 3-25.

Leonardo Boff, at the time a Franciscan friar (he has since left the order), to cease lecturing and publication and to observe a period of silence and reflection.[4] In the event, the period was less than a year (Boff wrote three books during the time), and the resulting publicity, which preceded Boff's resignation, suggests that the silencing was not a particularly astute policy.

Boff is best known for his work on liberation theology, which has been interpreted variously. "At the base of this theology for the poor," he has written, "there is a spiritual experience of protest and love. Above all, it is a holy ire, the very virtue of the prophets, against the collective misery of the poor." [5] This theology has for him "two principal tasks: first, to point out the theological relevance of freedom movements ... . Second, the theology of liberation deals with emphasizing the liberation aspects that are present in the Gospel, in the life and praxis of Jesus, and in the great tradition of the Church. Faith is salvific only when it is transformed into a praxis of love;

---

[4] These events were widely reported, but here I am indebted to Harvey Cox, *The Silencing of Leonardo Boff, The Vatican and the Future of World Christianity* (Oak Park, Ill.: Meyer Stone Books, 1988), *passim.* See the well-known examination of Boff's work signed by Joseph Cardinal Ratzinger and Archbishop Alberto Bovone, "Notificazione sul volume 'Chiesa: Carisma e Potere. Saggio di ecclesiologia militante' del padre Leonardo Boff, o.f.m.," *L' Osservatore Romano,* Anno CXXV, N. 66 (37.862), (20-21 March, 1985), pp. 1-2, which appeared in the same year as the English translation of Boff's most influential work, *Church: Charism and Power, Liberal Theology and the Institutional Chruch,* trans. John W. Diercksmeier (New York: Crossroad, 1985); the book was oiginally published in Brazil as *Igreja: Carisma e poder* in 1981. I am indebted too to Philip Berryman, *Liberation Theology* (London: I.B. Taurus & Co. Ltd., 1987), especially chapter 6, pp. 96-110. The process involved was a complex one by any standard: Boff's work was studied by officials of the Congregation who met and requested findings from experts and Professors; Boff was offered the opportunity to change or explain certain aspects of his writing (in the event, he took the initiative by sending to the Congregation the answer he had given to the Archdiocesan Commission for the Doctrine of the Faith of Rio de Janiero, which also had criticized the book); after more discussion, a vote was required from the Cardinal Members of the Congregation resident in Rome; the Prefect of the Congregation, Josef Cardinal Ratzinger (whose role in these procedure should be neither exaggerated nor underestimated) would have discussed the matter with the Pope, whose approval, with an order to publish, was required.

[5] Leonardo Boff, *Saint Francis. A Model for Human Liberation,* trans. John W. Diercksmeier (New York: Crossroad, 1982) p. 83. Subsequent references in the text, preceded by (SF). For a fine recent account of the fraternal orders in the medieval period which shows their impact on established authority and the response that challenge evoked, see Penn R. Szittya, *The Antifraternal Tradition in Medieval Literature* (Princeton: Princeton University Press, 1986), especially pp. 95-112. Boff is not the first Franciscan to create problems.

today, this praxis rises above the merely personal and must assume a structural and social character" (SF, 84-85).

Like Rolle, Boff is sensitive to the difficulties an institutional body can impose between the individual and truth, but it will hardly do to read him as a reconstructed Richard Rolle. Both share a higher regard for the individual than for the social setting in which he or she may be cast, but for Rolle, spiritual guidance guards against any abridgment of individual spiritual growth, but in doing so seeks merely to indicate direction, not to dictate a path. This is an important point, one which led Margaret Porete to difficulties when she sought to record her sense that the free but instructed soul did not need an alliance with virtue in the last stages of its ascent to the spirit.[6] Rolle's more considered focus indicates stages of spiritual growth, and concerns itself with the Christian who seeks to follow the path he indicates. For Boff, the free love of God is at the heart of religious action, and thus at the heart of any reconstruction of social identity. It is simply not true that he identifies self-realization with class struggle,[7] though his self is realized in appropriate association with others, and this social role, grounded in a carefully articulated consideration of the relationship between love and justice, is central to its development. Rolle's movement of self, on the other hand, is grounded in a reality which exists outside the self, one toward which the self can move and unite, thus coming into full being. But for Boff this realization emerges as a combination of heart, thought, mind, and will, in which love and justice, each hidden in the other, transform the self, and do not wink at the presence of exploitation and dictatorship. It is his realization of God's presence in the process of liberation, not the presence of repression alone, which causes and confirms his involvement on behalf of others.

Both men also give evidence of a radical rethinking of the difference between spiritual perfection and the fragmented world the individual experiences. Both have had a marked impact on the way religious values are perceived and articulated. But partly for these reasons, both reject individual accomplishment as a category of spiritual definition, and suggest instead a universalizing sense closer to the insight supplied by, for example, the Four Noble Truths of Buddhism

---

[6] See my account in *The Revelations of Margery Kempe,* pp. 35-37.

[7] A charge often made against him, but against which he has been defended by Cox, pp. 78-84, and Berryman, pp. 185-189.

than Western psychologizing categories. A sense of liberation from the suffering which is the world takes on a different character in each case, but a spirituality which emerges from the people violates neither Boff's praxis nor Rolle's singularity.

Rolle's *Form of Living* is one of the more sensitive guidebooks to emerge from the interest in individual spirituality which flourished in the fourteenth and fifteenth centuries.[8] But the word "guidebook" itself needs a gloss: it is no map and not a set of directions which, if followed, will lead to mystical union. It is more like the web of a net within which the subject is invited to find herself—or himself. That discovery begins in the acknowledgment of imperfection, in words, deeds, thoughts, but even that discovery is paradoxical, since the acknowledgment of imperfection, or even of sin, is also an acknowledgment of the self which that sin has helped to form. Grounded in academic philosophy as he is, Rolle insists that sinners "chesen" (3/12) the vile sin of this world. It is deviation from a form, he implies, that describes and defines a new self, and the confrontation of that new self with a different one, whether one lost or one which the future may hold out, brings an acute sense of loneliness and insecurity, which causes the changed believer, even while moving toward a higher spiritual state, to "fallen" (4/57), a word which can mean both "fall" and "fail." [9]

That is why the reminder of self, together with an abnegation of it, is an integral part of the process which surrounds, but by no means leads to, the experiences with which Rolle is concerned. But the acknowledgment of limitation is only a part of the awakening Rolle seeks. His intention, after all, is to give his follower him or her self, in the expectation that an awakened self can seek, can rise to, can

---

[8] *Richard Rolle: Prose and Verse Edited from MS Longleat 29 and Related Manuscripts*, by S. J. Ogilvie-Thompson, Early English Text Society, Original Series No. 293 (London and Oxford: Oxford University Press, 1988), pp. 3-25. the *Form of Living* is entitled in the Longleat manuscript *Tractatus Ricardi heremite ad Margaretam de Kirkby, reclusam, de Vita Contemplatiua* (p. 3). Subsequent references to the *Form* are in the text. Rolle's well-known interest in devotion to the Name of Jesus is in its way a form of spiritual direction. See Irénée Huasherr, *The Name of Jesus*. Trans. Charles Cummings, O.C.S.O. Cistercian Studies Series: Number 44 (Kalamazoo, Michigan: Cistercian Publicatuions, Inc., 1978), pp. 63-105.

[9] Ogilvie-Thompson, p. 193, note to l. 57, records that the word is a Northern form of "fail" which was possibly misunderstood by a Southern scribe who wrote the manuscript Ogilvie-Thompson prints as "fall." Either works in the context I have suggested.

become settled in a spiritual state that matters. In this process the fire of the Holy Spirit that "purgeth al syn" (6/126) leads and teaches, particularly if the believer is in that state of solitude which Rolle remarks "is most able of al othre to reuelaciouns" (6/138-9) which the Holy Spirit shall impart. These revelations shall not come quickly, but only through "longe trauaille and bisynesse to loue Ihesu Criste" (6/148-9). This effort can lead toward, but not to, divine revelation.

But even the three "stages" which are often cited as the heart of Rolle's mystical thinking—Insuperable, Inseparable, Singular—are not "steps" in any progressive sense. The stages both differ and do not differ, and their relationship is not only in kind, but also in degree. In this they differ from the careful delineation of steps and degree present in his source, Richard of St. Victor's *De Quattor Gradibus Violentae Charitatis.*[10] Insuperable, in Rolle's definition, implies strength, but it is a strength based on inclusiveness. Inseparable indeed stands for unity, but it is a stage that exists outside of time, "set and stablet in Ihesu" (16/539). But the stages exist together, or at least the devout Christian seeks to achieve each in itself, not (like steps) in turn, and each supports the other. From one point of view the two stages are almost identical; from another they are mutually intertwined. But neither has much to do with the third. Indeed the Singular stage is in its way far apart from the other two, "heghest, and most ferly to wyn" (16/549). It is a denial of inclusion and strength, since inclusion requires that something lies without, and strength implies resistance. "Ferly" has a connotation of something strange or marvelous, disconnected but pertaining to otherworldly events. The singular state is *sui generis*, attached to the others by no apparent links, but attached all the same. This sense of false starts, apparently unconnected associations, and spiritual questioning lies at the heart of his human, moving, mystical, and very popular document. It is a process that leads nowhere, an awakening of self that is also a denial, a love in which others both figure importantly and do not figure at all. It leads nowhere and everywhere. It seeks to define for the self a direction which the self must itself find out, and which is at the heart

[10] Identified in Hope Emily Allen, *Writings Ascribed to Richard Rolle* pp. 201-206, and Ogilvie-Thompson, p. 199, n. to l. 525 ff. Allen also suggests that Rolle adapted Gregory the Great's classification of contemplation into three movements, which Richard of St. Victor also used. But Rolle is turning not only to his authorities but also to his experience in what he writes, and the resulting lack of definite progression reflects this dialectic.

of the process, but that process is not finally what the tract is about. And this connection between process, act, and reality is what links the fourteenth-century mystic to the twentieth-century Franciscan.

I do not wish to exaggerate the significance or the courageousness of Boff's position in what follows, but what seems to me important about his silencing is not that the Congregation for the Doctrine of the Faith imposed it, but that Boff, then still a friar, accepted it. No doubt his options were limited. He wanted to act deliberately, and the conventions indicated calm. But what Boff had written about Church power might seem to have predicted, or perhaps even to have called for, a somewhat different course. In his most controversial work, Boff had cited Pope Gregory VII's *Dictatus Papae* (1075), as the moment that the pope "rose up against the secular practices of power," setting up instead "the ideology of the absolute power of the papacy. Support for this was not the poor, humble, and weak Jesus but rather God himself, omnipotent lord of the universe and sole source of power." [11] Against such historical absolutism, Boff insisted, stands the power of the individual Christian:

> Paul makes charism the structuring element of the community. His theology of justification rests on the belief that with the appearance of the church, the end-times had begun. This is why the fullness of the spirit had exploded in all its power. Charism is no longer extraordinary or unexpected but is the common rule for the structure of the community. For Paul charism means simply the concrete function that each person exercises in the community for the good of all (*cf.* 1 Cor 12:7; Rom 12:4; Eph. 4:7). Paul details this model by stating that the church is a body with many members, all springing from the spirit itself, each with its unique function. There is no noncharismatic member, no one is useless, everyone accepts a decisive place in the community. (157)

But if the source for the power which would blunt this charism is in the eleventh century, its champion is found in the thirteenth. Lest my linking of a medieval and a modern seem capricious, I indicate the connection offered by the founder of Boff's order, who supplies an

---

[11] Leonardo Boff, *Church: Charism and Power*, p. 51. Subsequent references are in the text. The bibliography is enormous, but see in particular Gustavo Gutierrez, *The Power of the Poor in History* in particular "Liberation Praxis and Christian Faith," pp. 36-74, and "The Historical Power of the Poor," pp. 75-107.

important connecting link between the spirituality the two share, and who influenced the young Franciscan deeply. St. Francis of Assisi was born about 1182, the son of Peter Bernardone, a wealthy cloth merchant.[12] He seems to have taken an evident pleasure in knighthood in his youth, but in 1205 he experienced the first of several divine revelations, after which he abandoned a military expedition he had joined and returned to Assisi. This awakening led toward his new life. Other revelations were not less dramatic and continued throughout his extraordinary but familiar career, which hardly seems to have ended with his death in 1226. But in 1210, Pope Innocent III, as absolutist a pontiff as any Boff indicted, approved his order, and did so at Francis' request.

Francis' order, like Boff himself, seemed born for social confrontation. The stories of the saint hammering a roof off a building where his followers were living too comfortably, chalking lines to indicate, in a particularly mean structure, where they might sleep, and identifying himself with beggars, all indicate an attachment to "the poor" his followers have subsequently embraced. But against such contempt for social convention stands an ecclesiastical orthodoxy which gave stability to those friars who embraced it, though not all of them did. Then as now, ecclesiastical stability maintains a certain dialogue with the love of poverty, and it is a tension which seems to live at the heart of Francis' order. But it is rarely the attachment to Rome which draws the friar closer to God.

Boff acknowledges this in his writing on Francis, whose attachment to poverty provided the theologian with an opening which was also a contradiction. It is the unconditional and free love of God which impels the love of the poor, Boff argues, and it was that love which directed Francis on his way. But love has another aspect too. All of the early accounts of Francis stress the physical suffering he and his followers constantly embraced, a suffering which found its fullest expression in Christ's passion. This sense of love and suffering points toward Francis' stigmata, perhaps the first of the medieval period, and one of the very few ever attributed to a man,[13] and the stigmata in turn provide a visible link between his mysticism and his social praxis. The experience of Christ's passion occurs frequently in me-

---

[12] The dates are those recorded in John Moorman, *A History of the Franciscan Order* (Oxford: Clarendon Press, 1968) pp. 4-80.

[13] Caroline Walker Bynum, "The Female Body and Religious Practice in the Later Middle Ages," in *Fragments for a History of the Human Body*, Part One, *Zone 3*

dieval spirituality (Rolle's meditations are among the best examples),[14] and in mystical texts like Julian of Norwich's *Showings*. For Francis, Richard Rolle, and Leonardo Boff the events surrounding Christ's death are what matter most about the Incarnation. They do so because they show the spiritual burden without disguising the suffering human frame into which it is born, and the mediation of the passion carries with it the same degree of suffering and self-definition present in Rolle's *Form of Living*. Boff points out that for Francis the Incarnation is "a mystery of divine sympathy and empathy ... thus, for Francis, to say God incarnate is to say God the child who cries, who is nursed, who smiles. It is to concretely represent ... his surrender on the cross" (SF 26). Boff goes on to insist that there is something of the Franciscan spirit implicit in the restraint (but not rejection) with which Francis treated the traditional theological formulation of the doctrine of the Incarnation in terms of nature and spirit, while favoring instead one which delights in sympathy and empathy. For both, it is the heart, not the mind, that best responds to, and best describes, the event.

The difficulty with Boff's own praxis does not lie—as is sometimes objected—in his inability to distinguish kinds of capitalism, the socially mediating elements of which have either self-interest or a contradictory impulse at their base. The contradiction that Francis' spirituality poses for Boff's praxis is that "the poor," in Francis' thought, are an isolated and changeless group, to be esteemed for the special spiritual insight which their poverty is thought, by itself, to supply. Boff retains the traditional Franciscan respect for the poor, but joins to it his praxis, grounded in a sense of the way capitalism has worked historically in Latin America. From this point of view a reformed society requires more than changed hearts and good intentions. The charism that can restructure the state may not be the uncommon or unexpected movement of grace which Rolle describes, but it does include a free binding of self to matters which engage the whole person. This sense of renewal links Boff to Rolle and forms one bridge to the new role Boff assigns to poverty. From this perspective, the task of pointing out "the theological relevance of freedom movements" is less

(1989), 165, reprinted in *Fragmentation and Redemption*, pp. 181-238, and developed in *Holy Feast and Holy Fast, passim.*

[14] Ogilvie-Thompson, pp. 64-68 (Meditation A), and pp. 69-83 (Meditation B), both on the passion the first also directed to Margaret Kirkby.

to justify any revolutionary practice than to understand the relevance of social change to the reconstructed community, a reconstruction which rests upon the same directed—but elected—freedom which Rolle encourages. The direction both men allow is finally dependent upon the spiritual order on which both philosophically depend, but there is a sense of individual awareness which equally both invite. This awareness is predicated upon a tradition of spirituality in which the presence of the Spirit is neither expected nor dismissed. They do not disguise their sense that the ground of being from which their perceptions spring is not an imaginary construct, nor one which can be easily conceptualized. The Franciscan sense of the Incarnation Boff describes is grounded in terms which do not deny the reality of the event, though what is imagined is based upon a settled spiritual reality which it partly, but not entirely, represents. That is why a spiritual dynamic, inconclusive but finished, continuing but only begun, moves Franciscan and mystic alike. The mystic's followers are directed to a state they cannot conceptualize, the Franciscan's poor to a world their suffering has transformed.

Perhaps the one criticism which can be made is that, given Boff's implied identification of liberation and the good, it is difficult to see from what vantage point his critique of liberation movements themselves would proceed. It is easy enough to proceed if the subject is, for example, the United Fruit Company, but what of Pol Pot? The appropriation of the language, but not only the language, of liberation, and also certain of its ends, makes it difficult to see how distinctions would be drawn or on what they would rest. But the revolutionary has this in common with the mystic, that she or he seeks to realize a limitless dynamic in a limited setting. But equally it is the effect of that experience, not just its power, that matters.[15]

The idea I have been examining here, that mysticism is otherworldly and limitless, is of relatively recent date, but it has had important implications for the study of the topic. As a concept it developed

---

[15] The main criticism of Boff which the Congregation made, however, had to do with what seemed to it his reduction of the sacraments to "production and consumption," in traditional Marxian terms, with the clergy expropriating the means of religious production from the people. The Congregation argued that the administration of the sacraments is not production in an economic sense, nor is their reception consumption, since all receive in them the grace of God. See the "Notificazone sul volume 'Chiesa: Carisma e Potere'," note 4, above.

more in common parlance than in other discourse and is inclined to emphasize the exclusiveness of the subject (there is sometimes an implied comparison with the artist); the exclusiveness of the act of knowing (it is said to be incommensurate with all human experience); and to require a particularly able student.[16] But other readings are possible, and the actual experience of encounter seems often to include an imperative to communicate it to others.

It is somewhat indelicate to ask a mystic what union with the Almighty was really like. We must attend, rather, to what we are told. And that act of telling is important. The love of God seems, on the basis of available evidence, to dispose the recipient to love others and to draw them into the mystic's world. But that world is not without its limitations. Like Buddha who turned back from Nirvana out of compassion for those whom he would otherwise leave in darkness, so the mystic addresses his or her followers, in terms which are an intimate part of the mystical experience. Union may have delights unknown to contemplation, but what does that matter? To the Christian at prayer, a new dimension emerges easily enough. And it is with that person, in the end, that the mystic is concerned. By definition, mysticism is not an entirely human experience, but the extent of its human attachments are not often explored. If religion is something added on to what it means to be human—whether for reasons of culture, psychology, or personal or devout inclination—then it is possible to view the mystics' association with others as arbitrary. But if religion is integral, whether realized by choice, insight, response, or the sum total of life experience, then it is useful to conceive of mysticism as linked to the same human roots.

Mystics themselves attest to a disjunction between their experience of God and their devotions, and this aspect of their subject leads to silence. On the other hand, mysticism also enters into the world, with all that that implies. It becomes entangled in the lives of all and becomes indistinguishable from them. But this is not a lessening of the force and the effect of the encounter; it is a development of it, even an accomplishment of it. In each, the link between spirit and

---

[16] See, for example, Robert Alfred Vaughan, B.A. (1823-57), *Hours with the Mystics. A Contribution to the History of Religious Opinions* 2 vols. (London: John W. Parker, 1856). A second edition, prepared by Vaughan's father, appeared in 1860, and a third, edited by his son Wycliffe from Littlemore near Oxford, in 1880. Vaughan was a Congregationalist minister.

mind, between an intractable and a transformed world, between a self realized and a self denied stands at the heart of the mystery. Rolle was no socialist, Boff is no mystic, but what's in a name? When Rolle left the chapel and took up his pen, they became fellows.

CHAPTER EIGHT

THE *ARMA CHRISTI* AND POWER MEDITATION, MOTIVATION AND DISPLAY

Nothing changes quickly in Gubbio. The traveler who alights from the Perugia bus is greeted, before anything else, by a Fascist monument of singularly unattractive proportions, a bronze soldier leaning arrogantly away from a carved stone which rises behind him to reveal, in relief, a medieval knight on horseback, an ideal on which the bronze soldier has evidently turned his back. Across the square the church of San Francisco testifies that the first mission the saint undertook was not to nearby Perugia, which had imprisoned him for some months when he had gone there under arms, but here, and it had been a success, so that in the end his monument puts Mussolini's in the shade.

Gubbio's great day is Good Friday, when its citizens and children take part in the famous Processione del Cristo Morto, a procession for the dead Christ, and in that procession they carry the instruments of his passion, the *arma Christi.* In earlier days the procession was preceded by a presentation of the passion in the central square, and as late as the 1940's "Pontius Pilate" still took part in the procession, as did a chorus of black-veiled women (40 in 1820, though there were then 120 male choristers) to sing songs in Umbrian; the "Great Miserere" was sung by men alone. Formerly too nobles and common people walked together (in silence: it was their office to *hear* the music) in the procession, though it tended to be the nobles who held office in the confraternities. Today there is but one confraternity left, that of Santa Croce, and its board consists of 15 councillors, a priest, and the head of the confraternity, who together are responsible not only for organizing the event, but for keeping the religious element, not the social element, central to the proceedings. For all of the good feeling, it is not folklore or tourism which guides the event, but the confraternity itself and its councillors. But as the number of confraternities began to shrink in the nineteenth century—Santa Croce alone now serves a city of about seven thousand—the ceremonies were curtailed. The dramatic presentation of the passion ended, though there are those who believe that Vatican pressure to limit such extra-ecclesiastical ceremonies also played a part.[1] But the remnant is still impressive in its way: a powerful, evocative, urban, and (by now) male ceremony, in which Christ is carried to his tomb by a band of hooded brothers, all in white, and by a city in mourning.

But before the burial, the wake. This takes place at Santa Croce, a small and not particularly distinguished church just outside the city walls, and occupies most of the afternoon. In the front of the church, before the altar, a life-size painted and plaster corpus of Christ, removed from a crucifix, is exposed for veneration. One by one the parishioners approach it, make an offering, kiss the exposed feet (the nails which fixed the corpus have been removed) and receive in return two gifts: a small holy card showing the corpus mounted on the cross with a like statue of Mary standing nearby, and a spring flower. The participant then returns to the nave of the church and sits with the others, in an atmosphere which can only be compared to that of a wake.

Outside, the mood quickens. The churchyard is small, and so fills easily, with parishioners, schoolchildren, officers and members of the Santa Croce confraternity in different dress, friars, policemen, local officials, and visitors to the town, most of them Italian. Fixed to the church wall is the traditional *ordo* for the evening's events:

ORDINE DELLA PROCESSION DEL CRISTO MORTO
[ORDER FOR THE PROCESSION OF CHRIST DEAD]

Uomini della Battistrangola [men of the Baptistry, confraternity officials]

Uomo con Teschio [a man with a skull]

---

[1] For the facts reported here I am indebted to a conversation on 2 April 1994 with Mr. Paolo Salciarini, Treasurer of the Confraternity of Santa Croce, which now organizes the procession, and which preserves in its archives records of earlier practices. Mr. Salciarini kindly informs me that the earliest record of the *arma Christi* in the confraternity records occurs in 1609, when certain of the *arma* are sent for repair (gold leaf is to be applied to the spear, etc.), though he believes this to be a relatively late record and considers a late medieval origin to be likely. The corpus of Christ carried in the procession is believed to be of the sixteenth century, and the white hoods of the confraternity participients are shown on a banner of 1525-28, which is still preserved; the statue of the Virgin is nineteenth century. I would like to thank Ms. Clare Brannon, who ably assisted me during this (and other) interviews in Gubbio; Dr. Piero Luigi Menichetti for gracious assistance; and my friends Mr. Caesar Morello and Mrs. Anna Ajo Morello, of Gubbio and Milan, for help and interest in many things pertinent to my stay in Gubbio.

Uomini con crocie [men with crosses]
Uomo con la croce [a man with the cross]
"Albero della Vita" ["The Tree of Life"]
Uomo con la croce elevata [man with a raised cross]
Uomo con il calice [the chalice]
Uomo con la borsa [the bag containing 30 pieces of silver]
Uomo con la corda [the cord: the whip]
Uomo con la colonna [the column at which Christ was beaten]
Uomo con il gallo [the rooster who reminded St. Peter]
Uomo con i flagelli [the flagellum with which Christ was beaten]
Uomo con la corona di spine [the crown of thorns]
Uomo con il bacile [the basin in which Pilate washed his hands]
Uomo con il bronzo (con la scritta INRI) [the INRI plaque fixed to the cross]
Uomo con il velo [the veil of Veronica on which Christ left his image]
Uomo con il sudario [the shroud]
Uomo con i chiodi [the nails]
Uomo con il martello [the hammer]
Uomo con il spugna [the sponge]
Uomo con la lancia [the lance of Longinus]
Uomo con la veste [Christ's vestments]
Uomo con i dadi [the dice which the soldiers cast for Christ's cloak]
Uomo con la scala [the ladder used at the deposition]
Uomo con le tenaglie [the tongs used to pull out the nails]
Uomini con torce [the torches]
Vescovo e clero [Bishop and priests]
CHRISTO MORTO [the statue of Christ dead]
lo coro dei "Cantori del Miserere" [the chorus]
Popolo [the people]
Donna del "Coro della Passione" [Lady of the chorus of the Passion]
Chierichetti [choirboys]
MARIA ADDOLORATA [the statue of Mary grieving]
lo coro del "Cantori del Miserere" [the chorus]
Popolo [the people]

The procession thus preserves a rare modern example of the medieval devotion known as the *arma Christi*, the "arms of Christ," the instruments used in Christ's passion which appear in visual and literary representations all across late medieval Europe. Happily, the gender specific designations called for by the *ordo* are no longer strictly observed, and many of the instruments are carried proudly by girls as well as by boys, or rather their representations are, since most of them are reproduced in painted plyboard, reduced in size, and fixed to maroon-colored cloth backgrounds. Thus the column to which Christ was bound during the flagellation is less than a yard long and has a length of cord fastened to the top, while the chalice (not always reproduced among the medieval *arma*) is one borrowed from the church and gains in standing and authority from the fact that, symbol though it may be, it also is real.

The instruments, and the representations of them, which the children and others hold have a long history. Berliner has traced a vigorous Western European tradition which flourished from the twelfth century on, though its roots he indicates, are Byzantine.[2] But whatever its antecedents—I shall return to a particularly revealing one in a moment—its broad popularity is late medieval, when it appeared all across Europe as a separate and distinct devotion, one which took innumerable forms, on parchment prayerbooks and on coats of arms; in churches, in palaces, and in less noble places; in glass and in wood and in stone. But its roots were earlier: Berliner notes passages in Bernard of Clairvaux and others which may anticipate the devotion, but which seem less connected to it than certain of the Byzantine texts to which I have already alluded.

There are a number of passages in the ninth-century homilies of Photius, Patriarch of Constantinople, which indicate that the tradition of isolating and identifying, in a connected sequence, a number of instruments associated with Christ's passion may have been Byzantine in origin. Thus in one Good Friday homily Photius exclaims

---

[2] Rudolf Berliner, "Arma Christi," *Münchner Jahrbuch der Bildenden Kunst*, 6 (1955), 35-153. On the Byzantine influence see p. 40 ff. The depictions of the *arma Christi* in art Berliner cites are primarily fourteenth century and later: in many ways, as a separate and distinct devotion, it is late medieval, whatever its earlier antecedents. See also Hans Belting, *The Image and Its Public in the Middle Ages. Form and Function of Early Paintings of the Passion*, trans. Mark Bartusis and Raymond Meyer (New Rochelle, N.Y.: Aristide D. Caratzas, 1990), especially chapters V and VI, "The Icon of the Passion in Byzantium," pp. 91-129, and "The Icon in the West: Its Reception during the Thirteenth Century in Italy," pp. 131-185. There are good examples in Schiller, *Iconography of Christian Art*, plates 654-680, and van Os, *The Art of Devotion*, plates 34-36.

"But let us reverence Him who has been crucified for us. Let us be ashamed of the lance, the nails, (Oh, what forbearance and long suffering! [Rom. 2.4]), the stripes, the blows, the buffeting, the spitting, the crown of thorns, which the Lord of all willingly suffered for our sake, so that by rising above passions and sin, we may conduct ourselves worthily of our proportion in paradise." [3] In a Holy Saturday sermon he asks "Who is not filled with wonder and astonishment at the spitting, the scoffing, the jeering, the flagellation, on seeing intact feet pierced through, and stainless hands being transfixed, and the side being wounded with a spear, and, wonder upon wonder, the body being stained red with blood therefrom, and that after death?" [4]

But the most detailed enumeration occurs in another Holy Saturday sermon, when the Patriarch exclaims:

> *Who* shall cause all his praises to be heard? *Nails* are piercing the Lord's hands, and they are tearing up, roots and all, the offshoots of our wickedness which had become implanted in our members, and by which human kind was laid waste and corrupted. A *crown of thorns* is bound round his head, and that encircling and painful collar of the ancient curse is cast off our neck. His side is transfixed with a *spear*, and the fount of our salvation opens up and is constantly widened, as blood and water, the cleanser of the universal transgression, well from the wound even after death. Who shall tell the mighty acts of the Lord? *Who* shall cause all His praises to be heard? A disgraceful death has delivered the world from shame, and, receiving in His face the *spital of the Jews*, He who has gathered the drops of dew [Job 38.28], and counts the drops of the sea [Cp. Sir. 18 .10], drains the flood of sin. Who shall tell the mighty acts of the Lord? *Who* shall cause all His praises to be heard? The Lord is covered with a *tomb*, but the Lord's providence for all things is not shut in with it, nor does He make the sin of His insulters *an occasion* for universal destruction. Nay, the Creator dwells in a tomb, yet steers the universe in goodly order. For it was not to wreak disaster that He willingly endured the cross, death, blows, spitting and every torment, but in order to deliver humankind from it.[5]

The connection between these texts and the later tradition are difficult to demonstrate, and it was probably the visual representations,

[3] *The Homilies of Photius Patriarch of Constantinople*, trans. Cyril Mango, Dumbarton Oaks Studies III (Cambridge: Harvard University Press, 1958), Homily VI, p. 126. I have incorporated Mango's identification of scriptural allusion in square brackets.

[4] *Ibid.*, Homily XII, p. 212.

[5] *Ibid.*, Homily XI, pp. 194-195. I have italicized the items which subsequently became identified with the *arma Christi*.

not the verbal, that leapt cultures. But at very least they offer a way of identifying which instruments a thoughtful inquiry into Christ's passion might fasten upon, and with what results. More importantly, the passages also show two attitudes which attach to the instruments, attitudes which would be repeated over and over again in the Latin West. The first of these was the way in which the perception of the instruments, whether actually or in the mind, drew forth a sense of devout recollection which moved shame, awareness of sin, punishment, the implication of Christ's sacrifice for "our promises, the deeds of our life." This not particularly obvious connection was supported by allegorical inference ("A crown of thorns is bound round His head, and that encircling and painful collar of the ancient curse is cast off our neck. His side is transfixed with a spear, and the fount of our salvation opens up and is constantly widened"), in a way that would become common in late medieval England. From the beginning, the instruments reached out to the spectator and engaged him or her in a prayerful recollection of Christ's passion, one in which he or she somehow participated.

But there was one other attitude present in Photius which likewise reappeared in the later tradition: this involved not so much a prayerful recollection, as an act of adoration. The instruments were viewed as proof of "the mighty acts of the Lord," and as such became the "arms of Christ," the *arma Christi* of late medieval culture. This aspect to the *arma* is present from the beginning and remains, in greater or less degree, throughout the centuries, until it received its most powerful expression in Michelangelo's *Last Judgment.* This double sense of intimacy and of spectacle is central to the *arma Christi*, and as much as anything accounts for the breadth of its appeal, and its ability to endure. The two are of course connected: showing the instruments with which Christ's passion was accomplished leads to a consideration of the reason he undertook it, and that consideration in turn leads the spectator back into recollection. But one is still public, the other private. One is demonstrative, the other reclusive. One reaches out, the other in.

In some ways these attitudes are more useful in identifying the purpose and effect of the *arma Christi* than identifying and listing the individual instruments which make it up—though the inclination to identify and list them is not only modern, but also medieval. Berliner prints illustrations from two fourteenth-century manuscripts, one in the Royal Library in Brussels, the other in the British Library, which represent the instruments so as to suggest an interest in determining which they are, and their relationship to Christ's passion.[6] The instruments carried or represented in the Good Friday procession at Gubbio are a fair example of what had become standard by the fourteenth century, and Berliner's illustrations of fourteenth-century coats of arms, including a particularly interesting one from Prague (Plate 8, p. 52) of 1320, a Czech reliquary of 1387 (Plate 16, p. 65), and a small selection from the numerous wood block prints which became popular in the sixteenth century (Plates 20-21, p. 73; plates 34-35, p. 100), show how the devotion quickly left its elevated position among the nobility and, absorbed into devotions like the Mass of Saint Gregory (particularly in England),[7] took root among what the Gubbio procession identifies as the people. In England, even more than elsewhere, the devotion quickly became involved with, even rolled into, other devotions, other practices, particularly those which required a degree of introspective meditation: the element of display was maintained by illustrations if in manuscript or by woodblock in a printed text. Examples are numerous, but each one has a particular emphasis and a particular effect, and it is difficult to generalize with confidence. But one print among many reveals the direction which the *arma* took, particularly when used in conjunction with others.

A gloryous medytacyon of Ihesus crystes passyon (STC 14550) is one such devout prayerbook, and in this case a related manuscript has been identified which contains the same devotional material.[8] The instruments include the vernicle, a pelican, thirty pieces of silver, a lantern, swords and clubs, the staff with which Christ was beaten, two hands

---

[6] Berliner, pp. 49-51: the manuscripts in question are Brussels, Bib. Royale: Ms. 4459-70, fols. 150v and 192v; London: British Library Ms. 6 E VI, fol. 15v.

[7] See Duffy, *The Stripping of the Altars*, pp. 238-48.

[8] MS Douce 1 (Bodleian Library, Oxford, *Summary Catalogue* 21575). See Douglas Gray, "The Five Wounds of Our Lord," *Notes and Queries*, 208 (1963), pp. 50-51, 82-89, 127-134, 163-168; the remainder of the Middle English prayer/poems in the manuscript were printed by me, "Two English Devotional Poems of the Fifteenth Century," *Notes and Queries*, n.s. 15 (1968), 4-11. The manuscript (but not the printed book) also contains a poem on the number of drops of blood which Christ shed, on which see also my "A Fifteenth-Century Commentary on 'Ihesu for thy Holy Name'," *Notes and Queries*, 215 (1970), 44-45 and J. T. Rhodes, "Syon Abbey and its Religious Publications in the Sixteenth Century," *The Journal of Ecclesiastical History*, 44 (1993), 11-25. The *arma Christi* is found as well in a number of Middle English roll manuscripts, on which see R. H. Robbins, "Arma Christi Rolls," *Modern Language Review*, 34 (1939), 415-21.

(which tore Christ's hair and which beat him), the cloth with which he was blindfolded, the dice, Christ's cloak for which the dice were cast, the rods and whips with which Christ was beaten, the crown of thorns, the column to which he was bound, the cross on which he was crucified, three nails, two hammers, two vessels holding the drink Christ was offered on the cross, the sponge by which it was offered, the spear which was thrust into his side, the ladder by which his body was taken down, the tongs which drew out the nails, Jews spitting in his face, the cross again, and the tomb in which his body was laid. The devotion is followed by another to Christ's five wounds.

What is extraordinary about the devotion in manuscript and printed text both is the way the illustrations take precedence over the text: indeed, the descriptions of the instruments are brief, conventional, and perfunctory, virtually footnotes to the illustrations which they serve. Their purpose, however, is not very different from Photius': they recall not only the existence of the instrument each one describes, but its purpose, and also its intended effect, less on Christ than on the viewer. Although the prayerbook opens with a prose prayer and a short poem on the number of drops of blood Christ shed, it is the *arma Christi* which, because of its length and numerous woodblock prints, dominates. I print it here, modernizing letter forms and adapting punctuation, with a brief description of the woodblocks illustrations which appear throughout.

Christ's face on Veronica's veil:

> The veronycle I honour in worshyp of the
> That made it through his preuyte [secret power]
> The clothe set ouer his face
> His mouthe / his nose / his eyen twayne [two]
> Shelde me lorde for that in my lyue
> I haue synned with my wyttes fyue [five wits]
> Namely with mouthe of sclaunderynge [slandering]
> Of fals othes and backebytynge [backbiting]
> And makynge boost [boast] with my tongue also
> Of grete synnes that I haue do [done]
> Lorde of heuen forgyue them me
> Thrugh vertu of the fygure [image] that I here se

A pelican with young in a nest:

> The pelycan his blode [blood] dooth blede

Therwyth his byrdes for to fede
It fygureth [represents] that god with his blode
Us fedde hangynge on the rode [cross]
whan he vs brought out of helle
In Joye and blysse with hym to dwelle
And be our fader and our fode [food]
And we his chyldren meke and good

The thirty pieces of silver:

The pens [pence] also that Judas tolde [was paid]
For the whiche our lorde was solde
Lorde kepe me from treason and couetyse [covetousness]
Therin to deye in no maner wyse

The lantern:

The lantren that they bare [carried] in the lyght
whan Cryst vwas taken in the nyght
Lorde kepe me fro [from] nyght synne
That I neuer deye [die] therin

Two swords:

The swerdes [swordes] and battes that they dyde bare
Therwith Jhesu cryste to tere [tear]
From fendes [fiends] lorde kepe thou me
Of therm aferde [afraid] neuere to be

A staff:

With a staffe thou had a stroke
Therwith Jewes thy heed [head] broke
with good chere [countenance] and mylde mode [disposition].
All this thou suffred and styll stode
whan I mysse do or ony [any(one)] me
It be forgyuen for thy pyte

Two hands, one holding a clump of hair, the other open as if about to strike:

The handes lorde that tare thyn heere [hair]
And the hande that smote the vnder thi eere [ear]
For that payne [pain] lorde be my socoure [help] there
That I haue synned with pryde [pride] of here

And oll [all] other synnes also
That I with eeres haue herkened to

The blindfold:

The cloth before thyn eyen two
They bobbed [slapped] the / they knytted [hit] so
Lorde kepe me fro vengaunce
Of chyldhod and of ygnoraunce
and of many synnes also
That I se [see] with myn eyn two
And my nose in smelles of swetenesse
By vanytes & wantonnesse

A cloak:

The Jewes also kest lote [cast lots]
On thy precious purple cote [coat]
A greet dysap[i]te [dispite] to thee alway
whan ony [any] with dyce [dice] playe
Lorde be thou my helpinge
yf I haue vsed mysclothyng
By vaynglory and vanitee
Gracious lorde pardon me

The crown of thorns, with two rods crossed:

with roddes grete thou were to dasshed
And with knotted whyppes all to lasshed
Socour me lorde of my grete synnes
Of slouthe and of ydlenesse gynnes [snares]

The crowne of thorne on thy heed fast. [fixed]
The heere to torne / thy skynne all brast. [broken]
Lorde kepe me from payne of hell pytte [hell's pit]
Neuer to deserue it by mysspent wytte

A column with a rope wound around:

To the pyller lorde also
with a rope men bounde the so
Herde drawne and strayned fast
That synewes from the bones brast [broke]
Lord lose me of [from] bandes in dystresse
Though I am vnkynde ayenst kyndnesse

Christ carrying a cross:

Thou bare the crosse vpon thy backe
Out of Iherusalem it ys no lacke
Thy fete [foot] steppes as thou forthe yode [went]
were seen thrugh shedynge of thy blode
Thou mettest [meet] with women of Bedleem
Also with women of Iherusalem
All they wept for thy grete tourment [torture]
To them thou sayd apertiment [openly]
Ne wepe ye not for my smerte [pain]
But for your chyldren wepe [weep] ye at herte
For they shal haue tourment and payne
And hondred yere here after certayne
The steppes of grace to vs the pardon
whan we go with deuocyon [devotion]
On pylgrymage with good mynde [disposition]
Of my synnes lorde thou me vnbynde [unbind]

The nails:

The nayles through fote [foot] & hande also
Lorde kepe me out [from] synne and wo
That I haue in all my lyfe done
with handes handled & fete mysse gone

Two hammers:

The hamers bothe stronge and grete
That perced [pierced] holes in handes and fete
Lorde be my socour [help] in al my lyfe
And kepe me harmles [harmless] from sworde or knyfe

Two vessels:

The vessell of eysell [vinegar] and gall
Lorde kepe me from symmes all
That to the soule be no venym [venom]
That I neuer be poysoned therin

The sponge on a pole:

whan thou had grete thyrst and nede [need]
They gaue the eysell and gall on a rede
Of that I haue wasted in glotonye
Lorde forgyue me whan I dye

The spear:

Lorde the spere so sharpe ygrounde [ground]
That in thy herte made a wounde
It quenche[t]he the synne that I haue wrought
And with my harte in ydelnesse thought
with my prydde and boost therto [pride and boast]
And myn vnbuxumness [disobedience] also

The ladder:

The ladder that was reysed hy [raised high]
From the crosse to take thy body
whan I am lorde in dedly synne
Gyue me repentaunce & shrifte to wynne.

The tongs:

The tonges that drewe the nayles [nails] out
Of fete and handes withouten dout
And losed thy body from the tre [tree: cross]
Of my synnes lorde lose thou me

Jews spitting in Christ's face:

The Jewes that spytte [spit] lord in thy face
All thou suffred & gaue them grace
That I haue offended or ony man me
Forgvue it lorde for thy pyte

Christ standing with the instruments of the passion around him:

The crosse behynde thy backe bone
That thou suffred passyon vpon
Lorde gyue me grace in my lyue
Clene of my synnes me to shryue
And therto veray [true] repentaunce
with space to perfourme my penaunce

Christ's body in a tomb:

The sepulcre wherin thou were layde
Thy blyssed body all to brayde [twisted]
Lorde graunt me or that [before] I deye
Sorowe of herte with teeres of eye
And clene remyssyon for to haue

Or I be buryed and layde in graue
And heuen to haue at my laste ende
Jesu cryst vs thyder sende
Amen.

The *arma* is followed by an indulgence, a Latin prayer, and then a prayer poem to Christ's five wounds (also illustrated with woodblocks), and finally three prayers in English prose to the Blessed Virgin Mary, St. George, and St. Sebastian. Taken together the devotions provide a coherent and not undisciplined way of prayer, one which emphasizes Christ's passion, and the Christian's participation in it, before all else, but one which also draws upon the reader's prior understanding of the events to which it refers in order to awaken understanding and involvement. The *arma Christi* is central to the prayerbooklet and to the program of meditation which it holds out; indeed the fixing of the woodblock illustrations in the *arma* has the effect of drawing attention not only to the instruments they represent, but also to the passion narrative to which they allude, so awakening the memory of the reader and engaging him or her in the activity of recreating Christ's death. Here as in most representations of the *arma Christi*, this recreation is more visual than literary, and the effect of the devotion springs as much from display as from implied biblical allusion. One result was that the *arma* spread erratically, and from opportunity and chance. There is little of the sort of descent we observe in manuscripts present in its dissemination, and departures from traditional representation often comprise its most revealing treatments. One of these is in Florence.

Perhaps the single most striking example of the *arma Christi* is the fifteenth-century fresco Fra Angelico executed in cell 7 of the east dormitory in the Dominican priory of San Marco in Florence.[9] Usually called the *Mocking of Christ*, it shows St. Dominic seated on a chair which is covered by his robes, his eyes fixed on a book, evidently engaged in the *lectio divina* which also would have occupied the cell's occupant for much of the time he spent there. Slightly behind him, on a raised platform and in painful contemplation, sits Mary, and

[9] For reproductions of the frescos to which I refer see William Hood, *Fra Angelico at San Marco* (New Haven and London: Yale University Press, 1993): the *Mocking of Christ* (cell 7): plate 10 (p. 6) and detail: plate 214 (p. 217); *Homo Pietatis* (cell 27): plate 212 (p. 214).

behind her on a dais covered with a white cloth, blindfolded, crowned with thorns, and dressed in white sits Christ, a wooden scepter in one hand, an indistinct orb in the other. Arrayed around his shoulders and head are four hands, all of them unattached to any body: one pulls his hair, one is in the act of striking him with a stick, and two are open to strike him in the face. To Christ's right the head of a Jew, again unattached to any body, spits in his face, the spittle clearly in evidence. A fifth hand lifts the Jew's hat from his head in mocking reverence.

The image of Christ seems sprung at once from the saint's reading as from Mary's contemplation, and it links the two together in a single act of thought and veneration. The hands and the head around Christ are clearly drawn from the medieval tradition of the *arma Christi*, though the artist has been selective, focusing upon the instruments associated with the mocking of Christ. Elsewhere in the priory, in cell 27, an assistant, perhaps influenced by the master's work (the saint and Mary appear again; the instruments seem to echo those in cell 7), had executed a traditional representation of the *arma*, but the fresco in cell 7 takes up and uses dramatically the very quality which sets the *arma Christi* apart from all other medieval devotions: its peculiar mixture of intimacy and display, its double sense of a series of images which exist at once discretely apart and yet in close association with a narrative context, which speak generally, but also specifically to the responsiveness of the individual Christian, and to that Christian's engagement in Christ's passion. Marcia Hall has remarked: "In the cells at San Marco that Angelico frescoed for his Dominican brethren, he adjusted his style to function. The painting style, like the Dominican preaching style, which was designated *devotus*, is easily understood, edifies and instructs simple people, and avoids elaboration." [10] But in the extraordinary fresco in cell 7, Angelico not only retained an essential simplicity, but preserved as well the devout appeal to the onlooker's meditation.[11]

[10] Marcia Hall, *Color and Meaning. Practice and Theory in Renaissance Painting* (Cambridge: Cambridge University Press, 1992), p. 46. The quote continues: "The frescos have been stripped of all elements of ornament to present images appropriate to the devotions of the friar who would inhabit the cell; no expensive ultramarine was used at all. Their didactic intent is apparent not only in their iconography, but in their color style as well."

[11] A simplicity conditioned by the Dominican liturgy, as Hood points out: "Fra Angelico's source was not a gospel text but a meditation from the *Legenda aurea.*

The appearance of the image of the spitting Jew's head exposes as well one other aspect of the *arma* which demands consideration—the way it preserves, in a particularly virulent form, a streak of anti-Semitism which seems integral to its purpose and effect. Because the fourteenth century was the period in which the devotion flourished, it is worth recalling, with the great Solomon Grayzel, the way in which, in 1290, Pope Nicholas IV (1288-1292) "urged Churchmen in France to cooperate with the Inquisition, and he repeated the charge that Jews were actively proselytizing among Christians. For a century now, Judaism was being called a threat and the Jews a malicious lot. Should the pope have been surprised when laymen and clerics anywhere made Jewish life as difficult as they could?" [12]

The image of the Jew spitting in Christ's face was well-established by the fourteenth century, and Fra Angelico broke no new ground when he took the image up and sought to revitalize it in the cell 7 fresco. But the novelty of the work is almost entirely formal: a realistic and monumental Christ is set against an almost cartoon-like head of a Jew, whose lifted hat indeed mocks Christ, but has as well the effect of offering reverence and pointing to him. Five disembodied hands are set against the powerful central figure, but they seem trivial in comparison, and draw the spectator's eye even more firmly

---

Although the *Legenda aurea* became a popular source for saints' lives in the later middle ages, it was originally intended to provide meditations on the feasts of the year for reading aloud in the chapter rooms or refectories of Dominican convents. By the fifteenth century, to be sure, the *Legenda aurea* was widely and even popularly known; but one can safely assume that for the preachers of Fra Angelico's day, as of Fra Jacobo's, the proper context was the Dominican liturgy. There one reads that Christ was blindfolded, struck, and spat on, all in the house of Annas, and that he was dressed in a white garment in the house of Herod. Clearly, therefore, Fra Angelico intended to prompt the beholder's memory of the whole action rather than to represent a single event. His *Mocking of Christ* thus telescopes a number of narrative episodes stretched over a long period of time into a single and remarkably non-dramatic image" (p. 216).

[12] Solomon Grayzel, ed. and trans. *The Church and the Jews in the XIIIth Century. Volume II 1254-1314,* edited and arranged by Kenneth R. Stow (New York and Detroit: The Jewish Theological Seminary of America and Wayne State Univ. Press, 1989/5749), p. 23. Grayzel shows how during the thirteenth century the papacy manifested a " new spirit, essentially suspicious and aggressive" which "animated the bull *Turbato corde,* issued and re-issued in the second half of the 13th century at the request of the Inquisition," and that this " new attitude was to characterize Christian-Jewish relations for centuries to come" (p. 3). The addition of the spitting Jew to the *arma Christi* is in complete accord with this regressive and oppressive historical development.

to Christ's head, haloed, crowned with thorns (though exceptionally in San Marco and in this period, the thorns draw no blood from this powerful and compelling representation of the divine), and blindfolded—though far from mocking, the blindfold, by obscuring Christ's face, seems only to contribute to the sense of mystery and majesty which surrounds the Godhead.

But the anti-Semitism of the fresco, at once latent and expressive, cheapens its effect. The spittle from the Jew's mouth (a convention of the *arma* tradition) indeed points to Christ's head and is balanced by the inclined staff on Christ's left, but, like the raised hat and the lifted eye of a head set a few inches below Christ's own, it qualifies, even defeats, the sense of divinity present elsewhere in the fresco. The *arma* tradition was especially rich in associations, and repeatedly called for the spectator to contextualize and draw implications. But here the only identification possible is with the saint who reads at Christ's feet, and though the Jew's head may defer to Christ's, it also creates a focus of its own, at once crude, reductive, and circular, and like the saint and the Virgin below, inside and outside of the world which Christ defines.

As we shall see, this aspect of the *arma* is intimately associated with the complex power which the tradition involves, and the sense of display and meditation present throughout the *arma* tradition resonates here as well. But the San Marco fresco also serves as a warning, a reminder of how exclusion corrupts even the best intentions, and the ways in which meditation fails when it only turns in upon the self.

But there is a powerful counterbalance to the *arma* in Florence, one painted not many years after, and not many miles away. Probably the most dramatic presentation which the *arma Christi* ever had was when they appeared in Michelangelo's *Last Judgment* (1534-41), where, presented by angels, the *arma* intrude dramatically into the larger composition. But years earlier he had connected the *arma* to a full-length statue of the risen Christ, who is represented standing and nude, holding not only the cross, but also the pole to which the sponge was attached but has now been removed, and one of the flagellum. Michelangelo executed the statue in 1519-21 in Florence to replace an earlier version which he had abandoned when he left Rome in 1516, in the face of which a disfiguring vein of black had appeared. The statue now stands in S. Maria sopra Minerva, in

Rome, where it was erected at Christmas, 1521, though not in the architectural setting which Michelangelo had envisioned.

The work is often dismissed by modern critics as an inferior copy in which the artist had lost interest, and Wilde reports that there were false rumors circulating when the statue was set up in Rome that it had been executed by the young assistant who had assisted with part of the surface work.[13] In fact it is a powerful and impressive work, remarkable not only for the serpentine form and the antique youthfulness of Christ's body, but also for the extraordinary use made of those instruments of the passion which the artist has selected. The cross, that perennial sign of Christ's passion, is diminished in size as if to emphasize his resurrection, and the almost Apollo-like face conveys divinity, albeit with a Platonic echo, more than humanity or suffering. But this young, risen Christ carries with him two reminders of his humanity: the cord with which he was whipped, and the sponge which he was offered when he affirmed his humanity with the words "I thirst" [Jn. 19.28]. Of the two, it is the representation of the sponge which shows the most originality: for one thing, it is not paired, as it usually is, with the spear which pierced Christ's side: in fact that wound, though present on the corpus, is decidedly underemphasized, again directing our attention toward Christ Risen, not Christ Crucified. Exceptional too is the way the sponge proper is represented detached from the hyssop pole [Jn. 19.29], which now has the appearance of a pilgrim's staff, while the sponge itself seems almost edible, a reminder of the Eucharist which the sour wine signified, and which Christ has become. It is a particularly brilliant display of the *arma*, in which two are selected to stand for Christ's human nature, even as his divine nature is equally insisted upon. But few as they are, it was probably the use of the *arma* in the statue that prepared the way for their even more spectacular use in the next decade, when the artist undertook the *Last Judgment*.

In the twenty-two years which had elapsed between the completion of the Sistine ceiling in 1512 and early stages of the *Last Judgment*

---

[13] Johannes Wilde, *Michelangelo. Six Lectures*. Oxford Studies in the History of Art and Architecture (Oxford: Clarendon Press, 1978), p. 147. Howard Hibbard is among those who dismiss the statue: "Some of the unsuccess of the statue probably derives from its status as a copy of another work—artists rarely do so well a second time, and Michelangelo in particular was by then already more interested in concepts than in final execution." Howard Hibbard, *Michelangelo* second edition (New York: Harper & Row, 1983), p. 168.

(1536), a work which the artist undertook only with the greatest reluctance, there had occurred both the Sack of Rome (May to December 1527), with its accompanying famine, torture, plundering, and finally plague, and the beginning of the Reformation, events which indeed may inform the anguish which the powerful fresco radiates. But in the two lunettes above the main body of the painting, angels bring down and display the *arma Christi*, which seem brought forward almost as if they were exhibits presented in a court of law, evidence both against the damned and in favor of the saved.

Here, as in the earlier statue, the cross figures prominently in the left lunette, as does the crown of thorns; in the right, the cross is balanced by the column to which Christ was bound during the flagellation, the deposition's ladder appears in the background as well. The sponge reappears; the nails are represented; even the dice are reliably reported to have been present in the past.[14] The *arma* often appear in "Last Judgments" and in other ecclesiastical wall art, though usually, as in the powerful and elaborate stained glass windows of the near-contemporary (1511-1531) representations in King's College Chapel, Cambridge, or the wall paintings in such remote country churches of the same period as that of St. Lawrence in Lohja, Finland, they are diminutive and unemphasized, useful, instructive, and interesting, but not the powerful, overhanging images which appear here.[15]

But with the images which do appear there is one decidedly unconventional omission: that of the spear. Here, even more than in the statue at S. Maria sopra Minerva, the omission seems particularly unaccountable, since the *Last Judgment* lunettes contain a number of the instruments, and even though the sponge (attached to its pole this

---

[14] Reported in Charles de Tolnay, *Michelangelo. The Final Period* (Princeton: Princeton Univ. Press, 1971). De Tolnay remarks "The Last Judgment is related to the Crucifixion, symbol of mankind's salvation through Christ's sacrifice, and a crucifix stood upon the old altar, as can be seen in the earliest engravings of the Chapel interior by Lorenzo Vaccaro" V, 42.

[15] H.G. Wayment, *The Windows of King's College Chapel, Cambridge* Corpus Vitrearum Medii Aevi, Great Britain, Supplementary Volume I (London: Oxford University Press for the British Academy, 1972), primarily in Window 14.3, the *Lamentation of Christ*: "The brassy bowl containing water and a sponge, and the nails and tools, like the cross and ladders behind, remain as reminders of the manner of Christ's death" (p. 86). But they are all but lost in the window as a whole. The wall paintings of St. Lawrence, Lohja, are reproduced in István Rácz, *Lohjan Kirkko* (Helsinki: Kustannusosakeyhyiö Otava, 1970), plates 56-57. See also Friedman, *Northern English Books*, pp. 151-174

time) is not managed particularly well, it is impossible to believe that any technical detail, like the length of the shaft, accounted for the omission. On the contrary, the omission of this most usual and conventional instrument seems quite deliberate, and also somewhat surprising, since along with its biblical associations it carries as well a connotation of authority appropriate to the occasion.

But the appearance of the *arma* above the *Last Judgment* testifies to the importance of the relationship of the inner lives of those who are being judged to what is taking place. I said that the *arma* are presented almost as though they are exhibits at a trial, and so they are. But they are exhibits which concern all involved in the trial, and in an important way they stand against the sense of predestination which has often been found in the work as a whole.[16] For while they at once testify to and display Christ's power, and also offer reason for his authority, they further serve to remind the viewer of the openings to divine grace still available to him or her, and suggest as well that those below are being judged according to whether their lives partook in the realities, at once spiritual, practical, and moral to which the *arma* allude. Though they are not often read this way, they are intimately a part of the great fresco, and so understood, deeply inform its meaning and effect.[17] Too often they have been all but ignored, perhaps in part because of their position on the wall and their distance from the viewer, but also because the relationship of the *arma* to spiritual perfectibility and to moral action is no longer as apparent as it once was.[18] But these instruments, which would have been familiar

---

[16] A widely held opinion: among many places, see Marcia B. Hall, "Michelangelo's *Last Judgment*: Resurrection of the Body and Predestination," *The Art Bulletin*, 58 (1976), 85-92.

[17] Changes having been made there may be a parallel between the *arma* in the *Last Judgment* and a series of drawings of the crucifixion which Michelangelo made toward the very end of his life, about the time he was considering carving, in wood, another crucifixion. Paul Joannides remarks that while "a wooden crucifix may have been in Michelangelo's mind, these drawings were also self-sufficient, not presentation drawings but spiritual exercises, aids to contemplation and prayer, intended to focus the old artist's attention on the redemptive sacrifice." " 'Primitivism' in the Late Drawings of Michelangelo: The Master's Construction of an Old-age Style," in *Michelangelo Drawings*, Studies in the History of Art 33 (Symposium Papers XVII) (Washington, D.C.: National Gallery of Art, 1992), p. 252. The same motives Joannides finds in the drawings were clearly present in the *Last Judgment* and in the (never completed) crucifix, and together these show how easily public display and private devotion could coexist in the artist's, and in many people's, mind.

[18] For example in Pierluigi de Vecchi, "Michelangelo's *Last Judgment*," in *The Sistine Chapel. The Art, the History and the Restoration* (New York: Harmony Books, 1986),

to the sixteenth-century viewer both from their presence in other such "Last Judgments" and from a host of other places, would have had a resonance and a significance by virtue of their size and position which would have been inescapable. Taken as a whole they qualify the powerful scene enacted below, partly by explaining its reason and purpose, partly by offering a way out to the still living.

II.

In what follows I am going to explore the relationship between the *arma Christi* and a series of connected images present to young persons in inner-city America, which I shall call, for the sake of balance and convenience, the *arma urbis*. These images appear frequently, sometimes in newspaper photographs, but more often on television and in the movies, in films like Ernest Dickerson's *Juice* (1992), Mario Van Peebles' *New Jack City* (1992), and even John Singleton's memorable *Boyz N the Hood* (1991). I understand that the formal pattern of conventional images found in the *arma Christi* does not exist here, though as I hope to show the repetition of certain associated images has a similar effect, and beneath the two *armas* there are other similarities, of expression, of ultimate meaning, which are instructive and mutually informative. But I understand as well that there will be those who will find the comparison inappropriate, disquieting, or worse, and I can only say that a judgment based on genteel decorum seems to me quite mistaken. The *arma Christi* was one of the most powerful (and ubiquitous!) images of late medieval Europe. Influenced by different cultures, it nonetheless crossed them, and by selection and addition artists repeatedly found in it a language appropriate to a number of occasions. Today moving images attract the most attention, and for many define value and articulate significance. It is true that here I am concerned with the values and attitudes of a particular group in a particular time and place, but the images I treat reveal concerns which seem to me strikingly like those addressed by the *arma Christi*, and to create a narrative context which establishes attitudes and defines objectives. The *arma Christi* is at once dependent upon,

---

176-207, which produces good (if pre-restoration: the cleaning of the *Last Judgment* was only completed in 1994, the Sistine Ceiling in 1984) reproductions of the lunettes, pp. 186-189, but fails to consider their significance.

but not entirely constrained by, biblical allusion, and invites not only recollection of what has happened, but also consideration of implication and significance. It is the collective assortment of images which binds these two *arma* together, though as we shall see, there are other things as well.

The kinds of images available to inner-city youth have three evident connections with those preserved in the complex tradition of the *arma Christi*. First, there is an implied narrative, one which describes a pattern which seeks to order events and inform attitudes. Second, there is the matter of prestige and status: the sense that the ordinary, the mundane, will be transformed and redeemed by actions which exist outside of the narrative, even apart from it; in this sense the visual representations exist against history, not in cooperation with it. And third, the *arma* and the television both carry with them a moral imperative, one which mediates between time and action, but which charges the viewer to participate in a series of events which are part ritual, part undetermined occurrence, but which taken together bestow meaning and assign significance.

In some ways the most complicated of these three propositions is the first one, the conventional narrative which is implied in each tradition. For the *arma*, that narrative is associated with the life, but particularly with the death, of Christ. The sponge, which was offered to Christ dipped in wine and gall in order to assuage his thirst, usually appears on a pole the length of the spear, with which it is often associated. These two items are in context really quite contradictory, since the sponge was employed to maintain Christ's life, however briefly, and was used to bring liquid to his lips; the spear was used to verify his death, and had the effect of drawing the last drops of liquid out of his body. The wine which is associated with the sponge has, again in context, eucharist associations, and these are not at all absent from the spear, which provided the last (of many!) openings out of which Christ's blood would flow to redeem humankind. In fact many representations of Christ on the cross show blood pouring from the wound on the side, a wound I have discussed in the chapter on Christ's blood. What is important in the context of the *arma Christi*, however, is the way in which they define power. The effect of both is at once suffering and redemption: the spear both represents Christ's death and also shows Death's failure: the sponge carries red wine to Christ's lips, and brings his now eucharistic blood to the mouths of those who wish to partake of it. As such, the imagery bears a certain parallel to certain icons present in inner-city America, where, however, the intention and effect are very different.

Gun and Police

The icons symbolic of suffering and redemption available to inner-city youth are several, and they are structured and identifiable in a narrative context just as the *arma* are. The primary icon—roughly equivalent, I suppose, to the cross—is the gun, today often an automatic handgun, but not otherwise identifiable. It is as famous for its results as for its presence, again like the cross, and carries with it a certain mystique which exists quite apart from its evident power. Although it takes many forms, at bottom all are one, and its presence informs the actions of all around it. Like the cross, the gun is a complex symbol, for it exists not only in the hands of standing authority, but also in the hands of those who oppose it. Just as the cross began as a sign of Roman power but was converted into the symbol of one who had been put to death upon it, so the gun, in the hands of the police a symbol of authority and power, becomes, in the hands of others, a sign for a new (if often false) identity, and the way to achieve it. In this context, the gun does not exist in isolation: rather it exists, like the *arma*, in a narrative setting which encodes meaning and inscribes significance.

That setting is communicated by a variety of media: the television primarily, but also, upon occasion, the newspapers, the radio, and (as important as any of these) common rumor and gossip. In what follows I am of course aware that I am drawing upon inner-city America of the late twentieth century as my primary point of reference, but I do so because the comparison I wish to explore seems to me to make it appropriate and revealing, revealing both of the late medieval and of the modern American community. But apart from the ubiquitous handgun, the second most available icon seems to me to be the police.

Victims and Power

If the gun projects power and, by extension, identity, other images convey an opposite effect: that of victimization. In the case of the *arma Christi*, the victim is sacrificial and innocent: but is the victim so carefully delineated in the popular media any different? Current American attitudes toward authority do not usually allow for the public representation of police weakness, even when they are said to be "out-gunned," a phrase which usually means that those whom they oppose carry automatic weapons, while the police do not. Paradoxically, the effect of the image is often to represent the police as embattled but strong, and to convey the impression that the armed persons who oppose them rely on "superior fire power" to make up for other deficiencies, in person, organization, and judgment.

The image, frequently repeated, of young African-American men lined up against a wall, presents a complex representation of both manliness and victimization. Children no longer, the young men are initiated into manhood by their capture and are treated now with the respect due to a dangerous opponent. But equally they are rendered powerless by their capture, and usually the overwhelming force associated with it further emphasizes their helplessness. Of course from the point of view of the police, a large force is calculated, by its numbers, to reduce violence, to give the impression that any resistance is futile. Power is seen as an alternative to violence, not as its instrument, and except in extraordinary cases, like the beating of Rodney King by a group of police in Los Angeles in 1993, the presence of police is usually represented as putting an end to violence, not bringing it about; the riots which followed in Los Angeles after the acquittal of the police officers who had beaten Mr. King were represented as showing (among other things) the foolishness of trusting to violence itself. In its own way the Rodney King beating contributed to the image of the young black man as victim and added another item, the police nightstick, to the list of repressive instruments through which power is maintained. Like the gun and the cross, the nightstick conveys power, but it does so in a particularly personal and sinister fashion, since it is of no use against an armed opponent and really can function only against the unprepared.

What these three items—the gun, the police line up, the nightstick—have in common is their ability to project power. I have already noted that one of these, the gun, is as often associated with the young black man as with the police, and so establishes a common vocabulary, even a common ground, although it is not a ground which appears to be particularly level. But that is why these icons have come to have such different resonances in the advantaged, and in the disadvantaged, communities. What is seen in the advantaged community as threatening, irrational, and violent can appear, to those being identified, as forbidden, challenging, empowering. Like the adjective *bad*, which, apart from its usual meaning, also can mean "Good, excellent, worthy of esteem or value," [19] these images can take on an inviting, if also frightening, aspect, one which identifies power and challenges the status quo, one which invites the observer to participate in some way in the narrative which they encode.

I believe that the image associations present in the modern *arma urbis* have implications for the way we interrogate the late medieval *arma Christi*. For one thing, they speak to the extraordinary popularity of the *arma Christi*, a popularity which, whatever its origins,[20] extended across much of Europe, and even found a home in nineteenth-century provincial America, as the publication in Albany of Peter Bauder's *The Spiritual Mirror* (1825) indicates.[21] But the comparison makes it somewhat easier to inquire about the connectedness of the items within the *arma Christi*, and to consider the effect of the *arma* as a whole. For the connections which exist, or at least are implied, are founded on a narrative, one which is only partly revealed in the gospel accounts of Christ's passion. Implied as well is the larger narra-

---

[19] *The Dictionary of American Regional English*, Frederic G. Cassidy, Chief Editor (Cambridge, Mass.: Harvard University Press, 1985-) vol. I, *s.v.* bad, adj., sense 6) notes the meaning as being found " *chiefly among Black speakers*" (a circumstance which certainly has changed since 1985), and reports one 1977 informant explaining "He is a bad dude would suggest to whites the idea of an undesirable character, whereas to blacks it would indicate a highly desirable person."

[20] Which were probably in Byzantium. See *The Homilies of Photius*, p. 127 above, and "Prayer and Meditation in Late Medieval England: MS Bodley 789," *Medium AEvum*, 48 (1979), 55-66, where I first noted this connection.

[21] The full title is *The Spiritual Mirror; or, Looking-Glass: Exhibiting the Human Heart as Being Either the Temple of God, or Habitation of Devils. Exemplified by a Series of Ten Engravings; Intended to Aid in a Better Understanding of Man's Fallen Nature.* (Albany: E. & E. Hosford, 1825). The *arma Christi* appear in plate 4 (facing p. 31) which shows "the heart of the sinner, who through Christ, is reconciled to God, and is determined to know nothing but Christ, and him crucified," and (in a modified version) in plate 6 (facing p. 44), which shows "the heart of a man whose spiritual life, has become cold, and again loves the world." Bauder notes (p. vi) the existence of five French editions, but reports that he translated from a 1732 German edition printed in Wertsburg (*non vidi*). I note too that the *arma Christi* is popular in contemporary Mexican folk art, functioning both as unusual decoration, and, particularly in the south in and around San Cristóbol de las Casas in Chiapas, as a devout protection which is often placed on roofs and house walls.

tive involving the engagement of the spectator, and his or her willingness to identify with the victim, who is Christ. The identification is partly dependent upon a knowledge of the gospels, partly on other devotional traditions to which many late medieval Christians, in one way or another, had access. But in its purest form the *arma Christi* involved taking the instruments of search (like the lantern), of capture, and of torture, and transforming them into instruments of power, a power which concerns Christ and the spectator alike. Thus items like the dice which the soldiers cast to see who would obtain Christ's seamless cloak, or the flagellum with which Christ was scourged, become transformed into images of power and authority. In the prayerbook context, such as that preserved in Bodleian Library MS. Douce 1 and its printed version, *A gloryous medytacyon* (STC 14550), the *arma* could invite intimacy, felt awareness of his suffering, and recollection of salvational nature of his sacrifice.[22] In a more public representation, like Michelangelo's *Last Judgment*, the images would testify at once to Christ's victory over death and to his power. In either case the representations are always on the verge of yielding a higher significance, one in which the innocent victim achieves power, and does so by transforming the instruments of secular authority which have been directed against him. What a comparison with the *arma urbis* reveals is the degree to which, collectively more than individually, the *arma* create context and supply motivation. And at the heart of that motivation is power.

Spirituality has indeed an integrating function in human life, and is in many ways concerned with the integrity of the individual. But it is not a panacea, and cannot function in the absence of the will: transformations of images can always be reversed. It is not unknown for secular institutions to appropriate sacred constructions, though the effect of their doing so is usually complex. It is not simply a case that that one image is substituted for another: it also happens that something of the earlier resonance remains, cheapened or informed or both in its new setting. Associate spirituality with arms and the result can as well be a bronze soldier as a devout Christian. But there are other possibilities as well.

---

[22] The *arma Christi* appear regularly in late medieval English woodcuts associated with meditation on the passion, and STC 5160 carries the legend "The declaracyon and power of the Chrysten fayth".

I would be less than candid if I said that my interest in identifying the connections that I have been concerned with was only to see what light the *arma urbis* could throw on the *arma Christi*: in fact, I am not less concerned to see if the process can be reversed. For one thing, it seems to me that as powerful a register of images as those contained in the *arma Christi*, informed by narrative context as they are, can help to identify the ways in which related images can (and do) link up to establish significance and supply motivation. The effect of a related group of images seems to me particularly complex, and, depending on narrative context, quite capable of creating an effect exactly opposite to the one which might be expected. My sense is that both *armas* are intimately concerned with the connections between victimization and power, and the ways in which the victim can, in turn, appropriate the images of power and authority which attend upon it. In the case of the *arma Christi* the victim is Christ, and the effect of the icons of power which attend upon him posits a religious transformation which the devout Christian is invited, somewhat ambiguously, to embrace. In the case of the *arma urbis* images of the sort I have been discussing equally have the power to dictate attitudes and to establish behavior, though, lacking any but an implied narrative context, their effect most often is secular and devisive. I am not arguing for censoring such images, but I am concerned that they be understood for what they are: not merely displays to divert or outrage the already advantaged, but signs fired deep into the community of the disadvantaged, signs which at once marginalize and stereotype, and which do nothing to assist in any search for identity or meaning.

CHAPTER NINE

THE NEW WORLD

> When our Captain and the Friar of the Order of Mercy saw that Montezuma was not willing that we should set up a cross on the Temple of Huichilobos nor build a church there, and because, ever since we entered this city of Mexico, when Mass was said, we had to place an altar on tables and then to dismantle it again, it was decided that we should ask Montezuma's stewards for masons so that we could make a church in our quarters.
>
> The stewards said that they would tell Montezuma of our wishes, and Montezuma gave his permission and ordered us to be supplied with all the material we needed. In two days we had our church finished and the holy cross set up in front of our apartments, and Mass was said there every day until the wine gave out. As Cortés and some of the other Captains and the Friar had been ill during the war in Tlaxcala, they made the wine that we had for Mass go too fast, but after it was all finished we still went to the church daily and prayed on our knees before the altar and images, for one reason, because we were obliged to do so as Christians and it was a good habit, for another reason, in order that Montezuma and all his Captains should witness our adoration and see us on our knees before the Cross, especially when we intoned the Ave Maria, so that it might incline them towards it.
> —Bernal Díaz del Castilo, *True History of the Conquest of New Spain*

Although it is doubtful that the spirituality displayed much impressed Montezuma, there is no doubt that the Spanish themselves took it seriously, repeatedly urging an end to human sacrifice[1] and what they described as "worshipping idols," and even thinking badly of one of their own, who had been with Montezuma when he died, because he had failed to convert him to Christianity. Desiring a better fate for those whom he had not killed, Cortés petitioned both king and pope

---

[1] Human sacrifice played a major role in pre-conquest religion: Montezuma sacrificed 5,100 prisoners of war at his elaborate coronation; a large numbers of children, almost all members of the lower classes, were taken, much against their parents' wishes, as sacrifice each year. See R.C. Padden, *The Hummingbird and the Hawk. Conquest and Sovereignty in the Valley of Mexico, 1503-1541* (New York: Harper and Row, 1970), pp. 76-99. For the instillation of the Virgin in Huichilobos' temple by the Spanish see pp. 182-188.

to send friars to his conquest, specifically requesting Franciscans.[2] The request was approved, though the usual hierarchy of parish priest and bishop was not instituted, since the spiritual conquest was not yet complete: rather the twelve Franciscans first dispatched were given powers usually reserved for bishops.[3]

The Franciscans, however, proved quite uncompromising with the Spanish military administration. From the very first they defended the interests of the native population and sought to avoid being identified with the military. When friars were sent to convert Yucatan, one of them, Friar Lorenzo de Bienvenida, traveled across the peninsula on foot and by canoe, studiously avoiding Spanish soldiers, and preaching and converting as he went. Nor did the friars concern themselves only with the faith of their congregations. In October 1550 the head of the Mexican mission, Friar Luis de Villalpando, wrote a long letter to the king in which he described the various depredations he had observed: the Indian woman tied naked to a post and whipped to death; the village chief who, beaten and in terror, had fled to Friar Luis' arms, only to be pulled away to sudden execution.[4] Multiply these scenes many times over and that was how the

---

[2] See Inga Clendinnen, *Ambivalent Conquests. Maya and Spanish in Yucatan, 1517-1570* Cambridge Latin American Studies 61 (Cambridge: Cambridge University Press, 1987), Chapter 4, "Missionaries," pp. 45-56. The quotation at the head of the chapter is taken from Bernal Díaz del Castillo, *The Discovery and Conquest of Mexico, 1517-1521*, trans. A.P. Maudslay (New York: Farrar, Straus and Cudahy, 1956), p. 225. On the military aspects of Cortés' invasion see Ross Hassig, *Mexico and the Spanish Conquest*, Modern Wars in Perspective (London and New York: Longman, 1994), which emphasizes the conditional quality of the Spanish victory, together with the massive restructuring of native life which followed. But throughout, my greatest debts are to Robert Ricard, *The Spiritual Conquest of Mexico. An Essay on the Apostolate and the Evangelizing Methods of the Mendicant Orders in New Spain: 1523-1572*, trans. Lesley Byrd Simpson (Berkeley, Los Angeles and London: University of California Press, 1966), John Leddy Phelan, *The Millennial Kingdom of the Franciscans in the New World. A Study of the Writings of Gerónimo de Mendieta (1525-1604)*, University of California Publications in History, volume 52, second edition (Berkeley, Los Angeles and London: University of California Press, 1971), and Deleno C. West, "Medieval Ideas of Apocalyptic Mission and the Early Franciscans in Mexico," *Americas*, 45 (1988/89), 293-313.

[3] The numbers were always small. By 1521 the Conquest was complete, and by 1536 the number had risen to about 60, by the late 1550s to about 380. Clendinnen, p. 47; West points out that on August 30, 1523, three friars arrived in Mexico led by Peter of Ghent, a relative of Charles V, but they were working without official recognition (306, n. 50). The first official group, commissioned on 25 January 1524, was chosen, West notes, "from Extremadure, Cortés' home, and a noted center for Franciscan reform with an unusually strict emphasis upon austerity and poverty" (306).

first Franciscans understood their role: as protectors not only of the souls but also of the bodies of those whom they believed to be their charges, though it probably should be remembered that, whatever their reservations and acts of opposition, friars usually acted under protection of Spanish arms, and that in opposing the casual brutalities of the place they were acting in the best spiritual interests of the Spanish soldiery as well, whose mortal sins they at once observed and sought to prevent.

The first institutions which the friars established were missions with schools attached, and it is the operation of these schools that other Franciscan attitudes emerge. Faced with the difficulty of instructing a population with no understanding of Christian doctrine, the Franciscans opted for external conformity rather than understanding. Inga Clendinnen quotes this passage from an early chronicle, detailing how the *Pater Noster* was taught:

> The word [in the Aztec language] which comes closest to the pronunciation of 'Pater' is 'pantli,' which means a little flag, which is their sign for the number twenty. So, in order to remember the word 'Pater' they draw the flag 'pantli' and so say 'Pater.' For 'noster' the closest word they have is 'nochtli,' which is the fruit called by the Spanish here tuna, and in Spain 'the fig of the Indies' [prickly pear] ... therefore to call to mind the word 'noster' they draw a tuna fruit alongside the little flag they call 'pantli,' and so they are able to continue along until they finish the prayer, and in the same way they find other similar characters and ways by which they are able to teach themselves those things they must commit to memory. (p. 48)

This method of instructing children is not unknown today—mosque schools in London usually teach children how to read and pronounce the Arabic script long before teaching them to translate it—but it also indicates the way certain of the Franciscans sought to preserve what they believed to be the innocence of their congregation by keeping their instruction simple, and preventing the discourse it occasioned

---

[4] Clendinnen, pp. 51-52 and 55-56. Friar Luis wrote: "the Indian, thus clinging to me and I to him, running with blood, filthy and stinking, [the *encomendero*] tore him away from me, dragging him by his hair from my arms, who could not help him, in front of all the people and a Spaniard who was standing there." He pointed out too how corrupt the legal system had become, "because one is a judge one year and the other one the next year, one sentences the other pay two *maravedis* for some offenses and for others they are set at liberty." In 1552 the Spanish Crown sent a royal judge to Yucatan in answer to Friar Luis' charges.

within what they took to be easily manageable bounds. In other places, however, the teaching was more orthodox. Ricard reports that all those baptized, offered communion, confession, and confirmation were obliged to know the sign of the cross, the *Credo*, the *Pater Noster*, the *Ave Maria*, and the *Salve Regina*. The catechism which the friars used contained also the fourteen articles of faith, the Ten Commandments, the five commandments of the Church, the seven sacraments, the seven deadly sins, venial and mortal sins, and teaching concerning general confession. A second part of the catechism contained, according to Ricard, "the cardinal and theological virtues, the works of mercy, the gifts of the Holy Ghost, the senses, the faculties of the soul, the enemies of the soul, the Beatitudes, the company of the Blessed, the duties of godparents." [5] But how much of this was understood and practiced by those whom the Franciscans instructed is unclear, as is the larger context into which the new teachings were cast. This last question is particularly important, since it is quite clear that the early Franciscans understood their mission against an apocalyptic background in which their conversions would not only win Mexico, but also restore the primitive church. Columbus had believed that his voyages were connected to apocalyptic prophecy, inclining toward a belief in a Christian monarch who would defeat the Muslims, before being himself defeated (he would flee to Jerusalem, where he would die); there would then follow a brief reign of the Antichrist, after which Christ himself would return in triumph. Columbus was drawn to these ideas by his association with the Franciscans (he took a Franciscan along with him on his second voyage, and between his third and fourth wrote a book, assisted by Friar Gaspar Gorritio, detailing his vision); and by his own reading, which included, among other sources, Psalms, apocryphal Esdras, certain of the church fathers and Joachim of Fiore—but he also referred to the Sybils and to Merlin. It may have been his apocalyptic beliefs which caused him to urge the Spanish crown to recapture Jerusalem without delay, and in a 1502 letter to Pope Alexander VI he reported that on his voyages he had seen the site of the Garden of Eden; two years

[5] Ricard, "The Catechism," pp. 96-108; quote from p. 102. Many of the catechisms used were printed in Spain, though at least one was adapted for use in Mexico, warning against veneration of objects, which brought down the charge of Protestantism on the heads of certain friars, and which has particular relevance in the case of the cult of Our Lady of Guadalupe.

later, in 1504, the first New World bishop was appointed, Friar Garcia de Padilla.[6]

Exactly how far apocalyptic expectations influenced New World spirituality is hard to say: most Franciscans would have been familiar with its parameters, and if it did not inform day-to-day intercourse it probably did influence larger issues and expectations. One of these may have been the extent to which the early Franciscans in Mexico engaged, or failed to engage, native Americans as co-participants in their work. The policy may have been predicated on the idea that Mexico would remain a colony indefinitely, and that it was possible to create the conditions of the primitive church in its operation, which was to be a radical departure from previous religious practices. The Franciscan attitude toward evangelization emerges too in the writings of a friar like Gerónimo de Mendieta, for whom Indian conversions could bring about a virtual rebirth of the primitive church, a circumstance indicated by what he believed to be the innocence of the native population. Thus, in spite of a 1550 royal directive which had enjoined the friars to teach Spanish to the native population so as to enable them to "acquire our Castilian social policy [*policía*] and our good customs," for decades the friars (who until 1583 enjoyed episcopal powers) did no such thing, isolating the native population from the Spanish in the belief that such a practice would help to protect both their lives and their innocence.[7] It is apparent that, for all of their abhorrence of atrocity, Franciscan practices were influenced as well by colonial institutions of the usual sort, which

---

[6] See Phelan, *The Millennial Kingdom of the Franciscans in the New World*, *passim*, and E. Randolph Daniel, *The Franciscan Concept of Mission in the High Middle Ages* (Lexington, Ky.: The University of Kentucky Press, 1975), especially pp. 76-100, "Apocalyptic Conversion," which treats the medieval intellectual background for the Franciscan practices. In "Medieval Ideas of Apocalyptic Mission," West points out that there were those who believed that the Mexican Indians were descended from the lost ten tribes of Israel, whom the apocryphal Esdras had prophecised would return at the end of time, and that certain of the religious practices in Yucatan (such as circumcision) were thought to be Jewish in origin, while certain symbols (the cross, the Trinity) were thought to be Christian (311). These circumstances had the effect of further reinforcing the apocalyptic nature of the Franciscans' mission.

[7] Daniel, *Franciscan Concept of Mission*; Phelan, *Millennial Kingdom*, *passim*; and Ricard, *Spiritual Conquest*, pp. 33-38 and 301-309. Ricard notes that he has not devoted a chapter to Mexican spiritual life in the sixteenth century, which he believes contained "all the basic and common elements of Catholic spiritual life" (p. 298). He remarks as well that the Augustinians in particular sought to develop a more contemplative spirituality among some at least of their converts, teaching some of the children to practice mental prayer (p. 301).

sought to impose a foreign structure on a native population and to adapt them to it, all in the interests of the colonial power. It is quite true that the Franciscans separated themselves from the brutal practices of the Spanish military, but in their attempted suppression of native religion, and in their redefinition of religious practice generally, they acted the part of a colonial power, and their reluctance to admit native Indians (as opposed to criollos, Spanish born in the Americas) into Holy Orders only confirms this attitude.

It was against (or perhaps with the memory of) this missionary background that in December 1531, the Virgin was said to have appeared to Juan Diego, universally identified as an Indian convert to Christianity. The early evidence for this apparition, as has recently been pointed out, hardly exists at all, and later accounts added considerably to what may or may not have taken place.[8] According to such accounts as there are, however, the Virgin was reported to have appeared to Juan Diego on the hill of Tepeyac near Mexico City, a place which earlier may have preserved a shrine to the pre-Hispanic goddess Tonantzin, a name which also became associated with the Virgin. The Virgin is said to have asked that a temple be built to her on the hill, and when, following some early skepticism, Diego subsequently asked her for a sign with which to convince the local bishop, she directed him to pick all the flowers then in bloom on the summit of the mountain. This he did, but when in the bishop's presence he opened his cloak to show the flowers which it contained, a painting of the Virgin miraculously appeared as well.[9] In time, it is

---

[8] See Jeanette Rodriguez, *Our Lady of Guadalupe. Faith and Empowerment among Mexican-American Women* (Austin: University of Texas Press, 1994), pp. 31-36, and an important revisionist account by Stafford Poole, C.M., *Our Lady of Guadalupe. The Origins and Sources of a Mexican National Symbol, 1531-1797*. (Tucson and London: University of Arizona Press, 1995). Poole argues that the devotion to the apparation sprang "as if out of nowhere" (126) in 1648, and that it is to be identified not with the Mexican Indians but with the criollos, Mexican-born Spanish, whose aspirations it is said to have legitimized. I am not entirely convinced even by Poole's searching account—no argument from silence is ever finally convincing, though in this case it may well indicate the popularity of the devotion was late rather than early; and the accounts of the devotion preserved in the Capitular Inquiry of 1665 (pp. 127-55) seem to me to point to an earlier origin for the cult than Poole is prepared to allow. But strictly speaking the position I am advancing here concerning the connections between late medieval devotions and those which subsequently emerged in the Americas both supports and gains from certain aspects of Poole's account.

[9] The bibliography on the cult of Our Lady of Guadalupe is enormous, as are the dimensions of the cult itself. See Gloria Grajales and Ernest J. Burrus, S.J., eds., *Bibliografía Guadalupana/Guadalupan Bibliography (1531-1984)* (Washington, D.C.:

said, the bishop championed the cult, which flourished, as did devotion to the new image, now universally known as "Our Lady of Guadalupe."

Early evidence for the attitude of the several religious orders then in Mexico is scarce, though the icon itself has been preserved and subjected to infrared photography, the results of which have been published. For all of its limitations, the photograph seems to reveal two images, one superimposed on the other, which have been described thus:

> 1. The original figure, including the rose robe, blue mantle, hands and face, is inexplicable. In terms of the infrared study, there is no way to explain either the kind of color pigments utilized, or the maintenance of color luminosity and brightness of pigments over the centuries. Furthermore, when consideration is given to the fact that there is no underdrawing, sizing or overvarnish, and that the weave of the fabric is itself utilized to give the portrait depth, no explanation of the portrait is possible by infrared techniques. It is remarkable that after four centuries there is no fading or cracking on the original figure on any portion of the agave tilma, which—being unsized—should have deteriorated centuries ago.
> 2. Sometime after the original image was formed, the moon and the tassel were added by human hands, perhaps for some symbolic reason since the moon was important to both Moorish-Spanish and Aztec mythologies.
> 3. Some time after the tassel and the moon were added, the gold and black line decorations, angel, Aztec fold of the robe, sunburst stars and background were painted, probably in the seventeenth century. The additions were by human hands and impart a Spanish Gothic motif to the painting. In all probability, at the same time the tilma was mounted on a solid support, the orange coloring of the sunburst and white fresco were added to the background. The entire tilma was for the first time covered with paint. It seems unlikely that Juan Diego could have worn a tilma stiffened with fresco on the fabric to the bishop's palace. Therefore, the original must have been the simple figure on the cloth.
> In all probability the Holy Image, especially at the bottom and around the edges, suffered some water damage, and the angel and other decorations, as well as the outer fresco white, were added to cover up the

---

Georgetown University Press, 1986), but see too Robert Ricard, "Les apparations de Notre-Dame de Guadalupe. A propos d'un ouvrage récent," *Revue d'Histoire des Missions* (June 1, 1931), 247-62, and the same author's *Spiritual Conquest of Mexico*, pp. 188-193.

damage. This is in no way different from the patches added to the Shroud of Turin to cover the fire damage to the Holy Relic." [10]

The reference to the Shroud of Turin, a medieval forgery still believed by many to be authentic in 1986, was not particularly happy, though as a cloth relic with a representation of a divine figure it would have seemed natural enough at the time. But early doubts about the authenticity of the icon seem to have come from the Franciscans. On September 8, 1556, the feast of the Nativity of the Blessed Virgin, friar Francisco de Bustamante, the Franciscan provincial, preached a sermon in which he denounced the cult, also asserting that it had no foundation and that the already-venerated image had been painted by an Indian. He further attacked Bishop Alonso de Montúfar, a Dominican, who recently had supported the cult, arguing that it was nothing more than a new form of idolatry, which was effectively undermining the work his friars had done in drawing the Indians away from their faith in wood and stone images.[11]

Ricard and now Poole have traced (with different emphases) the repercussions of the sermon, which were extensive. An investigation followed de Bustamante's sermon and indicated, among other things, that the Franciscan was not alone in his opinions, though it equally indicated that the cult was highly regarded among Indians, and that the sanctuary of Guadalupe was much visited by large numbers of them. It showed too that certain of the religious were not supporters of the cult, and there is every reason to believe that these included many, if not most, of the Franciscans.[12] The reasons revealed (largely

[10] Grajales and Burrus, note to the frontispiece (which shows the icon and a drawing of the infrared photograph). N.p., here citing Philip Serna Callahan, *The Tilma: Under Infra-Red Radiation*, CARA Studies on Popular Devotion, vol. 2 Guadalupan Studies, no. 3 (Washington, D.C.: Center for Applied Research in the Apostolate, 1981), p. 18. See also the analysis of the icon in Rodriguez, *Our Lady of Guadalupe*, pp. 19-30.

[11] Ricard, *Spiritual Conquest of Mexico*, pp. 102-103 and 188-193, and "Les apparitions," 247-62. See *contra* Poole, *Our Lady*, pp. 58-64.

[12] Ricard, *Spiritual Conquest*, p. 189, "Les apparition," 254, n. 2. Phelan, *Millennial Kingdom*, remarks that the "friars were afraid that too many miracles might confuse the neophytes and thus facilitate a relapse into magic, superstition, and idolatry" (48). And certainly by the seventeenth century the icon of Our Lady of Guadalupe became as important as that of the Annunciation, Our Lady of the Rosary, or the Immaculate Conception to artists producing *relicarios*, lockets containing mineature religious paintings or sculptures, which were widely venerated (and worn) across many Mexican classes. See Martha J. Egan, *Relicarios. Devotional Mineatures from the*

by hearsay) in the documents are not unfamiliar: some friars seem to have objected that many of the Indians had confused the painting with the Virgin, and that the cult had simply become another form of pagan idolatry. It is possible too, as Ricard indicates, that the visionary revelation was seen, by some Franciscans at least, to be at odds with the image of the primitive church reborn in the latter days of the world, which many of them were seeking to inculcate. It may be that the Dominicans and the Augustinians were less hostile than the Franciscans, but it seems clear that the cult flourished because it was supported by the local clergy and hierarchy, and, in some periods at least, by the native population.

But even when all this is said, it is difficult to believe that the cult would have assumed the proportions it did if it had been faced with unrelenting Franciscan opposition. Its continuing popularity, however, may indicate one reason that the painting has the quite extraordinary (and decidedly European) form which it now does. The last repainting, it will be remembered, may have done away with earlier representation of the Virgin on a hillside, and presented instead the woman clothed in the sun, which was the icon of the Immaculate Conception. This particular cult had been approved in 1476 (its origin in private devotion goes back to the twelfth century), though the dogma on which it was based, that Mary was conceived without Original Sin, was not proclaimed until 1854. It had for many years been a particular favorite of the Franciscans, for whom the Papal approval was nothing short of a triumph, and if there was one country where it took hold deeply, that country was Spain.[13] Thus the form which the later artist imposed on the icon both linked elements of the Indian tradition with others which were distinctly European—indeed distinctly Franciscan—as well. The reason for the repainting, and in

---

Americas (Santa Fe: Museum of New Mexico Press, 1993), pp. 54-56. Egan also points out that Cortés himself "wore religious jewelry, including medals and *relicarios*" (p. 33).

[13] See Rona Goffen, *Piety and Patronage in Renaissance Venice. Bellini, Titian and the Franciscans* (New Haven and London: Yale University Press, 1986), pp. 73-79, and Suzanne L. Stratton, *The Immaculate Conception in Spanish Art* (Cambridge: Cambridge University Press, 1994), especially pp. 35-66 for the iconographic link to the Virgin *tota pulchra*, and the *mulier amicta sole* of Rev. 12.1. Four years after the doctrine was promulgated Bernadette Soubirous reported seeing the Virgin at Lourdes, where she declared herself to be the Immaculate Conception. Sandra L. Zimdars-Swartz, *Encountering Mary. From La Salette to Medjugorje* (Princeton, N.J.: Princeton University Press, 1991), p. 55.

particular for the imposition of the Immaculate Conception on the native American icon, may well have been to reconcile Franciscan ideology to a devotion which was taking root, but which was as still supported by the local clergy, not the orders.

The contention between local clergy and the orders over an apparition has a strikingly modern parallel in the apparitions at Medjugorje, in Bosnia, which began on June 25, 1981, and which have not yet concluded. Initially, six children began to experience apparitions of the Virgin which took place almost daily. The number (and the frequency) have since declined, but the apparitions became organized by the Franciscans to include a daily program of confession, mass, and prayer, directed at the many tourists and pilgrims who have come in increasing numbers to Medjugorje, particularly between 1985 and the start of the civil war. Like most Marian apparitions of the nineteenth and twentieth century, the one at Medjugorje contains a number of secrets which Our Lady has entrusted to the children (who have grown up during the course of the apparitions) a total of ten secrets each, most of which have yet to be revealed, though some are said to concern the well-being of the church and the world, while others are more private, intended for specific persons. From the vantage point of the Guadalupean apparition, however, one other interesting point about the revelations at Medjugorje concerns the contention which has developed between the Franciscans and the local bishop, though now their roles are almost exactly reversed, with the Franciscans supporting the revelations, the local bishop expressing doubts.[14]

The development of "secrets" has become an important part of the new tradition, replacing the authority which formerly attached directly to the apparition itself with knowledge born of intimacy with the Godhead. While in political terms these secrets have often appeared to be markedly "conservative" (a lack of respect for the sacred order of things, a turning away from religion and, during the Cold War, the situation in Russia were frequent themes, as was the injunction that earlier messages had not been attended to),[15] it is worth

[14] See Chuck Sudetic, "Do 4 Behold the Virgin? Bishop is Not a Believer," *New York Times*, 28 September 1990, p. A4. The article reports that since 1985 the Franciscans have been distributing more than a million communion wafers a year, but that Cardinal Ratzinger, writing from the Holy Office, has not approved the cult, and has directed tour agencies associated with the Vatican not to send tours to the shrine. See also Zimdars-Swartz, *Encountering Mary*, pp. 233-44.

noticing that in many cases these requirements were predicated on a demand for social and economic justice. In the case of Our Lady of Guadalupe the message was entirely open and inclusive: all persons were invited to embrace a faith which served to unite Indian, criollo and Spaniard, and eventually Franciscan and secular as well. Whatever the origin of the Guadalupean icon, its effect has been extraordinary.

But the other political element, the division of interest and ideology between the secular and the regular clergy, offers another perspective. Although many Marian visionaries have encountered resistance from civil and ecclesiastical authorities, it has not been Vatican policy to approve private revelations even when they assume a public character, and usually, as we have seen, to support local hierarchies.[16] But apart from the evident local interests which the conflicts often point up, they sometimes show as well that there are two (or more) attitudes toward visionary experience involved, one emphasizing the witness and empowerment which the consequent notoriety brings with it, the other the need for continuity and stability as prerequisites for a developed spiritual life within a community. The Franciscan attitude toward pre-conquest spirituality stressed neither continuity nor accomplishment: Christianity was a break with the past—the past was full of pagan gods who didn't exist, and were up to no good. Yet there also was considerable continuity in the period, as the friars themselves certainly were aware.[17] What is of interest is the way, in the case of the vision of Guadalupe, the continuity seems pretty clearly to have sprung from Spanish and criollo roots. By the early sixteenth century the tradition of local visionary experience was well-established in Spain, and the conditions of vision would have been equally well- known in the New World. Juan Diego's personal circumstances, for example, were represented as simple, but no more so than many who had visions about the same time in Spain. Again, the Virgin was the usual divine figure to appear, and the request to build a shrine (and to hold processions) was

---

[15] See Zimdars-Swartz, *Encountering Mary*, pp. 245-50.

[16] *Ibid.*, p. 245 ff.

[17] There are numerous studies on this topic, but see in particular the recent study of Peru by Sabine MacCormack, *Religion in the Andes. Vision and Imagination in Early Colonial Peru* (Princeton, N.J.: Princeton University Press, 1991), and Gabrielle Palmer and Donna Pierce, *Cambios. The Spirit of Transformation in Spanish Colonial Art* (Santa Barbara: Santa Barbara Museum of Art, 1992), especially pp. 74-144.

not at all unusual.[18] Indeed, in most respects Guadalupe was a not uncommon expression of medieval Spanish culture and religion.

But that was not all it was. In Spanish visionary experience, it was unusual for an individual revelation to become associated with a physical object, like Juan Diego's tilma, and it was simply extraordinary for a religious object to assume the cross-cultural, and gender-related importance which the tilma quickly took on. The cross-cultural significance of the tilma probably went through at least two stages: the very representation of the Virgin was by itself an Indian concession to European attitudes, though perhaps conditioned by older memories as well. Even if the first image of the Virgin had not a miraculous origin, its evident popularity shows how deeply it became inscribed in the religiousness of a people. Unlike the early seventeenth-century painting of Our Lady of Copacabana, which also had miraculous interventions ascribed to it, the icon of Our Lady of Guadalupe is dark-skinned and evidently of native extraction, a *mestiza*, so that particularly in her most recent repainting, she assumes a role of importance in both cultures, and seems to offer to mediate between them. Certainly within a period she was worshipped quite unreservedly by all groups, and whatever adjustments to their code or practices the Franciscans had to effect, they did so in reasonably short order.[19]

Her other important attribute was her gender. In both cultures, medieval Christian and pre-conquest Indian, women enjoyed an important role, at least ideologically. The tassel ("cinta") or maternity band which the last repainting placed on the painting has upon it a

---

[18] William A. Christian, Jr., *Apparitions in Late Medieval and Renaissance Spain* (Princeton, N.J.: Princeton University Press, 1981), "General Themes in the Visions," pp. 188-222. Christian lists the occupations of the seers, 1399-1618 on pp. 208-09, which include servants, tenders of sheep or pigs, a plowman, and day laborer; he also notes that Mary appears far more often than any other saint, and to the question "What should [the people] do that they have not done?" offers this analysis for the visions he has surveyed: Masses (5), fasts (1), prayers (1), processions (10), pay tithes and other duties (1), build shrine (10), erect cross (2), set up brotherhood (2), punish lapses (2), general conversion (3)" (p. 212). The shrine and processions quickly became established at Guadalupe. On this topic see too Christian's *Local Religion in Sixteenth-Century Spain* (Princeton, N.J.: Princeton University Press, 1981).

[19] On Our Lady of Copacabana see Palmer and Pierce, *Cambios*, pp. 32-33, also citing the testimony, in 1568, of the English sailor Miles Phillips, who remarked of the shrine of Our Lady of Guadalupe, "Whensoever any Spaniards pass by this church, although they be on horseback, they will alight and come into the church, and kneel before this image, and pray to Our Lady to defend them from all evil" (p. 90).

small flower called a "nagvioli," which has been identified with the Aztec calendar, and which, on the Virgin's womb, would have had the same significance to the Nahuatl Indian that the band would have had to the Spanish, namely that she was pregnant.[20] The earlier painting did not present either symbol, and offered instead a woman alone, but one with supernatural powers.

It is sometimes said that one reason for the expansion of visionary experience in the Latin West during the late medieval period is the effect it had in empowering women, and giving authority to those who had, because of their gender, been prevented from acquiring standing is such academic disciplines as Canon Law. But in these circumstances women did not internalize their oppression and simply use access to the divine as another way of achieving the same end. Rather, as we already have seen elsewhere in this book, in many instances, women perceived and understood a sacred order to be present as well as a religious (and a secular) one, and this sacred order, available to men and women alike, became a way of developing and maintaining a spirituality which was at once personal and social, but not a part of the (usually patriarchal) social order itself. What we see in the case of Our Lady of Guadalupe, however, is an extension of this practice and perception. For in this case it is not too much to say that the Virgin came almost to partake of the Godhead itself. Springing from both Indian and Spanish stock (but it was her identification with Indian which was most remarkable); enthroned and powerful (at least in the last repainting); the representative of a teaching (the Immaculate Conception) which may have been added to make the devotion acceptable to those among the Franciscans who had other ideas of native piety, and which required a theological sophistication which not all who worshipped her enjoyed, the icon created a sense of the Holy, the Sacred, and carried with it something of the fear and awe which always accompany sacred mysteries. It was of course a woman who was venerated, and one, moreover, who had been firmly clamped into a doctrinally acceptable (if not yet formally approved) Western theological category, but that was not all. In some way too the Virgin represents an aspect of the divinity which is associated with a native woman, but also with Spain and power. She is indeed a representative of the marginalized, but not only of them: she

[20] Rodriguez, *Our Lady of Guadalupe*, p. 29, citing too an interview in March 1986 with Margarita Z. Parente-Martiniz in Mexico City.

also stands for all who claim faith in Christianity. It is not that Mary is God: but she stands for divine power, and becomes, as it were, an aspect of that divinity. She is of course powerful, but her power is sunk in mystery and implication. The lowered eyes see everything and nothing. But above all there is an extended sense of presence, of someone or something being there, an unavoidable and lasting manifestation of presence and love.

This is a considerably expanded role than the one usually associated with Marian apparitions in contemporary Spain. But the spirituality which attaches to Our Lady of Guadalupe has implications for the relationship between faith and activity which is so integral to the Christian tradition. The circumstances which existed in Mexico, after all, were far different from those which obtained in contemporary Europe. In Spain the visionary might indeed have some difficulty being believed, but he or she was speaking to and out of a settled and living tradition in which vision was one of several acceptable religious practices. In Mexico, on the other hand, the social context was one of cross purposes: Christianity was established by the Spanish, but not so much by the military as by members of the religious orders.

The larger issue here is a continuing concern for faith, and more particularly the ways in which faith—not icons, practices, conventions or even dogmas, but rather faith itself—is transmitted across cultures, and over time. There is of course both continuity and discontinuity in this transmission, and both, as we have seen, were involved in the complex process by which Christianity became rooted in the Americas. The faith which developed was thus no stranger to marginilization and persecution, and elements from its origins remain even today, even when its establishment seems fixed. A modern example may help to make this clear.

The political situation which has existed throughout Central America — and particularly in Guatemala — through the 1980's and beyond provides a particularly piquant parallel to the mix of culture and religion which took place in the early colonial period. Now as then, a powerful and aristocratic class, which held economic and military power, ruled, with great violence and brutality, an indigenous population, which they treated with contempt and exploited in whatever ways were convenient. Both the ruling elites and the Indian population were said to be Christian, primarily Roman Catholic, though this situation has now begun to change.[21] In Guatemala more than in any other country, the massacre of Indians in the countryside was encouraged as a way containing guerrilla activity, a policy which was abetted by the U.S. State Department at the direction of then President Ronald Reagan.[22] On March 23, 1982, a military coup in Guatemala brought to power General Efraín Ríos Montt, an evangelical Christian who expedited counter-insurgency greatly and in the most brutal fashion. Although many atrocities had taken place before Ríos Montt took office, there is little doubt that, in spite of his pretended ignorance,[23] the President was himself involved in the execution of the atrocities, some of the most brutal in a period known for its brutality. One institution which had begun before the coup, but expanded greatly after it, was the deployment of civil patrols, groups of civilians pressed into service by the army, and sent, at first unarmed, into areas where the insurgents were thought to be active. The army did not trust these patrols, whose members were Indians drawn from the very areas where the army had been committing atrocities, and membership was by no means a guarantee of safety.[24]

Although each country in Central America will have many such stories to tell, one in particular seems to me to have a certain interest in illustrating the nature of the spirituality still present among the people. The report in this case comes from Jean Marie Simon, a

---

[21] See David Stoll, *Is Latin America Turning Protestant? The Politics of Evangelical Growth* (Berkeley, Los Angeles and London: University of California Press, 1990). pp. 180-317. Probably the worst persecutions were in Guatemala, where certain members of the Catholic hierarchy were implicated in support for earlier repressive regimes, but where the worst programes were carried out under President Ríos Montt, an evangelical Christian. For a complex of reasons, Guatemala may be the first Central American country to emerge with a Protestant majority.

[22] Many of these have begun to be documented: among many places see Ricardo Falla, *Massacres in the Jungle. Ixcán, Guatemala, 1975-1982*, trans. Julia Howland (Boulder, San Francisco and Oxford: Westview Press, 1994), and James Dunkerley, *The Pacification of Central America. Political Change in the Isthmus, 1987-1993* (London and New York: Verso, 1994), which reports a "fair but conservative estimate would be 160,000 people killed and two million displaced during the decade [sc. the 1980's]," (p. 3).

[23] Noted by Stoll, pp. 204-206. The general, who professed the highest morality, claimed not to know of the massacres which took place during his presidency. When asked toward the end of his rule if a certain massacre had happened he equivocated: " 'It could have. I say it circumstantially because I can't be sure. I never authorized it. That's the truth ... They never come into my office and say "Today we burned such and such a village' " (p. 205).

[24] Stoll, *Is Latin America Turning Protestant*, pp. 198-203; Falla, *Massacres in the Jungle*, pp. 62-77; Dunkerley, *Pacification*, pp. 23-26. Enforced military service was not popular no matter which side was involved. On the issue in Nicaragua see Stoll, p. 238 ff.

photographer who is also a consultant to Americas Watch and Amnesty International:

A civil patroller told a Guatelaman nun about an incident which occurred in southern Quiché two months after the 1983 coup:

> Around November 1983, a man I know very well came to see me. He was crying, he was very upset. He told me that the army had come to his village and presented five men from that same village to the people there. They were prisoners. The villagers knew the men, they were their neighbors. The army commander told the people that they were guerrillas, and the civil patrol must "decide" what to do with them: they could kill them—that was their "business" —or they could let them go free. The army said it would return to see what their decision had been.
>
> The civil patrol did not know what to do. "How can we kill innocent people?" they anguished. They were very upset, they knew that the neighbors weren't guerrillas. And all this time, when they were deciding what to do, the five men were standing there, beside them, listening. Most of the patrollers were catechists, and they decided to pray to God to tell them what to do. Everyone began to pray—the patrollers and the condemned men too. They came to a community decision to kill their neighbors,because, "if we don't kill you the army will come back and massacre the entire village, and then the women and children will die as well." They already had experience with army killings.
>
> They told the prisoners that they were going to kill them not because they believed they were guerrillas, but simply to avoid a massacre. They asked the condemned men to forgive them for what they were about to do, and they asked God to forgive them too, for having to come to this terrible decision.
>
> Everyone in the village lined up and hugged the condemned men goodbye and they begged them for forgiveness. They asked the men to understand that they did it only for the good of the village, and that it was better for five to die than for the entire community to be massacred afterwards. One of the five, the next-door-neighbor of the man who told me this, asked him to "please take care of our widows and children, so they don't die from starvation, and please guard our crops and help our widows to harvest the corn."
>
> The men shot the five. To their surprise, the army showed up moments after the killing; they had been hidden nearby to see what the people would do. That day, there were five new widows and eighteen fatherless children in that community.[25]

[25] Jean-Marie Simon, *Guatemala. Eternal Spring, Eternal Tyranny* (New York: W. W. Norton, Co., 1987), p. 170.

I have quoted from her book, but when Jean-Marie Simon told the story some years ago she stressed the act of the people of the village and the condemned men praying together, all of them aware of what was to follow, yet bound together in a faith which quite separated them from the violence about them. In many ways this was the spirituality which Guadalupe taught them, a faith born of the power to see things clearly, to accept the rigors, unfairness, and grotesque uncertainties of life. The colonial Spanish were back again, perhaps not preaching the God of love this time, but doing everything else, convinced by the moral rectitude of their actions, and armed to the teeth.[26]

But between that certainty and those actions (carried out in this case by others) came the work of the spirit, informing and directing, creating an opening for future life in a world otherwise enclosed and grim and desolate. In the end the tale points to other realities: in particular to the world of politics, where the actions of the army appear as if in relief, and the behavior of the villagers becomes intelligible, moving and real. This attachment to the world of their ancestors and their children was at the heart of a faith which had its roots in Guadalupe.

In the end the spirituality of Guadalupe is based not only on the role and person of the Virgin and her effect on those who worship her, but like all spirituality, on how it affects the world. These effects are not only political, though they are that too, sometimes that most of all, but they also change forever the relationships which exist among people, so that some great things—like life and death—become not so great, and human relationships flourish. These things are hard to fix in the historical record, even though their results, attached to an idea of the sacred, are present everywhere. Still, they emerge here and there: Falla speaks of the religious quality to resistance and suffering present among those tortured by the Guatemala army, and cites the remark of one of them: " 'Thanks to the grace of God I am deeply convinced that it's better to give up one's life than to squeal on people' ." But he goes on to offer this explanation of what he calls

[26] The parallel between colonial and modern ideologies has often been put forward in liberation theology: see Gustavo Gutierrez, "the Historical Power of the Poor," in *The Power of the Poor in History*, pp. 75-107, and for an interesting study of political action and Catholicism in a traditional culture, Rowan Ireland, *Kingdoms Come. Religion and Politics in Brazil* (Pittsburg: University of Pittsburg Press, 1991), pp. 165-203.

"the liberation through death [which] is God's work: the witnesses' visions, which resemble those of charismatic Catholics, promise him liberation from the frightful dungeon, and this promise brings him comfort during such great suffering. When the promise becomes a possibility, trust in God's liberating force is symbolized by the sign of the cross the witness makes at the decisive moment between life or death, when he will either escape or be killed. The act of escaping is like a prayer, so the witness crosses himself before venturing forth." [27]

In the end Falla lists these hallmarks of the faith which persecution brought, the first three of which have evident links to the colonial period:

> 1. The experience of a God who is on the side of the just and persecuted and saves them from death at each step, and, to a lesser degree, the experience of being like Jesus, who was persecuted from childhood (as a refugee) and later massacred.
> 2. The experience of a saving, tangible and practical faith — a faith that does not undervalue the importance of security precautions, of human intervention, and of the people's struggle.
> 3. The experience of solidarity, which is so much stronger and more indispensable in times of great repression.
> 4. The experience of a grass-roots ecumenism that is not promoted from outside and an absence of or a reduction in the sectarian divisions that so plague Guatemala.
> 5. Faith in the institutional church, albeit with certain reserves, symbolized in the martyrdom of priests like William Woods." [28]

The radical and primitive teachings which the first Franciscans brought to the new world encountered, and no doubt also helped to create, a pattern of orthodoxy which, though it drew upon some Spanish practices, denied and rearticulated others, leaving openings both for traditional ecclesiastical practice, and (at least potentially) for spiritual and political renewal. The apparition at Guadalupe served, in later years especially, to redefine certain Christian ideals, and to incorporate some aspects of colonial ideology into a context of Christian spirituality which was by no means circumscribed by Hispanic culture, but which began at least to articulate a New World faith.

---

[27] Falla, *Massacres in the Jungle*, p. 164. See also pp. 187-88 for Falla's account of religious persecution during this period, which "involved persecution of the Catholic and Evangelical churches alike" (187).

[28] Falla, *Massacres in the Jungle*, p. 188, though as Stoll has shown, depending upon circumstances, the definition of "institutional church" is subject to change.

CONCLUSION

In sixteenth-century (and twentieth-century) America, as in medieval Europe, what distinguished faith was its powers of inclusion and integration. Not universally, but often, and at its best, spirituality engaged rather than selected, and in so doing added to those to whom it spoke—and not only to their numbers. It is quite useless to speak of the purity of spirituality. If there has been one theme in this book it has been that spirituality, like language itself, is never concluded, is always in process.

"Faith is, among other things, an attitude," Wilfred Cantwell Smith concluded in his study, "and for intellectuals, an attitude to truth. It involves, among other matters, the will; and for intellectuals, the will to know and to understand. It requires—or confers—among other virtues, integrity; and for intellectuals, the utmost intellectual honesty. Among different persons, as well as among different communities and different centuries, the element of understanding and particularly of conceptualization has played differing roles in faith, and by intellectuals has been envisioned as playing differing roles. Yet insofar as conceptualizing be involved at all, it must, we may affirm, if it is to be *faithful*, be *the closest approximation to the truth of which one's mind is capable.*

"In its intellectual dimension, faith is first of all recognition of truth, insight into reality; and its conceptualization (the 'belief' that goes with it) must be on the one hand sincere, subjectively, a close approximation to what one personally apprehends (is apprehended by), and on the other hand be valid, not only in the objective sense of being a significantly close approximation to Reality, to final Truth, but also in the dynamic and demanding sense (thus linking the subjective and the objective) of the closest approximation possible." [1]

It will no doubt have emerged in the preceding pages that I am more reluctant than Smith to distinguish intellectuals from others, or to assign quite the same degree of authority "to Reality, to final Truth." Any religious person is in some sense intellectual, and able to articulate a conditional reality, or an intermediate truth, as easily as any more ultimate reality. And yet it is certainly true that insight

[1] *Faith and Belief*, pp. 168-69.

and response are at the heart of the matter. That is why faith, so absolute in some of its appearances, is so conditional in others, residing as it does in a tension between attitude and action in which religious meaning both informs and is informed by the requirements of a world in which interconnection plays a central role.

There is a story from President William Clinton's undergraduate days at Georgetown which may help to reformulate the perspective Bernard Lord Manning brought to his reading of "the people's faith" with which I began. (I reveal no secrets in telling it, since Candidate Clinton himself told the story, very publicly and with great aplomb, during the 1994 presidential campaign: it was largely ignored by the press.)[2] But toward the end of his first year at Georgetown, young Mr. Clinton was taken to lunch by his theology teacher, a Jesuit scholastic, himself still a young man and in training for the priesthood. The scholastic said he had enjoyed having young Mr. Clinton in class; the young man referred to averred that he, too, had enjoyed the experience. The scholastic said he had something important to say: he believed that the young man had a vocation to become a Jesuit priest. A moment's pause. Then young Mr. Clinton, a lifelong Baptist, asked politely if perhaps it was not necessary first to be a Catholic. Near at hand, and particularly when represented by an esteemed person, religious attitudes are frequently congenial, and spiritual values have more than one face. (In the story I have just told, the scholastic had been reading Mr. Clinton's papers all semester, and had come to believe that the values represented there were his own: from that it followed, he thought, that the young man was indeed a Catholic.) One text yields to another easily, and a prayer is passed on; a Buddhist tale becomes Christian, retaining, however, something of its rich past; gender and spirituality form an alliance which clearly is born of something more than convenience; a devout habit of mind enters a romance or crosses an ocean, and is forever changed in the process; signs and symbols of the passion inform a later age—but in what ways? And of what? The ways of transmission are as many as the persons who embrace them, and just when the differences seem insignificant, or to have disappeared entirely, they emerge again, *pace* Mr. Manning, all too vividly: only ask young Mr. Clinton. Spirituality does not descend along a stemma, and has nothing to do with

2 See now David Maraniss, *First in his Class, A Biography of Bill Clinton* (New York: Simon and Schuster, 1995), p. 58.

lineage. Its relationship to theology and to history is problematic. The patterns of medieval spirituality are gone forever, except when they reach us, informing our choices or suggesting a way.

I wrote in the Introduction that the chapters which make up this book are a series of *exempla* which are also explorations, explorations concerned with the development and transmission of medieval religious faith. But I have been concerned as well with the nature of the engagement which religious interaction of whatever form occasions, and I have also tried to be sensitive to the nature of a phenomenon which represents itself as both fixed and responsive, implicated by context and able to transcend it, present in time, and yet apart from it. Development, transmission, and change are at the heart of spirituality: yet its attraction is often that they appear to be no such thing.

This book has been concerned with a number of topics which spirituality often takes up: the discernment of the inner person, and the ways of addressing him or her; the fluctuating representations of Christ and his mother as, over centuries, a prayer is copied and recopied; the movement into the West of one form of Eastern spirituality, and its only partial accommodation there; the ways in which popular literature appropriated mystical language to represent the sacred; the complex ways in which authors addressed gender, operating often with different agendas, but not always at cross purposes, and locating an ideal of the sacred in which to negotiate or create appropriate space; the extraordinary reception accorded devotions represented as Christ's blood, or the *arma Christi*, or mysticism itself.

Small wonder that any attempt, in the Americas, to limit, or focus, or restrict the faith on which that spirituality rested fell of its own weight. The practice of religion has always involved others, and that has meant accommodation and sometimes adaptation. The Spanish who sought, by processing, kneeling, and singing the *Ave Maria*, to impress Montezuma with their devotion were in a long tradition, one with descendants both in Central American armies and among intelligent persons of many persuasions, but obtusely, they had mistaken that tradition's meaning and effect. To be religious is to be human, and the study of spirituality begins with that.

BIBLIOGRAPHY

Aili, Hans. "St. Brigitta and the Text of the *Revelations*: A Survey of Some Influences Traceable to Translators and Editors," in *The Editing of Theological and Philosophical Texts from the Middle Ages.* Acts of the Conference Arranged by the Department of Classical Languages, University of Stockholm, 29-31 August 1984. Ed. Monika Asztalos. *Acta Universitatis Stockholmiensis, Studia Latina.* Stockholmiensia XXX. Stockholm: Almqvist & Wiksell International, 1986. Pp. 75-91.

Allen, Hope Emily. *Writing Ascribed to Richard Rolle, Hermit of Hampole, and Materials for his Biography.* The Modern Language Association of America, Monograph Series III. New York: D.C. Heath and Co., and London: Oxford University Press, 1927.

Alford, John A. "Richard Rolle and Related Works," in *Middle English Prose. A Critical Guide to Authors and Genres.* New Brunswick, New Jersey: Rutgers University Press, 1984.

Alston, William P. *Perceiving God. The Epistemology of Religious Experience.* Ithaca and New York: Cornell University Press, 1991.

Amore, Roy C. "The Concept and Practice of Doing Merit in Early Theravada Buddhism." Columbia University Dissertation, 1970.

Anderson, Bonnie S. and Judith P. Zinsser. *A History of their Own. Women in Europe from Prehistory to the Present.* vol. 1. New York: Harper and Row, 1988.

Arnould, E.J.F. "Richard Rolle and A Bishop: A Vindication," *Bulletin of the John Rylands Library*, 21 (1937), 3-25.

Arthur, Ross G. *Medieval Sign Theory and Sir Gawain and the Green Knight.* Toronto: University of Toronto Press, 1987.

Ashley, Kathleen and Pamela Sheingorn, eds. *Interpreting Cultural Symbols. St. Anne in Late Medieval Society.* Athens, Ga. and London: University of Georgia Press, 1990.

Asmussen, Jes P., ed. and trans. *Manichaean Literature. Representative Texts Chiefly from Middle Persian and Parthian Writing.* Persian Heritage Series No. 22. UNESCO Collection of Representative Works. Delmar, N.Y.: Scholars' Facsimiles & Reprints, 1975.

Aston, Margaret. *Faith and Fire. Popular and Unpopular Religion, 1350-1600.* London and Rio Grande, Ohio: The Hambledon Press, 1993.

Atkinson, Clarissa W. *Mystic and Pilgrim. The Book and the World of Margery Kempe.* Ithaca and London: Cornell University Press, 1983.

Aubert, Marcel. *La sculpture française au moyen-age.* Paris: Flammerion, 1947.

Audelay, John. *The Poems of John Audelay*, ed. Ella Keats Whiting. Early English Text Society, Original Series 184. London: Oxford University Press for the Early English Text Society, 1931.

Barb, A.A. "The 'Wound in Christ's Side'," *Journal of the Warburg and Courtauld Institutes*, 34 (1971), 320-21.

———, " 'Vidi Aquam...' and the Wounded Christ," *Faith*, 5 no. 1 (1979), 20-21.

Barré, Henri. *Prières anciennes de l' occident à la Mère du Sauveur des origines à saint Anselme.* Paris: P. Lethiellevx, 1963.

Bauder, Peter. *The Spiritual Mirror; or, Looking-Glass: Exhibiting the Human Heart as Being Either the Temple of God, or the Habitation of Devils. Exemplified by a Series of Ten Engravings; Intended to Aid in a Better Understanding of Man' s Fallen Nature.* Albany: E. & E. Hosford, 1825.

Beckwith, Sarah. *Christ' s Body. Identity, Culture and Society in Late Medieval Writings.* London and New York: Routledge, 1993.

Belenitskii, A.M. and B. I. Marshak, "The Nature of the Cultural Relations of Sogdiana," in *Sogdian Painting. The Pictorial Epic in Oriental Art.* Berkeley, Los Angeles and London: University of California Press, 1981. Pp. 26-34.

Belting, Hans. *The Image and Its Public in the Middle Ages. Form and Function of Early Paintings of the Passion.* Trans. Mark Bartusis and Raymond Meyer. New Rochelle, N.Y.: Aristide D. Caratzas, 1990.

Benedict. *RB: 1980. The Rule of St. Benedict in Latin and English with Notes.* Ed. Timothy Fry, O.S.B., *et al.* Collegeville, Minnesota: The Liturgical Press, 1981.

Bennett, J.A.W. *Poetry of the Passion. Studies in Twelve Centuries of English Verse.* Oxford: Clarendon Press, 1982.

Benson, C. David. *Chaucer' s Drama of Style: Poetic Variety and Contrast in the Canterbury Tales.* Chapel Hill: University of North Carolina Press, 1986.

Berliner, Rudolf. "Arma Christi," *Münchner Jahrbuch der Bildenden Kunst*, 6 (1955), 35-153.

Berryman, Philip. *Liberation Theology.* London: I. B. Taurus & Co. Ltd., 1987.

Bestul, Thomas H. "St. Anselm and the Continuity of Anglo-Saxon Devotional Traditions," *Annuale Mediaevale*, 18 (1977), 39-45.

———, *"British Library MS. Arundel 60 and the Anselmian Apocrypha," Manuscripta*, 35 (1981), 271-75.

Boff, Leonardo, O. F. M. *Saint Francis. A Model for Human Liberation*, trans. John W. Diercksmeier. New York: Crossroad, 1982.

———, *Church: Charism and Power. Liberal Theology and the Institutional Church*, trans. John W. Diercksmeier. New York: Crossroad, 1985.

Bornstein, Daniel E. *The Bianchi of 1399. Popular Devotion in Late Medieval Italy.* Ithaca and London: Cornell University Press, 1993.

Bowker, John. *The Sense of God. Sociological, Anthropological and Psychological Approaches to the Origin of the Sense of God.* Oxford: Clarendon Press, 1973.

Brandenbarg, Ton. "St. Anne and her Family. The Veneration of St. Anne in Connection with Concepts of Marriage and the Family in the Early Modern Period," in *Saints and She-devils. Images of Women in the 15th and 16th Centuries*, ed. Lène Dresen-Coenders, trans. C.M.H. Sion. London: The Rubicon Press, 1987. Pp. 101-127.

Brigden, Susan, *London and the Reformation.* Oxford: Clarendon Press, 1989, rpt. 1991.

Brittain, F. *Bernard Lord Manning. A Memoir.* Cambridge: W. Heffer & Sons, 1942

Brook, Christopher, *et al. David Knowles Remembered.* Cambridge: Cambridge University Press, 1991.

Brown, Andrew D. *Popular Piety in Late Medieval England. The Diocese of Salisbury 1250-1550.* Oxford Historical Monographs. Oxford: Clarendon Press, 1995.

Brown, Peter. *Augustine of Hippo. A Biography.* London: Faber and Faber, 1967.

———, "The Rise and the Function of the Holy Man in Late Antiquity," *Journal of Roman Studies*, 61 (1971), 80-101.

———, *Society and the Holy in Late Antiquity.* London: Faber and Faber, 1982.

———, *The Body and Society. Men, Women and Sexual Renunciation in Early Christianity.* Lectures on the History of Religions Sponsored by the American Council of Learned Societies, New Series, Number 13. New York: Columbia University Press, 1988.

Brown, T.J., G.M. Meredith-Owens and D.H. Turner, "Manuscripts from the Dyson Perrins Collection," *The British Museum Quarterly*, 23 (1960/61), 27-38.

Brundage, James A, *Law, Sex and Christian Society in Medieval Europe.* Chicago and London: University of Chicago Press, 1987.

Bryan, W.F. and Germaine Dempster, eds. *Sources and Analogues of Chaucer' s Canterbury Tales.* New York: Humanities Press, 1941, rpt. 1958.

Burrow, John. *A Reading of Sir Gawain and the Green Knight.* London, Henly and Boston: Routledge and Kegan Paul, 1967, rpt. 1977.

Bynum, Caroline Walker. "Did the Twelfth Century Discover the Individual?," *Journal of Ecclesiastical History*, 31 (1980), 1-17.

———, *Jesus As Mother. Studies in the Spirituality of the High Middle Ages*. Publications of the Center for Medieval and Renaissance Studies, UCLA, No. 19. Berkeley, Los Angeles and London: University of California Press, 1982, rpt. 1894.

———, *Holy Feast and Holy Fast: The Religious Significance of Food to Medieval Women*. The New Historicism: Studies in Cultural Poetics. Berkeley, Los Angeles and London: University of California Press, 1986.

———, " '...And Women His Humanity:' Female Imagery in the Religious Writing of the Later Middle Ages," in *Gender and Religion: On the Complexity of of Symbols*, eds. Bynum, Stevan Harrell and Paula Richman. Boston: Beacon Press, 1986. Pp. 257-88.

———, *Fragmentation and Redemption. Essays on Gender and the Human Body in Medieval Religion*. New York: Zone Books, 1991.

———, *The Resurrection of the Body in Western Christianity, 200-1336*. Lectures on the History of Religions Sponsored by the American Council of Learned Societies, New Series, Number 15. New York: Columbia University Press, 1995.

Capuzzo, Roberto. "Note sulla tradizione e sul culto del sangue di Cristo nella Mantova medievale," *Storia e arte religiosa a Mantova*. Mantova: Casa del Mantegna, 1991. Pp. 61-72.

Carroll, Michael P. *The Cult of the Virgin Mary. Psychological Origins*. Princeton: Princeton University Press, 1986.

Cassidy, Brendan, ed. *The Ruthwell Cross. Papers from the Colloquium Sponsored by the Index of Christian Art*. Index of Christian Art Occasional Papers I. Princeton, N.J.: Princeton University Press, 1992.

Cawley, A. C., ed. *Everyman*. Old and Middle English Texts. Manchester: Manchester University Press, 1961, rpt. 1970.

Charbonneau-Lassay, Louis. *La Bestiaire du Christ. La mystérieuse emblématique de Jésus-Christ*. Paris: Desclée, De Brouwer & Cie., 1940; rpt. Milan: Archè, 1980.

Chaucer, Geoffrey, *The Riverside Chaucer*, ed. Larry D. Benson. 3rd edition. Boston: Houghton Mifflin Company, 1987.

Chitty, Derwas J. *The Desert a City. An Introduction to the Study of Egyptian and Palestinian Monasticism Under the Christian Empire*. Oxford: Basil Blackwell, 1966.

Christian, William A., Jr. *Apparitions in Late Medieval and Renaissance Spain*. Princeton, N.J.: Princeton University Press, 1981.

———, *Local Religion in in Sixteenth-Century Spain*. Princeton, N.J.: Princeton University Press, 1981.

Clayton, Mary. *The Cult of the Virgin Mary in Anglo-Saxon England*. Cambridge Studies in Anglo Saxon England 2. Cambridge: Cambridge University Press, 1990.

Clendinnen, Inga. *Ambivalent Conquests. Maya and Spanish in Yucatan, 1517-1570*. Cambridge Latin America Studies 61. Cambridge: Cambridge University Press, 1987.

Coniglio, Giuseppe. *Mantova. La storia*. 3 vols. Mantua: Istituto Carlo D'Arco, 1958-63.

Conley, John. "The Doctrine of Friendship in *Everyman*," *Speculum*, 44 (1969), 374-82.

Colledge, Edmund, O.S.A. "Editing Julian of Norwich's Revelations: A Progress Report," *Medieval Studies*, 38 (1976), 404-27.

Congar, Yves, O.P. *I Believe in the Holy Spirit*. Volume I, *The Holy Spirit in the 'Economy.' Revelation and Experience of the Spirit*. Trans. David Smith. New York: The Seabury Press and London: Geoffrey Chapman, 1983.

Cook, Francis H. "Nirvana," in *Buddhism. A Modern Perspective*. Ed. Charles S. Prebish. University Park and London: Pennsylvania State University Press, 1975. Pp. 113-36.

Courtenay, William J. "Between Despair and Love. Some Late Medieval Modifications of Augustine's Teaching on Fruition and Psychic States," in *Augustine, the Harvest and Theology (1300-1650). Essays Dedicated to Heiko Augustinus Oberman in Honor of his Sixtieth Birthday*, ed. Kenneth Hagen. Leiden and New York: E. J. Brill, 1990. Pp. 5-20.

Cowdrey, H.E.J. *The Cluniacs and Gregorian Reform.* Oxford: Clarendon Press, 1970.

Cowell, E.B., gen. ed. and trans. *The Jātaka. Or Stories of the Buddha' s Former Births.* 7 vols. Cambridge: Cambridge University Press, 1895-1913.

Cox, Harvey. *The Silencing of Leonardo Boff. The Vatican and the Future of World Christianity.* Oak Park, Illinois: Meyer Stone Books, 1988.

Da Terrinca, Natale, O.F.M. *La Devozione al Prez, Mo Sangue di nostro Signore Gesu Cristo.* 2nd edn. Rome: Albano Liziale, 1987.

de la Potterie, Ignace, S.J. *Mary in the Mystery of the Covenant.* Trans. Bertrand Buby, S.M. New York: Alba House, 1992.

de Tolnay, Charles. *Michelangelo. The Final Period.* Princeton, N.J.: Princeton University Press, 1971.

de Vecchi, Pierluigi. "Michelangelo's *Last Judgment,*" in *The Sistene Chapel. The Art, the History and the Restoration.* New York: Harmony Books, 1986.

del Castillo, Bernal Díaz. *The Discovery and Conquest of Mexico, 1517-1521.* Trans. A.P. Maudslay. New York: Farrar, Straus and Cudhay, 1956.

Daniel, E. Randolph. *The Franciscan Concept of History in the High Middle Ages.* Lexington, Kentucky.: University Press of Kentucky, 1975.

Debroise, Olivier, Elisabeth Sussman and Matthew Teitelbaum, *El Corazon Sangrante/The Bleeding Heart.* Boston: Institute of Contemporary Art, 1991.

Despres, Denise L. "The Meditative Art of Scriptural Interpolation in *The Book of Margery Kempe,*" *Downside Review,* 106 (1988), 253-63.

Dickens, Bruce and A.S.C. Ross, eds. *The Dream of the Rood.* 4th edition. Methuen's Old English Library. London: Methuen and Co. Ltd., 1956, rpt. 1967.

Dickman, Susan. "Margery Kempe and the English Devotional Tradition," in *The Medieval Mystical Tradition in England.* Papers Read at the Exeter Symposium, July 1980, ed. Marion Glasscoe. Exeter Medieval English Texts and Studies. Exeter: University of Exeter Press, 1980. Pp. 156-72.

Dillon, John. "Looking on the Light: Some Remarks on the Imagery of Light in the First Chapter of the *Peri Archon,*" in *Origin of Alexandria. His World and his Legacy*, eds. Charles Kannengiesser and William L. Petersen. Christianity and Judaism in Antiquity, volume 1. Notre Dame, Indiana: University of Notre Dame Press, 1988. Pp. 215-30.

Dodds, E.R. *The Ancient Concept of Progress and Other Essays on Greek Literature and Belief.* Oxford: Clarendon Press, 1973.

Donnini, Giampiero. *I Legni Devoti.* Fabriano: Soprintendenza ai Beni Artistice e Storia delle Marche, Comune di Fabriano. 1994.

Duby, Georges, Xavier Barral i Altet and Sophie Guillot de Suduiraut. *Sculpture, the Great Art of the Middle Ages. From the Fifth Century to the Fifteenth Century.* New York: Skira\Rizzoli, 1990.

Duffy, Eamon. *The Stripping of the Altars. Traditional Religion in England 1400-1580.* New Haven: Yale University Press, 1992.

Dunkerley, James. *The Pacification of Central America. Political Change in the Isthmus, 1987-1993.* London and New York: Verso, 1994.

Dupré, Louis. "The Christian Experience of Mystical Union," *The Journal of Religion,* 69 (1989), 1-13.

Egan, Martha J. *Relicarios. Devotional Mineatures from the Americas.* Sante Fe: Museum of New Mexico Press, 1993.

Ellis, Roger. *Patterns of Religious Narrative in the Canterbury Tales.* London: Crome Helm, 1986.

Elm, Suzanna. *'Virgins of God.' The Making of Asceticism in Late Antiquity*. Oxford Classical Monographs. Oxford: Clarendon Press, 1994.
England, George and Alfred W. Pollard, eds. *The Towneley Plays*. Early English Text Society, Extra Series 71. London: K. Paul, Trench, Trubney and Co. for the Early English Text Society, 1897.
Ettlinger, L. D. *The Sistene Chapel Before Michelangelo. Religious Imagery and Papal Primacy*. Oxford-Warburg Studies. Oxford: Clarendon Press, 1965.
Erler, Mary. "Margery Kempe's White Clothes," *Medium AEvum*, 62 (1993), 78-83
Erler, Mary and Maryanne Kowaleski, eds. *Women and Power in the Middle Ages*. Athens, Ga.and London: University of Georgia Press, 1988.
Evans, Gillian. " *Mens Devota*. The Literary Community of the Devotional Works of John of Fècamp and St. Anselm," *Medium AEvum*, 43 (1974), 105-15.
Falla, Ricardo. *Massacres in the Jungle. Ixcán, Guatemala, 1975-1982*. Trans. Julia Howland. Boulder, San Francisco and Oxford: Westview Press, 1994.
Forsyth, Ilene H. *The Throne of Wisdom. Wood Sculptures of the Madonna in Romanesque France*. Princeton, N.J.: Princeton University Press, 1972.
Foster, Francis, ed. *The Northern Passion*. Early English Text Society, Original Series 145 and 147. London: Oxford University Press for the Early English Text Society, 1913 and 1916.
Fowden, Garth. "The Pagan Holy Man in Late Antique Society," *Journal of Hellenic Studies*, 102 (1982), 33-59.
Friedman, John B. *Northern English Books, Owners, and Makers in the Late Middle Ages*. Syracuse: Syracuse University Press, 1995.
Galliffet, Joseph de, S.J. *De Cultu Sacrosancti Cordis Dei ac Domini Nostri Jesu Christi*. Rome: Joannem Mariam Salvioni, 1726.
Gardner, Arthur. *Medieval Sculpture in France*. Cambridge: Cambridge University Press, 1931.
Giffords, Gloria Fraser, *et al*. *The Art of Private Devotion. Retablo Painting of Mexico*. Fort Worth and Dallas, Texas: Intercultura and SMU, 1991.
Glasscoe, Marion. *English Medieval Mystics. Games of Faith*. Longman Medieval and Renaissance Library. London and New York: Longman, 1993.
Goffen, Rona. *Piety and Patronage in Renaissance Venice: Bellini, Titian and the Franciscans*. New Haven and London: Yale University Press, 1986.
Gombrich, Ernst. "Arcaeologists or Pharisees? Reflections on a Painting by Maarten van Heemskerck," *Journal of the Warburg and Courtauld Institutes*, 54 (1991), 253-56.
Goodman, Anthony. "The Piety of John Burnham's Daughter, of Lynn," in *Medieval Women: Dedicated and Presented to Professor Roaslind M.T. Hill*, ed. Derek Baker. Studies in Church History, Subsidia I. Oxford: Published for the Ecclesiastical History Society by Basil Blackwell, 1978. Pp. 347-58.
Gougoud, Louis, O.S.B. *Devotional and Ascetic Practices in the Middle Ages*. Trans. G.C. Bateman. London: Burns, Oates and Washbourne, 1927.
Grajales, Gloria and Ernest J. Burrus, S.J., eds. *Bibliografía Guadalupana/ Guadalupan Bibliography (1531-1984)*. Washington, D.C.: Georgetown University Press, 1986.
Gransden, Antonia. *Legends, Traditions and History in Medieval England*. London and Rio Grande: The Hambledon Press, 1992.
Gray, Douglas. "The Five Wounds of Our Lord," *Notes and Queries*, n.s. 10 (1963). 50-51, 82-89, 127-34, 163-68.
Grayzel, Solomon, ed. and trans. *The Church and the Jews in the XIIIth Century. Volume II, 1254-1314*, edited and arranged by Kenneth R. Stow. New York and Detroit: The Jewish Theological Seminary of America and Wayne State University Press, 1989/5749.
Greene, R.L., ed. *The Early English Carols*. Oxford: Clarendon Press, 1935.
Griffin, Mary. *Studies on Chaucer and his Audience*. Québec: Les éditions l'éclair, 1956.

Günzel, Beate, ed. *AElfwine's Prayerbook (London, British Library Cotton Titus D.xxvi + xxviii)*. Henry Bradshaw Society vol. CVIII. London: Boydell Press, 1993.
Gurewich, Vladmir. "Observations on the Iconography on the Wound in Christ's Side, with Special Reference to its Position," *Journal of the Warburg and Courtauld Institutes*, 20 (1957), 358-62.
———, "*Rubens and the 'Wound in Christ's Side', A Postscript,*" *Journal of the Warburg and Courtauld institutes*, 26 (1963), 358.
Gutierrez, Gustavo. *The Power of the Poor in History. Selected Writings.* London: SCM Press, and Maryknoll, N.Y.: Orbis Books, 1983.
Haigh, Christopher, ed. *The English Reformation Revised.* Cambridge: Cambridge University Press, 1987.
———, *English Reformations. Religion, Politics and Society under the Tudors.* Oxford: Clarendon Press, 1993.
Hall, Marcia. "Michelangelo's *Last Judgment*: Resurrection of the Body and Predestination," *The Art Bulletin*, 58 (1976), 85-92.
———, *Color and Meaning. Practice and Theory in Renaissance Painting.* Cambridge: Cambridge University Press, 1992.
Hallinger, Kassius. "The Spiritual Life of Cluny in the Early Days," in *Cluniac Monasticism in the Central Middle Ages*, ed. Noreen Hunt. Readings in European History. London: Macmillan, 1971. Pp. 29-55.
Hanning, Robert W.. "From *Eva* to *Ave* to Eglentine and Alison: Chaucer's Insight into the Roles Women Play," *Signs*, 2 (1977), 580-99.
Hassig, Ross. *Mexico and the Spanish Conquest.* Modern Wars in Perspective: London and New York: Longman, 1994.
Hausherr, Irénée. *The Name of Jesus.* Trans. Charles Cummings, O.C.S.O. Cistercian Studies Series: Number 44. Kalamazoo, Michigan: Cistercian Publications, Inc., 1978.
Heiming, Odilo, O.S.B. "Ein Benediktinisch-Ambrosianisches Gebetbuch des frühen 11. Jahrhunderts, Brit. Mus. Egerton 3763 (ehemals Dyson Perrins 48)," *Archiv für Liturgiewissenschaft*, VIII 2 (1964), 325-424.
Herlihy, David. *Medieval Households.* Studies in Cultural History. Cambridge, Mass. Harvard University Press, 1985.
Hibbard, Howard. *Michelangelo.* 2nd edn. New York: Harper & Row, 1983.
Hirschfeld, Yizhar. *The Judean Desert Monasteries in the Byzantine Period.* New Haven and London: Yale University Press, 1992.
Hirsh, John C. "Two English Devotional Poems of the Fifteenth Century," *Notes and Queries*, n.s. 15 (1968), 4-11.
———, "*Providential Concern in the 'Lay le Freine',*" *Notes and Queries*, n.s. 16 (1969), 85-86.
———, "*A Fifteenth-Century Commentary on 'Ihesu for thy Holy Name',*" *Notes and Queries*, n.s. 17 (1970), 44-45.
———, "*Author and Scribe in The Book of Margery Kempe,*" *Medium AEvum*, 44 (1975), 145-150.
———, "*Reopening the Prioress' Tale,*" *Chaucer Review*, 10 (1975), 37-41.
———, "*The Experience of God: A New Classification of Certain Late Medieval Affective Texts,*" *Chaucer Review*, 11 (1976), 11-21.
———, "*The Politics of Spirituality: The Second Nun and the Manciple,*" *Chaucer Review*, 12 (1977), 129-37.
———, "*Prayer and Meditation in Late Medieval England: MS Bodley 789,*" *Medium AEvum*, 48 (1979), 55-66.
———, "*Margery Kempe,*" in *Middle English Prose. A Critical Guide to Major Authors and Genres*, ed. A.S.G. Edwards. New Brunswick, N.J.: Rutgers University Press, 1984. Pp. 109-119.

———, *Barlam and Iosaphat. A Middle English Life of Buddha.* Early English Text Society, Original Series 290. London: Oxford University Press, 1986.

———, *Hope Emily Allen. Medieval Scholarship and Feminism.* Norman, Oklahoma: Pilgrim Books, 1988.

———, *The Revelations of Margery Kempe. Paramystical Practices in Late Medieval England.* Medieval and Renaissance Authors, volume 10. Leiden and New York: E. J. Brill, 1989.

Hood, William. *Fra Angelico at San Marco.* New Haven and London: Yale University Press, 1993.

Hudson, Anne. *The Premature Reformation. Wycliffite Texts and Lollard History.* Oxford: Clarendon Press, 1988.

Hutton, Ronald. *The Rise and Fall of Merry England, The Ritual Year 1400-1700.* Oxford and New York: Oxford University Press, 1994.

Ireland, Rowan. *Kingdoms Come. Religion and Politics in Brazil.* Pittsburgh: University of Pittsburgh Press, 1991.

Pope John Paul II. *Mulieris Dignitatem*, authorised English translation. *Origins*, vol. 18, No. 17 (October 6, 1988), 262-83.

———, *Letter to Women*, authorized English Translation. *Origins*, vol. 25, No. 9 (July 27,1995), 137-143.

Joannides, Paul. " 'Primitivism' in the Late Drawings of Michelangelo: The Master's Construction of an Old-Age Style," in *Michelangelo Drawings*, ed. Craig Hugh Smyth. Studies in the History of Art 33. Center for Advanced Study in the Visual Arts, Symposium Papers XVII. Washington, D.C.: National Gallery of Art, 1992. Pp. 245-61.

Johnson, E. H., ed. and trans. *The Buddhacarita. Or, Acts of the Buddha.* Punjab University Oriental Publications No. 32. Lahore and Calcutta: Baptist Mission Press, 1936; rpt. New Delhi: Oriental Books Reprint Corporation, 1972.

Julian of Norwich. *A Book of Showings to the Anchoress Julian of Norwich*, eds. Edmund Colledge, O.S.A. and James Walsh, S.J. 2 vols. Studies and Texts 35. Toronto: Pontifical Institute of Medieval Studies, 1978.

Keene, D. J. "Surburban Growth," in *The Medieval Town. A Reader in English Urban History 1200-1540*, eds. Richard Holt and Gervase Rosser. Readers in Urban History. London and New York: Longman, 1990.

Kellogg, Alfred L. "An Augustinian Interpretation of Chaucer's Pardoner," *Speculum*, 26 (1951), 465-81.

———, "*St. Augustine and the Parson' s Tale*," *Traditio*, 8 (1952), 424-30.

Knowles, David. *The Historian and Character and Other Essays.* Cambridge: Cambridge University Press, 1963.

Kolve, V. A. " *Everyman* and the Parable of the Talents," in *The Medieval Drama. Papers of the Third Annual Conference for Medieval and Renaissance Studies.* New York: SUNY Press, 1972.

Kramarae, Cheris and Paula A. Treichler, eds. *A Feminist Dictionary.* Boston, London and Henley: Pandora Press, 1985.

Kuryluk, Ewa. *Veronica and her Cloth. History, Symbolism and Structure of a " True" Image.* Oxford: Basil Blackwell, 1991.

Ladner, Gerhart B. " *Homo Viator*. Medieval Ideas on Alienation and Order," *Speculum*, 42 (1967), 233-59.

———, "*Medieval and Modern Understanding of Symbolism: A Comparison*," *Speculum*, 54 (1979), 223-56.

Landrum, Graham. "The Convent Crowd and the Feminist Nun," *Tennessee Philological Bulletin*, 13 (1976), 5-12.

Lawrence, C.H. *Medieval Monasticism. Forms of Religious Life in Western Europe in the Middle Ages.* Second edition. London and New York: Longman, 1989, rpt. 1993.

Lerner, Gerda. *The Creation of the Patriarchy*. Women and History, vol. 1. New York: Oxford University Press, 1986.
Lieu, Samuel N.C. *Manichaeism in the Later Roman Empire and in Medieval China. A Historical Survey*. Manchester: Manchester University Press, 1985.
Lloyd-Jones, Hugh. *Greek Studies in Modern Oxford. An Inaugural Lecture Delivered before the University of Oxford on 23 May 1961*. Oxford: Clarendon Press, 1961.
Lochrie, Karma. " *The Book of Margery Kempe*: The Marginal Woman's Quest for Literary Authority," *Journal of Medieval and Renaissance Studies*, 16 (1986), 33-55.
Louis, Cameron, ed. *The Commonplace Book of Robert Reynes of Acle*. Garland Medieval Texts I. New York: Garland Press, 1980.
Louth, Andrew. *The Origins of the Christian Mystical Tradition. From Plato to Denys*. Oxford: Clarendon Press, 1981.
Lueck, Jeanmarie, O.S.B. "Three Faces of Cecilia: Chaucer's *Second Nun's Tale*," *American Benedictine Review*, 33 (1982), 335-48.
Manning, Bernard Lord. *The People's Faith in the Age of Wyclif*. Thirwall Essay 1917. Cambridge: Cambridge University Press, 1919; rpt. Hassocks, Sussex and Totowa, New Jersey: The Harvester Press and Rowman and Littlefield, 1975.
Marlow, Christopher. *Doctor Faustus*, ed. John D. Jump. The Revels Plays. London: Methuen & Co. Ltd., 1962, rpt. 1966.
Marrow, James H. *Passion Iconography in Northern European Art of the Late Middle Ages and Early Renaissance. A Study of the Transformation of Sacred Metaphor into Narrative Description*. Ars Neerlandica. Brussels: Ministerie van Nederlandse Cultuur, 1979.
McCarthy, Dennis J., S.J. "The Symbolism of Blood and Sacrifice," *Journal of Biblical Literature*, 88 (1969), 166-76.
McEntire, Sandra J., ed. *Margery Kempe. A Book of Essays*. Garland Medieval Casebooks 4. New York and London: Garland Publishing, Inc, 1992.
McGinn, Bernard. *The Presence of God. A History of Christian Mysticism*. Vol. 1 *The Foundations of Mysticism*, vol. 2 *The Growth of Mysticism*. New York: Crossroad, 1991, 1994.
Meech, Sanford Brown and Hope Emily Allen, eds. *The Book of Margery Kempe*. Volume 1. Early English Text Society, Original Series 212. London: Oxford University Press, 1940.
Miller, Robert. "Chaucer's Pardoner, the Scriptural Eunuch and the *Pardoner's Tale*," *Speculum*, 30 (1955), 180-99.
Moorman, John. *A History of the Franciscan Order from its Origins to the Year 1517*. Oxford: Clarendon Press, 1968.
Morey, Adrian, O.S.B. *David Knowles. A Memoir*. London: Darton, Longman & Todd, 1979.
Morris, Colin. "Individualism in Twelfth-Century Religion: Some Further Reflections," *Journal of Ecclesiastical History*, 31 (1980), 195-206.
Morris, Richard. "The Book of Birth-Stories," *The Contemporary Review*, 39 (1881), 728-49.
Mueller, Janel M. "Autobiography of a New ' Creatur:' Female Spirituality, Selfhood and Authorship in ' The Book of Margery Kempe'," in *The Female Autograph. Theory and Practice of Autobiography from the Tenth to the Twentieth Century*, ed. Domna C. Stanton. Chicago and London: University of Chicago Press, 1987. Pp. 57-69.
Muir, Bernard James, ed. *A Pre-Conquest English Prayer-Book (BL MSS Cotton Galba A.xiv and Cotton Nero A.ii (ff. 3-13)*. Henry Bradshaw Society vol. CIII. Woodbridge, Suffolk: The Boydell Press, 1988.
Newman, Brabara. *From Virile Woman to WomanChrist. Studies in Medieval Religion and Literature*. Middle Ages Series. Philadelphia: University of Pennsylvania Press, 1995.
Nichols, John A, and Lillian Thomas Shank, eds. *Medieval Religious Women: vol. 1:*

Distant Echoes and *vol. 2: Peace Weavers*. Cistercian Studies Series, Nos. 71 and 72. Kalamazoo, Michigan: Cistercian Publications, Inc.: 1984 and 1987.

Noetinger, Maurice, O.S.B. "The Biography of Richard Rolle," *The Month*, 147 (1926) 22-33.

Oates, J. C. T. "Richard Pynson and the Holy Blood of Hayles," *The Library*, Fifth Series, 13 (1958), 269-77.

Oberman, Heiko Augustinus. *The Harvest of Medieval Theology. Gabriel Biel and Late Medieval Nominalism.* Cambridge, Mass.: Harvard University Press, 1963.

———, *The Dawn of the Reformation. Essays in Late Medieval and Reformation Thought.* Edinburgh: T. & T. Clark, Ltd., 1986.

Padden, R. C. *The Hummingbird and the Hawk. Conquest and Sovereignty in the Valley of Mexico, 1503-1541.* New York: Harper & Row, 1970.

Paredi, Angelo, ed. *Vita e Meriti di S. Ambrogio. Testo inedito del secolo nono illustrato con le miniature del salterio di Arnolfo.* Fontes Ambrosiani in lucem editi cura et studio Bibliothecae Ambrosianae XXXVII. Milan: Casa Editrice Ceschina, 1964.

Partner, Nancy. " 'And Most of All for Inordinate Love': Desire and Denial in *The Book of Margery Kempe*, *Thought*, 64 (1989), 254-67.

Peter the Chanter (attrib.). *The Christian at Prayer. An Illustrated Manual Attributed to Peter the Chanter*, ed. Richard C. Trexler. Medieval and Renaissance Texts and Studies, volume 44. Binghamton, New York, 1987.

Petroff, Elizabeth Alvilda. *Body and Soul. Essays on Medieval Women and Mysticism.* New York and Oxford: Oxford University Press, 1994.

Phelan, John Leddy. *The Millennial Kingdom of the Franciscans in the New World. A Study of the Writings of Gerónimo de Mendieta (1525-1604).* University of California Publications in History, volume 52. Second edition. Berkeley, Los Angeles, and London: University of California Press, 1971.

Photius. *The Homilies of Photius Patriarch of Constaninople.* Trans. Cyril Mango. Dumbarton Oaks Studies III. Cambridge, Massachusetts: Harvard University Press, 1958.

Pieris, Aloysius, S.J. "Western Christianity and Eastern Religions (A Theological Readings of Historical Encounters)," *Cistercian Studies*, 1 (1980), 50-66 and 2 (1982), 150-71.

———, "Interculturation in Non-Semitic Asia," *The Month*, 2nd N.S. 19 (1986), 83-87.

———, *An Asian Theology of Liberation.* Faith Meets Faith Series. Edinburgh and Maryknoll, New York: T. & T. Clark and Orbis Books, 1988.

Poole, Stafford, C.M. *Our Lady of Guadalupe. The Origins and Sources of a Mexican National Symbol. 1531-1797.* Tucson and London: University of Arizona Press, 1995.

Porete, Margaret (or Marguerite). *The Mirror of Simple Souls. A Middle English Translation*, ed. Marilyn Doiron, with an Appendix: "The Glosses by ' M.N.' and Richard Methley to 'The Mirror of Simple Souls'," ed. Edmund Colledge and Romana Guarnieri, *Archivo Italiano per la Storia della piettà*, 5 (1968), 241-382.

Principe, Walter, "Toward Defining Spirituality," *Sciences Religieuses/Studies in Religion*, 12 (1983), 127-41.

Rácz, István. *Lohjan Kirkko.* Helsinki: Kustannusosakeyhyiö Otava, 1970.

Rahula, Walpola Sri. *Zen and the Taming of the Bull. Towards the Definition of Buddhist Thought.* London: Gordon Fraser, 1978.

Ratzinger, Joseph Cardinal and Archbishop Alberto Bovone. "Notificazione sul volume 'Chiese: Carisma e Potoere. Saggio di ecclesiologia militante' del padre Leonardo Boff, o. f. m.," *L' Osservatore Romano*, Anno CXXV, N. 66 (37.862), 20-21 March, 1985, pp. 1-2.

Reames, Sherry. "The Sources of Chaucer's *Second Nun' s Tale*," *Modern Philology*, 76 (1978), 111-35.

———, "The Cecilia Legend as Chaucer Inherited It and Retold It: The Disappearance of an Augustinian Ideal," *Speculum*, 55 (1980), 38-57.

———, "A Recent Discovery Concerning the Sources of Chaucer's 'Second Nun's Tale'," *Modern Philology*, 87 (1990), 337-361.

Reilly, Cyril A. "Chaucer's *Second Nun's Tale: Tibruce's Visit to Pope Urban,*" *Modern Language Notes*, 69 (1954) 37-39.

Rhodes, J. T. "Private Prayers in England on the Eve of the Reformation Illustrated from Works Printed or Reprinted in the Period 1530-1540." Ph.D. Thesis, University of Durham, 1974.

———, "Prayers of the Passion: From Jordanus of Quedlinburg to John Fewterer of Syon," *Durham University Journal*, n.s. 54 (1993), 27-38.

———, "Syon Abbey and its Religious Publications in the Sixteenth Century," *Journal of Ecclesiastical History*, 44 (1993), 11-25.

———, The Body of Christ in English Eucharistic Devotion, *c.* 1500-*c.* 1620," in *New Science out of Old Books, Studies in manuscripts and Early Printed Books in Honour of A.I. Doyle*, edd. Richard Beadle and A.J. Piper. Aldershot: Scolar Press, 1995, pp. 388-419.

Ricard, Robert. "Les apparations de Notre-Dame de Guadalupe. A Propos d'un ouvrage récent," *Revue d'Histoire des Missions*, June 1, 1931, pp. 247-62.

———, *The Spiritual Conquest of Mexico. An Essay on the Apostolate and the Evangelizing Methods of the Mendicant Orders in New Spain: 1523-1572.* Trans. Lesley Byrd Simpson. Berkeley, Los Angeles and London: University of California Press, 1966.

Riehle, Wolfgang. *The Middle English Mystics.* Trans. Bernard Standring. London, Boston and Henly: Routledge and Kegan Paul, 1981.

Ries, Julien. "Jésus-Christ dans le religion de Mani," *Augustiana*, 14 (1964), 437-54.

Rodriguez, Jeanette. *Our Lady of Guadalupe. Faith and Empowerment Among Mexican-American Women.* Austin: University of Texas Press, 1994.

Robbins, Rossell Hope. "Arma Christi Rolls," *Modern Language Review*, 34 (1939), 415-21.

Rohling, Joseph Henry, C.PP.S. *The Blood of Christ in Christian Latin Literature Before the Year 1000.* Washington, D.C.: Catholic University of America Press, 1932.

Rolle, Richard. *Richard Rolle: Prose and Verse Edited from MS Longleat 29 and Related Manuscripts*, ed. S. J. Ogilvie-Thompson. Early English Text Society, Original Series 293. London and Oxford: Oxford University Press, 1988.

Rosenthal, Joel T., ed. *Medieval Women and the Sources of Medieval History.* Athens, Ga. and London: University of Georgia Press, 1990.

Rosenwein, Barbara H. *Rhinoceros Bound. Cluny in the Tenth Century.* The Middle Ages: A Series Edited by Edward Peters. Philadelphia: University of Pennsylvania Press, 1982.

Ross, Thomas W. "Five Fifteenth-Century 'Emblem' Verses from Brit. Mus. Addit. 37049," *Speculum*, 32 (1957), 275-84.

Rowell, Geoffrey, ed. *The English Religious Tradition and the Genius of Anglicanism.* Wantage, Oxon. and Oxford: IKON and Keble College, Oxford, 1992.

Rubin, Miri. *Corpus Christi. The Eucharist in Late Medieval Culture.* Cambridge: Cambridge University Press, 1991.

Ryan, Lawrence V. "Doctrine and Dramatic Structure in *Everyman*," *Speculum*, 32 (1957), 722-35.

Schiller, Gertrud. *Iconography of Christian Art.* Trans. Janet Seligman. 2 vols. Greenwich, Connecticut: New York Graphic Society, Ltd.: 1972.

Seidel, Linda. *Songs of Glory. The Romanesque Facades of Acquitaine.* Chicago: University of Chicago Press, 1981, rpt. 1987.

Shahar, Shulamith. *The Fourth Estate. A History of Women in the Middle Ages.* London and New York: Methuen, 1983.

Sheedy, C. E. *The Eucharist Controversy of the Eleventh Century*. Washington, D.C.: Catholic University of America Press, 1947.

Simon, Jean-Marie. *Guatemala: Eternal Spring, Eternal Tyranny*. New York: W. W. Norton, Co., 1987.

Sleeth, Charles R. " 'My Dames Loore' in the *Canterbury Tales*," *Neuphilologische Mitteilungen*, 89 (1988), 174-84.

Smart, Ninian. *The Science of Religion and the Sociology of Knowledge. Some Methodological Questions*. Princeton, N.J.: Princeton University Press, 1973.

Smith, H. Maynard. *Pre-Reformation England*. London: Macmillan & Co. Ltd., 1938, rpt. 1963.

Smith, Sidonie. *A Poetics of Women' s Autobiography. Marginality and the Fictions of Self-Representation*. Bloomington and Indianapolis: Indiana University Press, 1987.

Smith, Wilfred Cantwell. *Faith and Belief*. Princeton: Princeton University Press, 1979.

Smithers, G. V., ed. *Havelok*. Oxford: Clarendon Press, 1987.

Sommerville, C. John. *The Secularization of Early Modern England. From Religious Culture to Religious Faith*. New York and Oxford: Oxford University Press, 1992.

Spalding, Mary Caroline, ed. *The Middle English Charters of Christ*. Bryn Mawr College Monographs vol. XV. Bryn Mawr, Pennsylvania: Bryn Mawr College, 1914.

Staahl, Frits. *Exploring Mysticism. A Methodological Essay*. Publications of the Center for South and Southeast Asia Studies. Berkeley, Los Angeles and London: University of California Press, 1975.

Staley, Lynn. *Margery Kempe' s Dissenting Fictions*. University Park, Pennsylvania: The Pennsylvania State University Press, 1994.

Stoll, David. *Is Latin America Turning Protestant? The Politics of Evangelical Growth*. Berkeley, Los Angeles and London: University of California Press, 1990.

Stratton, Suzanne L. *The Immaculate Conception in Spanish Art*. Cambridge: Cambridge University Press, 1994.

Sturges, Robert S. " *The Canterbury Tales*' Women Narrators: Three Traditions of Female Authority," *Modern Language Studies*, 13 (1983), 41-51.

Sudwtic, Chuck. "Do 4 Behold the Virgin? Bishop is Not a Believer," *New York Times*, 28 September 1990, p. A4.

Szittya, Penn R. *The Antifraternal Tradition in Medieval Literature*. Princeton, N. J.: Princeton University Press, 1986.

Tanner, Norman P., S.J. *The Church in Late Medieval Norwich, 1370-1532*. Studies and Texts 66. Toronto: Pontifical Institute of Medieval Studies, 1984.

Tawney, C.H.. "The Buddhist Original of Chaucer's *Pardoner' s Tale*," *The Journal of Philology (formerly The Cambridge Journal of Philology)*, 12 (1883), 202-8.

Tolkien, J.R.R., E.V. Gordon and Norman Davis, eds. *Sir Gawain and the Green Knight*. 2nd edn. Oxford: Oxford University Press, 1967, rpt. 1972.

Turner, D. H. "The Prayer-Book of Archbishop Arnulph II of Milan," *Revue Bénédictine*, 70 (1960), 360-92.

Tuttle, Lisa. *Encyclopedia of Feminism*. London: Arrow Books, 1987.

van der Meer, F. *Augustine the Bishop. The Life and Work of a Father of the Church*. Trans. Brian Battershaw and G.R. Lamb. London and New York: Sheed and Ward, 1961.

van Os, Henk, *et al. The Art of Devotion in the Late Middle Ages in Europe 1300-1500*. Trans. Michael Hoyle. Amsterdam and London: Rijksmuseum Amsterdam in Association with Merrell Holberton, 1994.

Vaughan, Robert Alfred. *Hours with the Mystics. A Contribution to the History of Religious Opinions*. 2 vols. London: John W. Parker, 1856, rpt. 1860, 1880.

Wach, Joachim. *The Comparative Study of Religions*, ed. Joseph M. Kitagawa. Lectures on the History of Religion Sponsored by the American Council of Learned Societies. New Series, Number 4. New York and London: Columbia University Press, 1961.

Watson, Nicholas. *Richard Rolle and the Invention of Authority.* Cambridge Studies in Medieval Literature 1. Cambridge: Cambridge University Press, 1991.
Wattie, Margaret, ed. *Lai le Freine. Smith College Studies in Modern Languages* 10:2. Northampton, Massachusetts and Paris: Smith College and E. Champion, 1928.
Wayment, H.G. *The Windows of King's College Chapel, Cambridge.* Corpus Vitrearum Medii Aevi, Great Britain, Supplementary Volume I. London: Oxford University Press for the British Academy, 1972.
West, Deleno C. "Medieval Ideas of Apoclyptic Mission and the Early Franciscans in Mexico," *Americas*, 45 (1988/89), 293-313.
Wickham, Chris. *Early Medieval Italy. Central Power and Local Society, 400-1000.* New Studies in Medieval History. Totowa, New Jersey and London: Barnes & Noble Books and Macmillan Press, Ltd., 1981.
Wilde, Johannes. *Michelangelo. Six Lectures.* Oxford Studies in the History of Art and Architecture. Oxford: Clarendon Press, 1978.
Wilmart, André, O.S.B. *Auteurs spirituels et texts dévot du moyen age latin: études d' histoire littéraire.* Paris: Etudes Augustiniennes, 1932, rpt. 1971.
———, "Le Manuel de prières de Saint Jean Gualbert," *Revue Bénédictine*, 48 (1936), 259-99.
———, *Precum Libelli Quattuor Aevi Karoloini. Prior Part.* Rome: Ephemerides Liturgicae, 1940.
Windeatt, Barry A. "Julian of Norwich and her Audience," *Review of English Studies*, n.s. 28 (1977), 1-17.
———, " 'Privytes to us': Knowing and Re-vision in Julian of Norwich," in *Chaucer to Shakespeare. Essays in Honour of Shinsuke Ando*, edd. Toshiyuki Takamiya and Richard Beadle. Cambridge: D.S. Brewer, 1992, pp. 87-98.
Woolf, Rosemary. *The Middle English Religious Lyric.* Oxford: Clarendon Press, 1966.
Zimdars-Swartz, Sandra L. *Encountering Mary. From La Salette to Medjugorje.* Princeton, N.J.: Princeton University Press, 1991.

INDEX OF NAMES AND SUBJECTS

Studies in the History of Christian Thought

EDITED BY HEIKO A. OBERMAN

1. McNEILL, J. J. *The Blondelian Synthesis.* 1966. Out of print
2. GOERTZ, H.-J. *Innere und äussere Ordnung in der Theologie Thomas Müntzers.* 1967
3. BAUMAN, Cl. *Gewaltlosigkeit im Täufertum.* 1968
4. ROLDANUS, J. *Le Christ et l'Homme dans la Théologie d'Athanase d'Alexandrie.* 2nd ed. 1977
5. MILNER, Jr., B. Ch. *Calvin's Doctrine of the Church.* 1970. Out of print
6. TIERNEY, B. *Origins of Papal Infallibility, 1150-1350.* 2nd ed. 1988
7. OLDFIELD, J. J. *Tolerance in the Writings of Félicité Lamennais 1809-1831.* 1973
8. OBERMAN, H. A. (ed.). *Luther and the Dawn of the Modern Era.* 1974. Out of print
9. HOLECZEK, H. *Humanistische Bibelphilologie bei Erasmus, Thomas More und William Tyndale.* 1975
10. FARR, W. *John Wyclif as Legal Reformer.* 1974
11. PURCELL, M. *Papal Crusading Policy 1244-1291.* 1975
12. BALL, B. W. *A Great Expectation.* Eschatological Thought in English Protestantism. 1975
13. STIEBER, J. W. *Pope Eugenius IV, the Council of Basel, and the Empire.* 1978. Out of print
14. PARTEE, Ch. *Calvin and Classical Philosophy.* 1977
15. MISNER, P. *Papacy and Development.* Newman and the Primacy of the Pope. 1976
16. TAVARD, G. H. *The Seventeenth-Century Tradition.* A Study in Recusant Thought. 1978
17. QUINN, A. *The Confidence of British Philosophers.* An Essay in Historical Narrative. 1977
18. BECK, J. *Le Concil de Basle (1434).* 1979
19. CHURCH, F. F. and GEORGE, T. (ed.) *Continuity and Discontinuity in Church History.* 1979
20. GRAY, P. T. R. *The Defense of Chalcedon in the East (451-553).* 1979
21. NIJENHUIS, W. *Adrianus Saravia (c. 1532-1613).* Dutch Calvinist. 1980
22. PARKER, T. H. L. (ed.) *Iohannis Calvini Commentarius in Epistolam Pauli ad Romanos.* 1981
23. ELLIS, I. *Seven Against Christ.* A Study of 'Essays and Reviews'. 1980
24. BRANN, N. L. *The Abbot Trithemius (1462-1516).* 1981
25. LOCHER, G. W. *Zwingli's Thought.* New Perspectives. 1981
26. GOGAN, B. *The Common Corps of Christendom.* Ecclesiological Themes in Thomas More. 1982
27. STOCK, U. *Die Bedeutung der Sakramente in Luthers Sermonen von 1519.* 1982
28. YARDENI, M. (ed.) *Modernité et nonconformisme en France à travers les âges.* 1983
29. PLATT, J. *Reformed Thought and Scholasticism.* 1982
30. WATTS, P. M. *Nicolaus Cusanus.* A Fifteenth-Century Vision of Man. 1982
31. SPRUNGER, K. L. *Dutch Puritanism.* 1982
32. MEIJERING, E. P. *Melanchthon and Patristic Thought.* 1983
33. STROUP, J. *The Struggle for Identity in the Clerical Estate.* 1984
34. 35. COLISH, M. L. *The Stoic Tradition from Antiquity to the Early Middle Ages.* 1.2. 2nd ed. 1990
36. GUY, B. *Domestic Correspondence of Dominique-Marie Varlet, Bishop of Babylon, 1678-1742.* 1986
37. 38. CLARK, F. *The Pseudo-Gregorian Dialogues.* I. II. 1987
39. PARENTE, Jr. J. A. *Religious Drama and the Humanist Tradition.* 1987
40. POSTHUMUS MEYJES, G. H. M. *Hugo Grotius, Meletius.* 1988
41. FELD, H. *Der Ikonoklasmus des Westens.* 1990
42. REEVE, A. and SCREECH, M. A. (eds.) *Erasmus' Annotations on the New Testament.* Acts — Romans — I and II Corinthians. 1990
43. KIRBY, W. J. T. *Richard Hooker's Doctrine of the Royal Supremacy.* 1990
44. GERSTNER, J. N. *The Thousand Generation Covenant.* Reformed Covenant Theology. 1990
45. CHRISTIANSON, G. and IZBICKI, T. M. (eds.) *Nicholas of Cusa.* 1991
46. GARSTEIN, O. *Rome and the Counter-Reformation in Scandinavia.* 1553-1622. 1992
47. GARSTEIN, O. *Rome and the Counter-Reformation in Scandinavia.* 1622-1656. 1992
48. PERRONE COMPAGNI, V. (ed.) *Cornelius Agrippa, De occulta philosophia Libri tres.* 1992
49. MARTIN, D. D. *Fifteenth-Century Carthusian Reform.* The World of Nicholas Kempf. 1992

50. HOENEN, M. J. F. M. *Marsilius of Inghen.* Divine Knowledge in Late Medieval Thought. 1993
51. O'MALLEY, J. W., IZBICKI, T. M. and CHRISTIANSON, G. (eds.) *Humanity and Divinity in Renaissance and Reformation.* Essays in Honor of Charles Trinkaus. 1993
52. REEVE, A. (ed.) and SCREECH, M. A. (introd.) *Erasmus' Annotations on the New Testament.* Galatians to the Apocalypse. 1993
53. STUMP, Ph. H. *The Reforms of the Council of Constance (1414-1418).* 1994
54. GIAKALIS, A. *Images of the Divine.* The Theology of Icons at the Seventh Ecumenical Council. With a Foreword by Henry Chadwick. 1994
55. NELLEN, H. J. M. and RABBIE, E. (eds.). *Hugo Grotius – Theologian.* Essays in Honour of G. H. M. Posthumus Meyjes. 1994
56. TRIGG, J. D. *Baptism in the Theology of Martin Luther.* 1994
57. JANSE, W. *Albert Hardenberg als Theologe.* Profil eines Bucer-Schülers. 1994
58. ASSELT, W.J. VAN. *The Covenant Theology of Johannes Cocceius (1603-1669).* An Examination of its Structure. *In preparation*
59. SCHOOR, R.J.M. VAN DE. *The Irenical Theology of Théophile Brachet de La Milletière (1588-1665).* 1995
60. STREHLE, S. *The Catholic Roots of the Protestant Gospel.* Encounter between the Middle Ages and the Reformation. 1995
61. BROWN, M.L. *Donne and the Politics of Conscience in Early Modern England.* 1995
62. SCREECH, M.A. (ed.). *Richard Mocket, Warden of All Souls College, Oxford, Doctrina et Politia Ecclesiae Anglicanae.* An Anglican Summa. Facsimile with Variants of the Text of 1617. Edited with an Introduction. 1995
63. SNOEK, G.J.C. *Medieval Piety from Relics to the Eucharist.* A Process of Mutual Interaction. 1995
64. PIXTON, P.B. *The German Episcopacy and the Implementation of the Decrees of the Fourth Lateran Council, 1216-1245.* Watchmen on the Tower. 1995
65. DOLNIKOWSKI, E.W. *Thomas Bradwardine: A View of Time and a Vision of Eternity in Fourteenth-Century Thought.* 1995
66. RABBIE, E. (ed.). *Hugo Grotius, Ordinum Hollandiae ac Westfrisiae Pietas (1613).* Critical Edition with Translation and Commentary. 1995
67. HIRSH, J.C. *The Boundaries of Faith.* The Development and Transmission of Medieval Spirituality. 1996
68. BURNETT, S.G. *From Christian Hebraism to Jewish Studies: Johannes Buxtorf (1564-1629) and Hebrew Learning in the Seventeenth Century.* 1996
69. BOLAND O.P., V. *Ideas in God according to Saint Thomas Aquinas.* Sources and Synthesis. 1996.
70. LANGE, M.E. *Telling Tears in the English Renaissance.* 1996